WITHDRAWN

D0874001

372.12
G914s

The Sex Factor and the Management of Schools

Neal Gross
University of Pennsylvania

Anne E. Trask
Educational Testing Service

A Wiley-Interscience Publication
JOHN WILEY & SONS
New York • London • Sydney • Toronto

Copyright © 1976 by John Wiley & Sons, Inc.

All rights reserved. Published simultaneously in Canada.

No part of this book may be reproduced by any means,
nor transmitted, nor translated into a machine language
without the written permission of the publisher.

Library of Congress Cataloging in Publication Data:

Gross, Neal, 1920–
    The sex factor and the management of schools.

    "A Wiley-Interscience publication."
    Includes bibliographical references and index.
    1. School superintendents and principals.
2. Sex role.   I. Trask, Anne E., joint author.
II. Title.

LB2831.9.G76   372.1′2′012   75-34337
ISBN 0-471-32800-6

Preface

This book reports the findings of an inquiry that focused on men and women who occupied an identical managerial position, the elementary school principalship, in school systems of major American cities. The basic objectives of the study were to determine if the sex of administrators influenced their role performance, their conception of their tasks, their orientations and reactions to managerial responsibilities, their career histories and aspirations, as well as the operation and productivity of their organizations.

These issues are of concern to many groups in our society: social scientists who are interested in organizational leadership and functioning, role performance, and reactions to work; educators, school board members, and parents who are concerned about the educational implications of the recent tilting of the sex ratio in the elementary principalship in favor of males; women who are uncertain about whether they should aspire to careers in educational administration; individuals who are in a position to decide whether or not women will be appointed to jobs with important responsibilities; and women's organizations and other groups that are committed to equal opportunities for women in the world of work.

Our investigation was conducted as part of the National Principalship Study, a research program that was carried out at Harvard University during the 1960s and that was supported by the U.S. Office of Education. The Study was designed to explore a number of problems of interest to both social scientists and educational practitioners. The results of a study of the effects and determinants of the professional leadership exhibited by principals as the executives of their schools were published in Neal Gross and Robert E. Herriott, *Staff Leadership in Public Schools: A Sociological Inquiry* (New York: John Wiley & Sons, Inc., 1965). Additional monographs have examined the following issues: the effects and determinants of selected dimensions of administrative performance such as closeness of supervision, support of innova-

CAT Jul 3 '78

15.30

6-6-78 B-D

iii

77-8074

tion, and client involvement in school affairs; the incidence and correlates of role conflicts in the principalship; and the job and career satisfaction and the level of aspiration of school administrators.

A report of the findings of the "sex differences" study was completed and submitted in 1964 to the U.S. Office of Education. Our decision to write a book based on this study was due to our belief that its findings had direct relevance to basic issues about the effects of sex roles that would become the subject of wide, and frequently heated, debate in public education, university and governmental circles, and in the women's movement for equal rights. The initial work on the book was started in 1965; its completion was delayed because of the pressure of other more immediate responsibilities and personal exigencies.

We acknowledge with pleasure our indebtedness to the senior staff members of the National Principalship Study: Peter C. Dodd, Robert Dreeben, Robert E. Herriott, Joseph L. Hozid, Paul E. Kelley, Keith W. Prichard, and Dean K. Whitla. In addition to participating in the design of the overall Study they prepared research materials, supervised field work activities in many cities, and conducted most of the interviews. The senior staff also served as editors and coders (or supervisors of coding) for both the questionnaire and the interview data. Robert Dreeben assumed major responsibility for coding the open-ended interview materials and Peter C. Dodd and Joseph L. Hozid worked closely with him. Robert E. Herriott coordinated the development of the many research instruments and supervised the extensive computer programming, data reduction, and statistical analyses for the many parts of the Study. Keith W. Prichard and Paul E. Kelly reviewed relevant bodies of social science and educational literature with considerable skill. Dean K. Whitla had primary responsibility for developing and carrying out the sampling procedures. He also served as Associate Director of the Study during the first two years of the research program.

We express our appreciation to the following individuals who augmented the senior staff in the data collection phase of the Study: John Clark, James M. Coffee, Mario D. Fantini, Harold L. Hodgkinson, and Miriam Lieber.

We were advised on various statistical problems by the following individuals: Hubert Blalock, William G. Cochran, Robert E. Herriott, Howard Raiffa, John Tukey, and Dean K. Whitla. Their cooperation and advice is acknowledged with much gratitude.

For their critical appraisal of sections of earlier drafts or of the entire manuscript, we wish to express our sincere thanks to members of the senior staff and to Larry Weiss. Marion L. Crowley served as the secretary of the Study, and we are indebted to her for her many valuable contributions throughout the entire period of manuscript preparation. Theresa Divers, Irma Kienitz, Adele Lechowicz, Olive Molder, Rebecca Nestor, Darl Walter, and Louise Zahn, ably carried out their many secretarial and related responsibilities. For her valuable editorial assistance on the initial draft of this manuscript, we are indebted to Helen G. Hughes.

We wish to express our thanks to Harvard University, the University of Pennsylvania, the University of Illinois, and the Educational Testing Service for the generous support and cooperation they gave us while we were preparing this manuscript.

One hundred and eighty-nine principals and 1303 teachers in 41 large American cities participated in this inquiry. Without the cooperation and interest of these educators it would not have been possible to undertake the study. We are greatly appreciative of the time and effort they were willing to devote to the inquiry. We acknowledge our indebtedness to them with special gratitude.

Philadelphia, Pennsylvania   NEAL GROSS
Princeton, New Jersey   ANNE E. TRASK
October 1975

Contents

1

Introduction to the Study

The women and men selected to administer and to offer leadership to public elementary schools in large cities of the United States are the subjects of this book. The fact that a substantial number of females and males occupy the identical managerial position, the school principalship, in these educational establishments provides an opportunity to examine a set of largely unexplored and intriguing questions about ways in which the sex factor may influence the careers of administrators, their role performance, the functioning and productivity of their organizations, and their orientations and responses to their work.[1]

We present in this book the findings of an inquiry designed to shed light on these questions. They bear on issues of concern to many groups: social scientists, educators, members of school boards, personnel managers, women with an interest in professional careers, and individuals vexed by sex discrimination in the world of work. The data required to examine them were secured in the early 1960s through interviews and other techniques from a national cross section of 189 elementary principals in 41 large city school systems in all parts of the United States as well as from their administrative superiors and a sample of teachers in each of their schools.[2]

OBJECTIVES OF THE STUDY

Our inquiry had four specific objectives. The first was to examine the impact of the sex factor on important career decisions of principals, for example, their decision to enter teaching, their later decision to become a principal, and their career aspirations for the future.

The second was to determine if the sex factor influenced their orientations and reactions to their work. We wanted to find out if men and women who serve as principals differ in the following respects: their educational values, the importance they assign to their major responsibilities, their evaluation of their own performance, their job satisfaction, and the worry they experience in performing their administrative responsibilities.

The third objective was to ascertain if men and women principals perform their roles differently. We wanted to determine if male and female educational administrators differ in the degree of control they exercise over their faculties, the emphasis they place on the responsibility of teachers to provide maximum service to their pupils, the way they relate to faculty members within and outside of the school, and the extent to which they involve parents in school affairs.

The final objective was to examine whether the sex of principals had any bearing on the functioning and productivity of their organizations. It led us to inquire if the morale of teachers, their classroom behavior, and pupils' academic performance were influenced by the gender of the administrator of a school.

MOTIVATING CONDITIONS FOR THE STUDY

A number of circumstances motivated us to focus on these objectives. One was our acute awareness that sociologists had largely ignored how the gender of managers of organizations might influence their operation and the careers of incumbents of these positions themselves. Our examination of the social science literature with reference to the central questions of our inquiry led us to conclude that sociologists had largely neglected the sex factor as a potentially important determinant of behavior in organizational settings. We could discern little progress in filling in the knowledge gap that Gouldner had identified in 1957 in his appraisal of the sociological literature on organizational functioning:

> ... many sociologists who study factories, offices, schools, or mental hospitals take little note of the fact that the organizational role-players invariably have a gender around which is built a latent social identity. One does not have to be Freudian to insist that sex makes a difference, even for organizational behavior.[3]

In sociological perspective, our inquiry constitutes an attempt to increase our limited understanding of ways in which the gender of role incumbents may influence administrative behavior, reactions to work, organizational performance, and career patterns. We not only gave explicit recognition to the fact that administrators of organizations have a gender, but highlighted this attribute in our investigation.

A second motivating condition was our puzzlement over the educational effects and other consequences of the dramatic shift that had occurred in the sex ratio among elementary school principals over the last four decades. In 1928 the majority (55%) of the administrators of public primary schools were women; three decades later, in 1958, the proportion of women in the elementary principalship had dropped to 38%. This downward trend persisted during the 1960s with the result that in 1971 only one out of five (21%) of elementary school principals were women.[4] The fact that the principalship of an elementary school has turned into a job largely reserved for males is a development that has received little notice either in or outside of educational circles. What is especially perplexing is that the decline in women in the principalship persisted during the sixties, a decade in which strong demands were being made by the leaders of the women's rights movement for equality of occupational opportunity for members of their sex. Moreover, Title VII of the Civil Rights Act which was passed by Congress in 1964 forbids sex discrimination in the hiring and promotion of personnel.

Since 85% of American elementary school teachers are women, it might have been expected that the wide publicity received by the feminist movement and the forceful pronouncements of its leaders during the sixties would have led large numbers of female teachers to seek elementary principalships and many school systems to promote women to these administrative posts. However, as noted, the proportion of women in the principalship declined during this period.

A number of explanations have been offered to account for this perplexing state of affairs. One attributes it primarily to "outright discrimination against women [that] exists in the promotion practices, if not in the official policies, of many school districts."[5] A second views the decline in the number of female principals as the consequence of an informal male preference policy of school boards that is based on the belief that more men need to be retained in and attracted to primary schools, the segment of public education in which the teaching force is largely dominated by women. These school boards assume that men teachers usually seek and generally need greater income and prestige from their work than do women teachers, and therefore they have disproportionately appointed men to fill vacancies in the principalship.

A third explanation is that school boards overreacted to one of the major criticisms to which elementary schools were exposed in the sixties: boys lacked male role models and authority figures. The culture of the school and its mode of operation, it was alleged, were dominated by a general orientation that has been described as "momism." Appointing men to the principalship served as a strategic way to cope with the criticism.

A fourth explanation places the blame on the colleges and universities that prepare educational administrators. It has been maintained that these institutions have shown little concern for the sex imbalance in the principalship and other educational administrative positions. Their policies of recruitment and financial aid, it is claimed, have been biased in favor of males.[6] Another possible explanation is that the proportion of women teachers who aspire to the principalship, in comparison to the percentage of men teachers, may have markedly dropped during the 1960s.

Whatever its causes, the consequences of the imbalanced sex ratio in the principalship for pupils and the operation of schools are issues that require intensive examination. Leaving aside the equity issue for competent and qualified women who have aspired to, but have been denied, the principalship (and we view this as an important matter), we need to determine whether it is reality or myth that reserving the principalship primarily for men will have an impact on the leadership climates to which teachers are exposed, their morale, their performance, and the learning of their pupils. The answers to these questions have direct and important implications for personnel policies of school systems.

A third motivating condition was our belief that our inquiry might be of value to both unmarried and married women with professional aspirations who have speculated about careers in educational administration. We thought that these women, as well as female teachers who are wondering whether they should strive for the principalship, would benefit from a consideration of sex differences in career timetable, in work gratification, in task performance, and in job-related worry.

Moreover, we believed that conclusions that emerge from a comparison of the performance of men and women as administrators of schools would also be useful for them since they would shed light on whether widely held beliefs about sex differences in the behavior and capabilities of principals have any factual basis. In short, we hoped to provide a body of information that would be of use to women vexed by these questions as they confront the world of work in public education.

The fourth and final motivating circumstance was our interest in a set of questions that bear on an issue of growing concern to the top management of business, governmental, and other types of organizations: the manner in which women will perform if appointed to managerial and professional positions. As noted, Title VII of the 1964 Civil Rights Act forbids sex discrimination in the hiring and promotion of personnel in large sectors of the American economy. One of its consequences is that some large-scale organizations, for example, A.T. & T., have been "stimulated" to develop programs to prepare women to assume managerial or executive positions. However, most corporations continue to drag their feet in viewing women as a source of executive talent. Beyond question, unfavorable prejudgments of the following kind about women have impeded their chances in competing for responsible supervisory positions: women will not commit themselves to their jobs and careers; they are reluctant to assume supervisory responsibilities; they become too emotionally involved; they lack the ability to work effectively with subordinates, and so on. As Gardner observed nearly 30 years ago:

> . . . there is the general belief that women make poor supervisors, that they are too emotional and "take things personally," that they cannot command the loyalty and respect of their subordinates nor the cooperation of their equals. In the face of such beliefs, which appear among executives as well as workers, women are rarely given a chance at supervisory positions. And when occasionally one is given such an opportunity, her supervisors are always doubtful, as if to say, "We know women don't usually make good supervisors, so we really don't expect you to succeed."[7]

At a time when increased consideration is being given to the use of female talent at the managerial level in industry, in government, and in other areas, it is especially important to inquire if views of this kind simply reflect prejudices or if they have any real basis. Although our examination of men and women in management will be limited to the public schools, our findings *may* be suggestive for executives who select managers in other types of organizations.

WOMEN AND MEN IN THE WORLD OF WORK

Our inquiry is concerned with women and men who occupy an identical managerial position in one sector of the occupational structure. To place it in the larger setting of which it is a part, women and men in the world of work, we briefly examine four topics: (1) recent developments about the sex composition of the labor force; (2) men and women in executive positions in American society; (3) men and women administrators in public education; and (4) constraints on women in the world of work.

Women and Men in the Labor Force: Recent Developments

Since the turn of the century striking changes have occurred in the participation of American women in the world of work. Whereas in 1890 women represented about one-sixth of the working population, in 1970 over 30 million women were employed in any average month and they accounted for approximately one-third of the civilian labor force.[8] Nearly half of the adult women in 1900 had never engaged in paid employment, but as early as 1957 it was estimated that at least 90 out of every 100 women would be employed outside their homes at some time during the course of their lives.[9] Furthermore, the number of years that adult women participate in the labor force has substantially increased: they worked an average of 11 years at the close of the century. Girls in school today can expect to spend an average of over 25 years in employment outside the home.[10]

Dramatic changes have also occurred in the age and marital status of women in paid employment, as evidenced by the following findings of the National Manpower Council:

> In 1890, out of every ten women who did work, seven were single and five were under 25 years old. Today, only one fourth of the female labor force consists of single women. About six out of every ten women now working are married, and five out of ten are over 40 years of age. Three out of every ten married women are now working. Even more striking is the fact that nearly two out of every five mothers whose children are of school age are in the labor force.[11]

Shifts in the types of occupations women enter have accompanied these changes. As in the case of men, the proportion of women in white-collar employment has materially increased while their participation in unskilled and semiskilled work has markedly declined. Nearly one-fourth of all working women, according to the 1970 Census, were employed in secretarial, clerical, and sales work; in 1890, approximately 5% of women in the labor force were employed in these jobs. At that time, over 80% of employed women who did not work on farms were engaged in teaching, domestic and personal service, or in the clothing and textile industries. Today, only about one out of every four women who are employed work in these occupations. In 1970 less than 6% of employed women were engaged in domestic service; 50% held jobs of this kind in 1890.

Anthropologists stress that in every society, be it primitive or modern, sex is important in the allocation and selection of work. There is "men's work" and "women's work." This certainly applied to American society in the early 1900s, and Degler contends that this condition largely persists today. He states that ". . . the fact remains that the occupations in which the vast majority of women actually engage are remarkably similar to those historically held by women."[12] The 1970 Census showed that the number of women classified as professional workers increased substantially during the previous decade; women, however, are still generally concentrated in a narrower band of occupations than men.[13] In 1970 nearly eight million women were employed in professional services, primarily in the fields of health, education, and public administration. They represented approximately one-fourth of the females in the labor force. Women employed in retail trade and as factory workers accounted for an additional one-third, while only one-sixth of the women in the labor force were employed as service workers.

The occupations in which women are concentrated continue on the whole to be dominated by them: nearly one-half of all working women are found in occupations in which three-quarters or more of those employed are women. Some occupations such as nursing and household work are almost entirely staffed by women. Moreover, as the National Manpower Council has noted, in occupational categories that include substantial numbers of both men and women, specific jobs tend to be allocated primarily to one of the sexes. For example, although men comprise approximately 33% of the 2.1 million teachers in the public schools, only 15% of teachers in the elementary schools are male.[14]

Some women, of course, do hold positions in highly paid professions, in industry, in business, and in government. However, most of the jobs they hold in these fields tend to be less remunerative than those held by men. The difference in the kind of occupations that men and women tend to specialize in partly explains why the earnings of all women working full time in 1970 averaged only about 55% of those of all men working full time. Furthermore, where both males and females were employed in identical occupations, the level of earnings of women was substantially lower than that of men.

Men and Women in Executive Positions in American Society

The sex factor has been critical in the selection of executive and managerial personnel. A crude measure of changes in the proportion of women in managerial positions between 1960 and 1970 can be obtained from comparing the number of women at these points in time in the broad census category, "Managers and Administrators, Except Farm." Between 1960 and 1970 the number of women in this category increased by nearly 25%, from 794,000 to 1,055,400. During the same decade the number of male managers increased by approximately 12%, from 4,695,000 to 5,315,800. Approximately 20% of the administrators and managers were female in 1970 as compared to nearly 15% in 1960. Thus, although the increase in the absolute number of female executives during the decade was double that of males, the proportion of total managers and administrators that was female rose only by 5%.[15]

The census category "Managers and Administrators, Except Farm," however, is extremely broad in scope and covers a wide range of incomes. The use of this classification for comparison of females with males is also open to the additional objection that the median income for the men included in it is considerably higher than that for the women: $11,802 versus $6030.

A more useful comparison for our purposes is one that is based on male and females classified as "Managers and Administrators, Except Farm," who have incomes that are $10,000 or more. The data reveal that between 1960 and 1970 the number of women in the category more than quadrupled, from 25,457 to 109,493. During the same period the number of men in this classification increased by more than 250%, from 1,156,817 to 2,943,558. The number of female managers and administrators earning $10,000 a year or more in 1960 was approximately 2% of the males in this income bracket. In 1970 the number of females in this category had risen to slightly more than 3% of the males with such incomes.

If this more restricted criterion for defining an executive is employed, it would appear appropriate to conclude that while the rate of increase in the number of female executives has been greater than that of males, the proportion of female to male executives in the labor force has increased only slightly between 1960 and 1970.[16]

Men and Women Administrators in Public Education

What about the ratio of women to men in management positions in American public education? We noted earlier that there has been a steady decline in the percentage of women employed as principals of elementary schools, from 55% in 1928 to only 21% in 1971. The proportion of women serving as secondary school administrators, however, has increased in recent years. In 1960-1961 the percentage of women principals in *all* public *secondary* schools was 3.8%; in 1971 the proportion had risen to 6.5%.

The percentage of women who serve as the top administrators of local public school systems is insignificant: less than 1% of all school superintendents in the United States were female in 1971. Women served with greater frequency in lower positions in the central administration of school districts: nearly 8% of the deputy superintendents and 15% of the administrative assistants to superintendents were female. According to the National Education Association, women also held a substantial proportion of the middle management positions in the central offices of school systems: 46% of the administrators responsible for instruction and supervision in American school systems were women in 1971 and 48% of the officials in charge of general administration and 38% of those responsible for pupil personnel services were female.[17]

These data, in combination with those about the sex ratio in the principalship, reveal that the top administrative positions of school systems and of individual schools are disproportionately filled by men.

Constraints on Women in the World of Work

Parsons attributes many of the problems to which females are exposed in the world of work to, as he puts it, "the asymmetrical relationship of the sexes to the occupational structure."[18] He points out that an approved occupational role is fundamental to the status of an adult male in American society since his economic and social standing, and that of his family if he is married, are primarily determined by the socioeconomic status of his occupation or profession. The situation is different, however, for most women. In the case of married women, whether they are employed or do not work, their social and economic status is generally a function of their husbands'. Although females who identify with the women's liberation movement reject these notions, most women apparently continue to subscribe to them. Unmarried adult working women, a minority of their sex, are still generally identified by their marital status, that is, as "single"; they are infrequently evaluated in terms of the status of their occupations.

Circumstances confronting men and women in their work careers are frequently dissimilar. For one thing, the occupational careers of women are usually not continuous. While men generally work from the termination of their formal education until retirement or death, most women absent themselves from paid employment shortly before the birth of their first child and return to the labor force, if they decide to do so, only after their last child has entered school. In the second place, a substantial proportion of women are secondary breadwinners: their earnings, if not devoted to their own support, generally supplement the income of parents, husbands, or other relatives. Third, married women tend to move about less freely than men. They generally seek employment in or near the communities in which their husbands work. Fourth, at any given time a much larger proportion of qualified women than of men are out of the labor force. For example, many women who are qualified to teach do not work in the schools; in the case of nursing, only a relatively small proportion of the trained personnel exercise their professional skills at any given time.[19]

Another problem confronting women who work in occupations or professions dominated by men is that females pose a "status contradiction" to their male colleagues. Hughes has observed that "people carry in their minds a set of expectations concerning the auxiliary traits properly associated with many of the specific positions available in our society. These expectations appear as advantages or disadvantages to persons who, in keeping with American social belief and practice, aspire to positions new to persons of their kind."[20] Women in predominantly male work groups can be perceived as threats to their male associates because of the manner in which sex roles are generally defined in our society. This is one reason why top positions are generally reserved for men and accounts in part for the obstacles that confront women who strive for advancement. Caplow has argued that prevailing norms concerning male-female relationships at work are women's greatest handicap in this connection:

> Women are barred from four out of every five occupational functions, not because of incapacity or technological unsuitability, but because the attitudes which govern interpersonal relationships in our culture sanction only a few working relationships between men and women, and prohibit all the others on grounds that have nothing to do with technology.[21]

He stresses the importance of the general norm that a man is not expected to be directly subordinate to a woman and notes that intimate groups, except those based on family or sexual ties, are composed of one sex or the other, but never of both.[22] He also notes that it is common knowledge that men accept women superiors with great reluctance and that this circumstance largely explains why the majority of women in supervisory positions have women subordinates only or are assigned to technical or staff jobs involving little exercise of authority. Whyte's finding that male countermen in restaurants resent and resist taking orders from female waitresses is a case in point.[23] It has been argued that the customary opposition of male workers to the introduction of a women in their midst reflects their attempt to avoid pangs of guilt; that is, society has taught them—and the women as well—not to enter into occupational competition with each other.[24]

RESEARCH METHODS*

We now turn to the research techniques that were used to obtain and analyze the data of our inquiry. We focus on three major facets of its

---

*The remainder of this chapter presents the major methodological issues of the study and how we dealt with them. Readers with little interest in issues of this kind may wish to proceed directly to Chapter 2.

research design: the population and the sample, the collection of data, and their processing and reduction for purposes of data analysis.

Our investigation was designed as part of the National Principalship Study.[25] The target population of school principals for the Study consisted of all supervising principals in cities of 50,000 or more in the United States during the 1960–1961 school year. Through the use of a cluster sampling procedure that was designed to secure a 5% sample of the 10,956 principalships in large-size cities, a sample of 508 secondary and elementary principals in 41 cities was chosen. To select the specific sample of schools in each of the communities, the schools in each city were classified by grade level and by the socioeconomic composition of their student bodies.[26] The schools in our study represent the sample of 189 *elementary* schools that were identified by the cluster sampling procedure. The small number of female principals in junior and senior high schools precluded the involvement of secondary school principals in the study design.

Following the development and the pretesting of the research instruments, the data collection phase was initiated. To satisfy the data requirements of its several research projects, the National Principalship Study required the collection of data from school principals, their administrative superiors, and their teachers.

Three steps were involved in collecting data from the principals: (1) the completion of a mailed Personal and School Background Questionnaire prior to the arrival of the study staff in the community; (2) the completion of an extensive Role Questionnaire in group sessions with local administrators under the supervision of the field staff; and (3) three- to five-hour personal interviews conducted by members of the field staff.

The higher administrators in the local school systems completed a lengthy Superior's Questionnaire, similar in many respects to the instruments answered by the principals, but drawn up from the perspective of the central administration. The higher administrators completed their questionnaires at the three-hour group meetings held during the field staff's visit in each community. Responses were received from 172 higher administrators of whom 128 were later classified as the immediate superiors of the 501 principals in the total sample.

The several investigations also used teachers as a source of data. In the spring of 1961 a random sample of 10 teachers in each of the elementary, junior high, and senior high schools whose principals were included in the study were asked to respond to a 21-page Teacher Questionnaire that included sections on how they viewed their own role and that of their principals, their principals' performance, satisfactions in their jobs and careers, and their personal and occupational histories. They were also asked to report their observations about the performance of their fellow teachers and their own pupils.[27]

To obtain the highest possible rate of return, after two and then four weeks, follow-up letters were sent to teachers who still had not sent in the questionnaires. Out of 4760 teachers 3367 (71%) returned usable questionnaires. Of special relevance to our inquiry is the fact that 1303 of the 1750 elementary school teachers, or 74%, returned the Teacher Questionnaire in usable form (see Appendix B).

From 14 schools we have no data from the teachers because the higher administration in the local school system would not consent to their participation. Therefore, of the analyses of principals that involve data from teachers—for example, their observations on the performance of their principals—the maximum number of cases is 175; but when analyses required only data obtained from principals—for example, reports on their level of aspiration—the maximum number of cases is 189.

A great deal of the data were precoded: the Background Questionnaire, the Role Questionnaire, the Superior's Questionnaire, and the Teacher Questionnaire. After being edited by staff members to clarify dubious replies, the responses were punched directly on IBM cards by professional operators and then verified.

The open-ended data from the personal interview were handled differently. We followed standard methods of content analysis[28] in devising codes to categorize responses which then were coded by two independent coders. After each coder had coded the replies of some 50 principals, his work was checked against the second coder's. If they were in substantial agreement, no further checks were made until all coding was completed; if not, the coders discussed their differences and clarified their definitions of the categories, after which a new sample of replies was checked for reliability. A final verification was carried out on a random sample of the completed questionnaires. Following this, the coded data were punched on IBM cards and verified in the same way as the precoded questionnaire materials.

The chief statistical techniques used to reduce the data from a series of responses to a single score were factor analysis and Guttman scaling. Wherever it appeared feasible, we first tried to devise a Guttman scale as an index of a variable. When the data did not meet the requirements of Guttman scaling, a principal components factor analysis was undertaken. If the factors that emerged could be interpreted clearly, their loadings were used as weights in computing factor scores; if not, the significant factors were rotated following Kaiser's Varimax criterion, which maximizes or minimizes factor loadings within the restriction of orthogonality.[29] The factor loadings resulting from the Varimax solution were converted to factor score coefficients using Harman's shortened method, and the new coefficients were used as weights in computing factor scores used in the analysis.[30]

On a number of the instruments, principals and teachers were asked to respond to the same questions. Since the major focus of the National Principalship Study was on principals, all factor analyses were carried out on the correlation matrices computed from their responses. When factor scores were also required for the teachers, the item means, standard deviations, and factor weights resulting from the principals' matrix were applied to the teachers' data in computing their factor scores, thereby making certain that the operational definition of all scores developed from a given set of items would be identical.[31]

To establish a "best estimate" of the behavior of the principals on a particular dimension, the reports of the from four to ten teacher-observers in each school as to the behavior of their principal were averaged. Before employing this procedure for the elementary schools that were the central focus of this and another investigation, studies of the reliability of the reports of the 1303 elementary teachers who served as observers of the principals were undertaken. Based on the analysis of the responses of the elementary teachers about the Executive Professional Leadership of men and women principals, it was concluded that the reports were both reliable and relatively free from any bias referable to the personal characteristics of the teachers.[32]

Some of the inquiries of the National Principalship Study concerned 501 elementary, junior, and senior high schools while others, such as this one, pertained only to elementary schools. Thus we faced the alternative of using scores operationally derived from an analysis of data secured in all 501 schools, or of repeating the lengthy and expensive task of Guttman scaling and factor analysis of the data obtained from personnel in the elementary schools alone. An examination by Gross and Herriott of the difference between factor scores defined from factor analyses of the data from the entire 501 schools and from the 175 elementary schools showed that the Pearsonian product-moment correlation coefficients computed from scores developed from the 501 and 175 cases on teachers' morale, teachers' professional performance, and pupil academic performance were in excess of .999.[33] Since these findings indicated that there would be no appreciable advantage in duplicating the factor analysis and scaling procedures to obtain a new set of measures specifically for the elementary schools, we decided on the first alternative.

Another methodological matter deserves emphasis: for purposes of coming to a conclusion about whether a hypothesis, prediction, or assumption to be tested receives empirical support, we have adopted as our standard that a relationship be significant statistically at below the .05 level.

The Use of Third Variables

In many of our analyses we introduce third variables in ways in which sociologists have conventionally used them:[34] to determine if we are making a spurious interpretation of a relationship, to determine if findings from the total sample are internally replicated in subclassifications of the sample, and to explore conditional relationships. A fourth use of third variables that we employ in our study, however, deserves special comment.

In specifying the reasoning on which hypotheses to be tested are based, we posit in each instance that one or more third variables *may* intervene as links in a causal chain between the sex of principals and a specified dependent variable, accounting in part for the relationship between the two. If the reasoning underlying the hypothesis has any justification, then two necessary conditions should exist: first, the variable(s) posited as intervening between the independent and dependent ones should be related to both of them; second, if this condition is met, then when the effects of the intervening variable(s) are removed (through partial correlation, for example) the strength of the relationship between the independent and dependent variables should diminish[35]—for if the relationship between the independent and dependent variables remains the same, then the explanatory variable being held constant could have had no bearing on the relationship, since it had no effect on it. However, when our analyses indicate empirical support for third variables serving as links between an independent and dependent variable as specified by our reasoning, such findings of course indicate only *the possibility* that the third variables *could* serve in a causal manner. Conclusive evidence in support of the existence of such relationships can only be obtained from research designs in which the time order specified for the linkage of the several variables (independent, intervening, and dependent) can be observed.

Despite this handicap of cross-sectional studies, we believe it is important to attempt to test the reasoning underlying a hypothesis as well as the hypothesis itself, since only in this way can we begin to distinguish between explanations of relationships that are invalid and those that *may be* tenable.

A Note on Sex as the Major Independent Variable

Our decision to focus on the sex factor as the primary independent variable of our inquiry and to use other personal characteristics of principals, for example, their age and their marital status, primarily as "specifying" variables was based on both theoretical and pragmatic considerations.[36] The major theoretical problem arose in regard to the age variable. As Strodtbeck and Mann have noted: "there are no clear *a priori* expectations" of how behavior will vary within the adult range.[37] A pragmatic consideration, lack of data for analytic purposes, precluded using marital status as an independent variable, either singly or in combination with gender. The sample included only a handful of single men and a relatively small group of married women. In addition, only 11 of 189 principals were divorced, separated, or widowed. In short, the data required to examine the effects of marital status, singly or in combination with sex, were unavailable.

NOTES AND REFERENCES

1.   In her 1974 review of the literature on the performance of women in the field of school administration, particularly elementary school principals, Meskin identified only

three studies, in addition to our own research, that have dealt with one or more aspects of this problem area (Joan D. Meskin, "The Performance of Women Administrators—A Review of the Literature," *Administrator's Notebook*, XXXIII, 1 (1974). The first is the Florida Leadership Project that was initiated in 1952 (Hulda G. Grobman and Vynce A. Hynes, "What Makes a Good School Principal?", *Bulletin of the National Association of Secondary School Principals*, 40 (November 1956). The second is Barter's inquiry that was published in 1959. Barter examined whether there was any evidence to indicate that sex discrimination existed in the appointment of elementary principals in one Michigan county and if there were circumstances that might bear on the imbalanced sex ratio in the principalship. She concluded that the official hiring practices of the school districts did not indicate discrimination even though women principals were in the minority. She found that there were sex differences among teachers with respect to their preferences for men and women principals and their evaluation of their personal characteristics and abilities. Her major conclusion was that women teachers generally display too little interest in the elementary principalship and that more of them need to be stimulated to aspire toward the position. (Alice S. Barter, "The Status of Women in School Administration: Where Will They Go From Here?", *Educational Horizons*, 38 (Spring 1959), pp. 72–75.

The third investigation Meskin reviews is John K. Hemphill, D. E. Griffiths, and N. Frederiksen, *Administrative Performance and Personality* (New York: Teachers College, Columbia University, 1962). This simulation study examined a number of dimensions of the behavior of elementary principals and presents the scores of men and women principals on a number of variables. In their abbreviated consideration of the influence of the sex factor on administrative performance they conclude, on the basis of their "in-basket" findings, that "the women involved teachers, superiors and outsiders in their work, while men tended to make final decisions and take action without involving others." They also found that in projective learning situations, women tend to place greater emphasis than men on teaching objectives, pupil involvement, and assessment of teaching (*ibid.*, pp. 332–334). On the basis of these and other findings, they concluded that there probably was no justification for appointing men rather than women to the elementary principalship.

2.   Two characteristics of the sample need to be kept in mind in interpreting the findings or drawing generalizations from them. The first is that the principals represent a stratified random sample of principals from large cities, that is, of cities with a population of 50,000 and over. The second is that the data were obtained from them, their teachers, and other sources during 1960–1961. Whether the findings apply to communities of smaller size or to principals in communities with a population of 50,000 and over at earlier or later dates is of course problematic; only replication studies can provide answers to questions of this kind.

We believe that the timing of our inquiry was fortuitous because the early 1960s was a period of relative tranquility in sex relations in the United States. The "modern" women's movement was in its infancy and strenuous efforts to obtain *equality* of opportunity for women in the occupational and professional worlds and in other aspects of American life developed later in the decade. Hence the time frame of our inquiry permits us to examine how men and women who occupied the same managerial position behaved and reacted to their work during a period when sex discrimination in the world of work was especially widespread and when attempts to "liberate" women were relatively infrequent.

Another point deserves emphasis. It is empirically problematic whether sex difference findings based on data obtained during one year, for example, 1973, are applicable to a later time period, for example, 1976 given the fast pace of change in American society. This points to the need for replication studies conducted at regular intervals.

3. Alvin W. Gouldner, "Organizational Analysis," in Robert K. Merton, Leonard Broom, and Leonard S. Cottrell, Jr., (Eds.), *Sociology Today* (New York: Basic Books, Inc., 1959), p. 412.

4. National Education Association, *Research Bulletin,* XLIX (October 1971), p. 68. See also *Wanted—More Women in Educational Leadership* (Washington, D.C.: National Education Association, National Council of Administrative Women in Education, 1965), pp. 7–12 and "The Elementary School Principalship—A Research Study," Thirty-seventh Yearbook, *The National Elementary Principal,* Department of Elementary School Principals, National Education Association (1958), p. 110.

5. Suzanne S. Taylor, "Educational Leadership: A Male Domain?", *Phi Delta Kappan* (October 1973), p. 125.

6. See Barter, *op. cit.* Also see Catherine D. Lyon and Terry N. Saario, "Women in Public Education: Sexual Discrimination in Promotions," *Phi Delta Kappan* (October 1973), pp. 120–121.

7. Burleigh B. Gardner, *Human Relations in Industry* (Chicago: Richard D. Irwin, Inc., 1945), p. 269.

8. Margaret Mead and Frances B. Kaplan (Eds.), *American Women* (New York: Charles Scribner's Sons, 1965), pp. 45–46. See also U.S. Department of Commerce, Social and Economic Statistics Administration, Bureau of the Census, *1970 Census of the Population, Industrial Characteristics,* issued January 1973.

9. National Manpower Council, *Womanpower* (New York: Columbia University Press, 1957). It deserves note that women leave and enter the labor force in large numbers and that census data on the employment of women are based on weekly estimates. *Ibid.,* pp. 59–60.

10. *Ibid.,* Chapter 2.

11. *Ibid.,* p. 10.

12. Carl N. Degler, "Revolution without Ideology: The Changing Place of Women in America," *Daedalus* (Spring 1964), p. 661.

13. Mead and Kaplan, *op. cit.,* pp. 45–46. See also U.S. Department of Commerce, Social and Economic Statistics Administration, Bureau of the Census, *1970 Census of Population, Earnings by Occupation and Education,* issued January 1973.

14. National Education Association, "Estimates of School Statistics, 1970–71," *Research Division Report,* pp. 13–14. See also U.S. Department of Commerce, Social and Economic Statistics Administration, Bureau of the Census, *1970 Census of Population, Earnings by Occupation and Education,* issued January 1973.

15. See G. W. Bowman, N. B. Worthy, and S. A. Greyser, "Are Women Executives People?" *Harvard Business Review* (July-August, 1965), p. 22. For a more detailed consideration of the proportion which women constitute of all managerial personnel, see National Manpower Council, *op. cit.,* pp. 124–125.

16. U.S. Department of Commerce, Social and Economic Statistics Administration, Bureau of the Census, *1970 Census of Population, Occupation by Industry,* issued January 1973.

17. National Education Association, *Research Bulletin,* XLIX (October 1971), p. 68.

18. Talcott Parsons, "Age and Sex in the Social Structure of the United States," in *Essays in Sociological Theory* (Glencoe: The Free Press, 1954), pp. 88–103; also Talcott Parsons et al., *Family, Socialization and Interaction Process* (Glencoe: The Free Press, 1955), Chapter 1.

19. Theodore Caplow, *The Sociology of Work* (Minneapolis: University of Minnesota Press, 1954), pp. 234–237.

20. Everett C. Hughes, *Men and Their Work* (Glencoe: The Free Press, 1958), p. 106.

21. Caplow, *op. cit.,* p. 237.

22. *Ibid.,* p. 238.

23. William F. Whyte, *Human Relations in the Restaurant Industry* (New York: McGraw-Hill Book Co., 1948).

24. Caplow, *op. cit.,* p. 239.

25. For the findings of the National Principalship Study on the effects and determinants of the professional leadership of principals, see Neal Gross and Robert E. Herriott, *Staff Leadership in Public Schools* (New York: John Wiley and Sons, 1965). Findings on the determinants and effects of selected dimensions of the principals' administrative performance are presented in Robert Dreeben and Neal Gross, *The Role Behavior of School Principals,* Final Report No. 3, Cooperative Research Project No. 853, April 1963; those on role conflict are reported in Peter C. Dodd, *Role Conflicts of School Principals,* Final Report No. 4, Cooperative Research Project No. 853, October 1965.

26. The breakdown of the 501 schools by actual level included in the total study was: elementary—189; junior high—150; and senior high—162. Principals supervising more than one building as well as first year principals were excluded from the sample.

27. Forty of the 41 school systems participated in this phase of the study.

28. See William J. Goode and Paul K. Hatt, *Methods in Social Research* (New York: McGraw-Hill Book Co., 1952), Chapter 19; and Marie Jahoda, Morton Deutsch, and Stuart W. Cook, *Research Methods in Social Relations* (New York: The Dryden Press, 1951), Chapter 16.

29. Henry F. Kaiser, "The Varimax Criterion for Analytic Rotation in Factor Analysis," *Psychometrika,* XXIII (1958), pp. 187–200; and Henry F. Kaiser, "Computer Program for Varimax Rotation in Factor Analysis," *Educational and Psychological Measurement,* XIX (1960), pp. 413–420.

30. For an excellent treatment of factor analysis, see Harry H. Harman, *Modern Factor Analysis* (Chicago: University of Chicago Press, 1960).

31. See Appendix C for the item means, standard deviations, and factor weights used in arriving at the summary measures of the principals' behavior based on the reports of teachers.

32. See Gross and Herriott, *op. cit.,* Chapter 2.

33. *Ibid.,* Appendix B.

34. For an introduction to the logic and problems of introducing third variables into the analysis of the relationship between two variables, see Patricia L. Kendall and Paul F. Lazarsfeld, "Problems of Survey Analysis," in Robert K. Merton and Paul F. Lazarsfeld (Eds.), *Continuities in Social Research* (Glencoe: The Free Press, 1950), pp. 148–167; also see Hubert M. Blalock, *Social Statistics* (New York: McGraw-Hill Book Co., 1960).

35. Blalock, *op. cit.*

36. *Ibid.*

37. Fred L. Strodtbeck and Richard Mann, "Sex Role Differentiation in Jury Deliberations," *Sociometry,* XIX (1956), pp. 3–11.

2

Personal Characteristics
and Family Background

The similarities and differences in the backgrounds of individuals in the same vocation or in different occupations and professions have long been of interest to sociologists and other social scientists, bearing as they do not only on the study of work, but on questions of social mobility and the relationships among the family, the educational and the occupational systems.[1] Due largely to the sex-typing of occupations, the subjects of most studies that have examined a single occupation or profession have been restricted to one sex. The relatively balanced sex ratio in the elementary principalship at the time we conducted our inquiry permits us to examine an issue infrequently investigated in the sociology of work: in what respects are the backgrounds of men and women who serve in the *identical* managerial position similar and in what ways are they different? More specifically, did the men and women in our inquiry who serve as principals of elementary schools in large American cities differ on the average in their age, marital status, or social class backgrounds? Is there a sex difference in their family backgrounds or in the type of community in which they attended elementary school?

In addition to their relevance to sociological issues, these questions concerned us for two other reasons. First, a number of the hypotheses examined in later chapters are based on assumptions about sex differences in personal and family backgrounds of the principals and it was essential that we find out whether the evidence available from our study supported them. Our second concern was the possibility that findings about sex differences in areas such as reactions to work or role performance might simply be an artifact of personal background characteristics associated with sex. Assume, for example, that it turned out that women principals worry more than men. If the data also revealed that older principals worry more than younger ones and if the women were older than the men, then the relationship between sex and worry might simply be due to the age difference between the men and women. To determine whether this possibility could be discarded or needed to be given serious consideration required evidence about the age difference between the female and male administrators. With this background, we now turn to the findings.

PERSONAL CHARACTERISTICS

Age

The 91 women in our sample of 189 elementary principals were, on the average, older than the 98 men: the mean age of the women was 54.3 years and of the men 49.2 years. Their median ages were 54.1 and 48.5 years, respectively. A comparison of the age distributions of the men and women points up this sex difference more sharply (Figure 2-1). Approximately four-fifths (79%) of the women were 50 years of age or older in contrast to less than one-half (47%) of the men. Over three

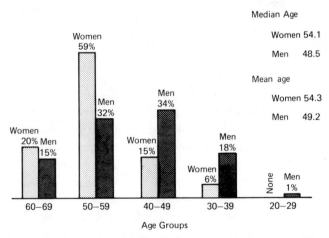

Figure 2-1. Age distribution of women (N = 91) and of men (N = 98) elementary school principals in the study.

times the proportion of the men as the women (19% vs. 6%) were 39 years of age or younger. In an investigation of elementary school principals in 1968, the Department of Elementary School Principals of the National Education Association reported a 13-year difference in the *median* ages of the female and male elementary principals in its sample: the median age of the women supervising principals was 56 and of the men, 43.[2]

Marital Status

The difference in the marital status of the men and women principals in our sample is striking: the men were predominantly married while the women were predominantly single.[3] Over 9 out of 10 of the men were married, but almost two-thirds of the women were single, a difference that exists in all age groups (Table 2-1). Our findings are similar to those Warner reported for high-level civil servants. He found that 65% of the women but less than 5% of the men were not married.[4]

Race

There was only a slight sex difference in the racial characteristics of our sample: 96% of the women in comparison with 92% of the men were white; with one exception, the remainder were black.

FAMILY BACKGROUND

Parents' Birthplace

When we asked the principals about the birthplace of their parents, 76% of the men and 70% of the women reported that both were native-born (Figure 2-2).[5] When we classified their responses by the age and sex of the principals, however, a sex difference finding of considerable interest emerged: for the women principals, a larger proportion of those in the youngest than in the oldest age group had parents who were native-born; in the case of the men, the finding is just the opposite. Ninety-one percent of the youngest versus 63% of the oldest women principals came from families in which both parents were born in the

TABLE 2-1. Percentage Distribution of Marital Status of Women and Men Principals by Age

Marital Status	Age							
	Young (25–45)		Middle (46–55)		Old (56–70)		All Cases	
	Women (N = 11)	Men (N = 37)	Women (N = 37)	Men (N = 32)	Women (N = 43)	Men (N = 29)	Women (N = 91)	Men (N = 98)
Single	64%	8%	57%	3%	67%	4%	63%	5%
Married	27	92	30	97	26	86	27	92
Other (divorced or widowed)	9	–	13	–	7	10	10	3
	100%	100%	100%	100%	100%	100%	100%	100%

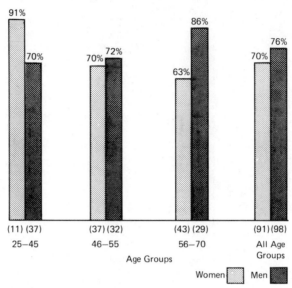

Figure 2-2.   Percentage of native-born parents of women and men principals by age.

United States. Among the men principals, however, 86% of the oldest as compared to 70% of the youngest had native-born parents. These findings indicate that the principalship in recent years has attracted a relatively greater number of sons of foreign-born parents and a relatively smaller number of daughters of parents born abroad.[6]

Socioeconomic Backgrounds

Studies of the medical and academic professions have shown that the women in these vocations tend to come from higher socioeconomic backgrounds than the men.[7] Is there a similar sex difference in the social origins of elementary principals as indexed by their fathers' occupation? Our findings reveal that there is: a greater proportion of women than men principals (51% vs. 36%) had fathers who were in the professions or white-collar occupations; a smaller proportion of the women than the men (30% vs. 38%) had fathers who were blue-collar workers (Table 2-2). Seventeen percent of the women and 22% of the men reported that their fathers' occupation was farming. These findings

TABLE 2-2. Percentage Distribution of the Occupations of the Fathers of Women and Men Principals by Age

| | Age | | | | | | All Cases | |
| | Young (25–45) | | Middle (46–55) | | Old (56–70) | | | |
Father's Occupation	Women (N = 11)	Men (N = 36)	Women (N = 37)	Men (N = 32)	Women (N = 43)	Men (N = 29)	Women (N = 91)	Men (N = 98)
Professional or scientific	18%	6%	22%	16%	23%	10%	22%	10%
Managerial or executive	18	14	16	16	16	14	17	15
Clerical or sales	9	14	19	18	7	–	12	11
White Collar	45	34	57	50	46	24	51	36
Skilled craftsman or foreman, semi-skilled, protective	28	42	22	22	30	31	26	32
Unskilled worker	9	8	5	–	3	10	4	6
Blue Collar	37	50	27	22	33	41	30	38
Farmer	18	11	11	25	21	31	17	22
Other	–	5	5	3	–	4	2	4
	100%	100%	100%	100%	100%	100%	100%	100%

25

are similar to those of other studies that have reported data on the occupations of the fathers of school principals and of teachers, the group from whose ranks principals are recruited.[8]

If we classify the men and women principals by age and then examine their fathers' occupations, we can determine whether this sex difference is a recent or long-standing phenomenon. The findings indicate that for at least a generation the fathers of women principals have engaged, on the average, in occupations that are of higher status than those held by the fathers of the men (Table 2-2). Within each age category, a greater proportion of the women than the men administrators were children of fathers with professional or white-collar backgrounds. For example, 45% of the women principals as compared to 34% of the men in the youngest age group (25–45) had fathers who occupied professional or white-collar positions. In the age group 46–55, the difference between men and women is least pronounced, but the direction of the trend is still the same.

To secure a comparative perspective on our findings about sex differences in the occupational backgrounds of the principals, we compared them with those obtained by Warner in his study of men and women government executives. The data are presented in Table 2-3. Elementary school principals, both men and women, tend to be

TABLE 2-3.   Percentage Distribution of Selected Occupations of the Fathers of Women and Men Principals and of Women and Men Government Executives

Occupation	Principals		Government Executives	
	Women	Men	Women	Men
Professional	22%	10%	34%	25%
Managerial and executive	17	15	18	29
Skilled and unskilled worker	30	38	13	21
Farmer	17	22	14	15

recruited more frequently from families of lower occupational levels than the higher civil servants; furthermore, the government officials came with much greater frequency from families in which the father held middle or upper-status occupations. In addition, the women and men executives in government were much more similar in their "occupational origins" than male and female principals. A greater proportion of the women in the principalship tend to come from lower socioeconomic backgrounds than the women in executive positions in the Federal government (Table 2-3): a smaller proportion of the female principals came from professional families (22% vs. 34%) and a larger proportion from working class homes (30% vs. 13%). The differences in father's occupational status between the men in the principalship and those in government are even sharper: over twice as many Federal executives as principals had fathers with professional or managerial backgrounds (54% vs. 25%); 21% of the Federal executives but 38% of the principals were from working class homes; and 22% of the principals had fathers who were farmers in comparison with 15% of the executives in the Federal government.

If we assume that the principalship has a higher occupational status than that of a clerk, salesman, blue-collar worker, and farmer, then 71% of the men administrators, in contrast to 59% of the women, had experienced upward occupational mobility. That is, they had attained an occupational status higher than that of their fathers'. If we accept a more limited criterion for specifying whether a principal has been upwardly mobile, applying it only to those instances in which their fathers were semiskilled or unskilled workers, then 30% of the women and 38% of the men had been upwardly mobile. Whichever criterion is used, we may conclude that a substantial proportion of the school principals had been upwardly mobile and that a larger proportion of the men than the women had achieved a social status that was higher than that of their parents.[9]

The proportion of the principals with mothers who were or had been teachers provides an index of the extent to which maternal occupational inheritance had occurred among the administrators.[10] Did a greater proportion of the women than the men principals whose mothers had been gainfully employed hold teaching jobs? The answer is yes: almost twice the proportion of the women as the men with employed mothers were children of teachers (46% vs. 24%). Of the total sample of principals,

TABLE 2-4. Percentage Distribution of the Occupations of the Employed Mothers of Women and Men Principals

Mother's Occupation	Women (N = 33)	Men (N = 38)
Teaching	46%	24%
Nursing	–	–
Secretarial	12	13
Sales	6	5
Industrial	6	–
Domestic	30	55
Other	–	3
	100%	100%

17% of the women as compared to 9% of the men had mothers who were teachers (see Table 2-4). In his study of beginning teachers, Mason reported that 10% of the women and 7% of the men had mothers with teaching experience.[11] We conclude that occupational inheritance of this kind occured more frequently among the women than the men administrators and appears to be somewhat greater for principals than for beginning teachers.[12]

In view of our findings about sex differences in fathers' occupations and the fact that occupation and education are positively related, we expected that the level of education completed by the fathers of the female principals would be higher than that obtained by the fathers of the male principals. Table 2-5 bears out this expectation: 28% of the women had fathers who had attended institutions of higher learning in comparison with 17% of the men; 44% of the women's fathers as compared to 32% of the men's fathers had attended or graduated from high school; and 27% of the women, but 49% of the men, reported that their fathers had completed or attended elementary school.

TABLE 2-5. Percentage Distribution of the Education of the Fathers of Women and Men Principals

Father's Education	Women (N = 91)	Men (N = 97)
No formal education	2%	2%
Completed elementary school or some elementary school	27	49
Graduated from high school or some high school	44	32
Some college	9	12
Graduated from college	10	–
Graduate or professional school	9	5
	100%	100%

TABLE 2-6. Percentage Distribution of the Education of the Mothers of Women and Men Principals

Mother's Education	Women (N = 91)	Men (N = 98)
No formal education	5%	3%
Completed elementary school or some elementary school	33	37
Graduated from high school or some high school	45	47
Some college	14	10
Graduated from college	3	2
Graduate or professional school	–	1
	100%	100%

The findings, however, did not reveal a sex difference in the level of education attained by the mothers of the men and women administrators. They indicated that the largest proportion of the mothers of both the men and women principals had attended or graduated from high school: 45% of the women's mothers and 47% of the men's had achieved this level of education (Table 2-6). A similar proportion of the female and male principals' mothers had attended college or engaged in post-high school training: 17% of the women principals' mothers and 13% of the men's.

Parent Income Level

To obtain a general indicator of the economic status of their families when the principals had been adolescents, we asked them, "What was the income position of your parents in *your* community at the time of your graduation from high school?" Table 2-7 reveals that 48% of both the men and women principals classified their families as being in the second lowest of four categories of family income. Forty-two percent of the women and 37% of the men principals reported that their families were in the two highest income categories. The tendency for women principals to come from families of somewhat higher socioeconomic status than the men appears again, although the sex difference in

TABLE 2-7. Percentage Distribution of the Income Position of the Parents of Women and Men Principals at Time of Principal's High School Graduation

Income Position of Parents	Women (N = 90)	Men (N = 98)
Highest 25% of community	9%	12%
Second highest 25% of community	33	25
Third highest 25% of community	48	48
Lowest 25% of community	10	15
	——	——
	100%	100%

TABLE 2-8. Percentage Distribution of Type of Community in Which Women and Men Principals Spent Most of Their Youth by Age

Type of Community	Age						All Cases	
	Young (25–45)		Middle (46–55)		Old (56–70)			
	(N = 11)	(N = 36)	(N = 37)	(N = 32)	(N = 43)	(N = 28)	(N = 91)	(N = 96)
Farm	18%	11%	11%	15%	14%	36%	13%	20%
Small town	27	25	16	22	26	21	22	23
Small city	9	19	11	22	23	14	17	18
Large city	46	45	62	41	37	29	48	39
	100%	100%	100%	100%	100%	100%	100%	100%

this instance is quite small and not as pronounced as in the case of father's occupation and education.

Our findings about the level of education attained by the mothers and fathers of the educational administrators in our sample, along with the findings about the occupation of their fathers and their parent's income, highlights the social mobility that had been experienced by a substantial proportion of both the men and women principals. They also indicate that generally the men's vertical mobility had been somewhat greater than that of the women principals.

Size of Community

Did the men and women who serve as elementary principals grow up in communities of different sizes? The findings show that a slightly larger proportion of the women than the men came from large cities (48% vs. 39%), and that slightly more men than women (20% vs. 13%) spent their youth primarily on farms (Table 2-8). When we classify the men administrators by age and examine the type of community environment in which they grew up, the findings show what could be expected in view of the steady decline of the farm population: the proportion of men principals who grew up on farms had decreased over the years. Thirty-six percent of the men principals who were 56 years or older grew up on farms as compared to only 11% of those in the 25–45 age group. Table 2-8 also reveals that the percentage of male principals who came from large cities had increased: 45% of the youngest, in comparison to 29% of the oldest, men administrators were products of big cities. Among women principals, surprisingly enough, a slightly larger percentage of the youngest than the oldest (18% vs. 14%) had grown up on farms. However, a smaller proportion of the youngest than the oldest women principals had come from small cities. Perhaps the most unexpected finding in Table 2-8 is that the majority of both men and women principals had grown up in urban communities. In view of this finding, and since nearly all of the principals in our inquiry were former teachers, our data raise questions about the validity of the "persistent belief that teachers are drawn heavily from small town and rural communities."[13]

NOTES AND REFERENCES

1. See for example Natalie Rogoff, "The Decision to Study Medicine" and Wagner Thielens, Jr., "Some Comparisons of Entrants to Medical and Law School," in Robert K. Merton, George Reader, and Patricia L. Kendall, *The Student-Physician* (Cambridge: Harvard University Press, 1957), pp. 109–129 and pp. 131–152; also Howard S. Becker et al., *Boys in White* (Chicago: University of Chicago Press, 1961). For a general discussion of the characteristics of recruits to different occupations, see Edward Gross, *Work and Society* (New York: Thomas Y. Crowell Co., 1958), Chapter 5.

2. Department of Elementary School Principals, National Education Association, *The Elementary School Principalship in 1968–A Research Study* (Washington, D.C.: National Education Association, 1968), Table 2, p. 10.

3. The DESP study did not cross-tabulate the marital status of supervising principals in their sample by sex.

4. W. Lloyd Warner et al., *The American Federal Executive* (New Haven: Yale University Press, 1963), p. 187.

5. The same overall pattern of sex differences in nativity is reported by Warner et al.: a larger percentage of the women than the men federal executives had both fathers and grandfathers who were native-born; data concerning nativity changes over time are not presented. *Ibid.,* p. 184.

6. Warner's study of a 1952 sample of business leaders found that 24% were first-generation, indicating that business was at least as accessible as education to this group. (W. Lloyd Warner and James Abegglen, *Occupational Mobility in American Business and Industry* [Minneapolis: University of Minnesota Press, 1955], p. 93.) Janowitz's study of the military suggests that it is much more restricted in nativity and that "there can be no doubt that a long native-born background of many generations has been a distinguishing characteristic of the professional soldier." (Morris Janowitz, *The Professional Soldier* [Glencoe: The Free Press, 1960], p. 85.)

7. Josephine J. Williams, "The Professional Status of Women Physicians" (unpublished Ph.D. dissertation, University of Chicago, 1949) and Jessie Bernard, *Academic Women* (University Park: The Pennsylvania State University Press, 1964), pp. 77–78.

8. See John K. Hemphill et al., *Administrative Performance and Personality* (New York: Bureau of Publications, Teachers College, Columbia University, 1962), p. 65; Ward S. Mason, *The Beginning Teacher: Status and Career Orientations* (Washington: U.S. Government Printing Office, 1961), pp. 11–13; Lindley J. Stiles (Ed.), *The Teacher's Role in American Society* (New York: Harper and Brothers, 1957), Chapters 2–4; and W. W. Charters, Jr., "The Social Background of Teaching," in N. L. Gage (Ed.), *Handbook of Research on Teaching* (Chicago: Rand McNally and Company, 1963), pp. 719–722.

9. A study which directly examines teacher mobility arrived at a similar conclusion: in a comparison of the social class positions attained by teachers and other school system personnel with that of their parents, McGuire and White found that slightly over one-half of the sample had been upwardly mobile. (Carson McGuire and George White, "Social Origins of Teachers—In Texas," in Stiles, *op. cit.,* pp. 23–41.)

10. Since the appropriate response alternative listed in the question on father's occupation for teaching was the category "professional or scientific," we could not determine the proportion of men and women in our sample whose fathers had been educators.

11.   Mason, *op. cit.,* p. 12.

12.   Adams' data on a sample of physicians showed that 12% of them had fathers who were doctors. Taking into account that the omission of fathers who were teachers from the analysis results in underestimating the overall proportion of occupational inheritance, it would seem that education is somewhat similar to medicine in this respect. See Stuart Adams, "Trends in Occupational Origins of Physicians," *American Sociological Review,* XVIII (August 1953), p. 407.

13.   W. W. Charters, Jr., *op. cit.,* p. 719.

3

Educational Backgrounds
and Career Experiences

In this chapter we focus on two additional aspects of the backgrounds of men and women principals that could influence their behavior and attitudes as school administrators: their formal educational experiences and their career histories prior to their appointment to the principalship. In examining the educational backgrounds of the principals we consider the following questions: Is there a sex difference with respect to the type of elementary and secondary schools that the principals attended? Did the women and men differ in their academic performance when they were students? When they were undergraduate and graduate students did they attend similar types of institutions of higher learning? Were there any notable differences in the professional training of the women and the men for teaching or administration?

Later in the chapter we consider several dimensions of the career experiences of the administrators prior to their becoming principals: the amount and type of their teaching experience, the length of time it took them to obtain a principalship, their administrative experience prior to their appointment to an elementary principalship, and the average age of the men and women when they obtained their first principalships. Findings about differences in the educational backgrounds and career experiences of the men and women principals provide data that bear on important issues in the sociology of work and on a number of assumptions involved in hypotheses that are tested in later chapters. They also may be of interest to those concerned with the issue of equal employment opportunities for women at the managerial level. If, for example, the data reveal that it takes women much longer to obtain a principalship than men, this information would support the position of those who maintain that women have frequently been denied equal opportunities in the management of public education.

EDUCATIONAL BACKGROUNDS

Elementary and Secondary Schooling

Both the men and women principals were predominantly products of the type of organizations they managed: 87% of the women and 93% of the men received most of their elementary education in the public schools. Furthermore, 94% of the women and 88% of the men reported that they had attended public secondary schools (Table 3-1).

To obtain an indicator of the overall quality of the principals' academic work when they were secondary school students we asked them: Which of the following phrases ("way above average," "above average," "average," and "somewhat below average") best describes the quality of your academic work when you attended secondary school? The quality of academic performance of the women principals was higher, on the average, than that reported by the men (Table 3-2): 86% of the women, in contrast to 68% of the men, responded that their school work was "way above average" or "above average." In addition, twice the proportion of men as women (31% vs. 14%) described their work as "average." We conclude on the basis of their self-reports that

TABLE 3-1. Percentage Distribution of Type of Elementary and Secondary School Attended by Women and Men Principals

| Type of School | Women | | Men | |
	Elementary (N = 91)	Secondary (N = 91)	Elementary (N = 98)	Secondary (N = 97)
Public	87%	94%	93%	88%
Parochial	12	3	5	5
Private	1	3	2	7
	100%	100%	100%	100%

TABLE 3-2.   Percentage Distribution of Quality of Academic Work in Secondary School of Women and Men Principals

Quality of Academic Work	Women (N = 91)	Men (N = 97)
Way above average	23%	12%
Above average	63	56
Average	14	31
Somewhat below average	-	1
	100%	100%

women principals, on the average, appear to have been the better students. This finding is consistent with one that is frequently cited in the educational psychology literature; in high school, girls generally secure better grades than boys.[1]

Undergraduate Education

The men and women principals attended a variety of institutions of higher learning when they were undergraduates. We now consider three aspects of their experience at college on which we anticipated sex differences: the types of institution attended, number of education courses taken, and quality of their academic performance.

Did the type of undergraduate institutions they attended differ? Our findings indicate they did (Table 3-3). Three major differences can be identified. First, nearly twice the proportion of women as men (60% vs. 31%) had attended state teachers' colleges or normal schools. Second, nearly twice the percentage of men as women attended state universities (24% vs. 13%).[2] Third, twice the proportion of men as women (29% vs. 14%) had been enrolled at private institutions.

When these findings are viewed in combination with the finding that the occupational status of the fathers of the men principals was lower than that of the fathers of the women (see Chapter 2), an interesting issue arises. We have seen that although the socioeconomic status of the

TABLE 3-3.   Percentage Distribution of Type of Undergraduate Institution Attended by Women and Men Principals

Type of Undergraduate Institution	Women (N = 91)	Men (N = 98)
State university	13%	24%
State teachers college or normal school	50	29
Other public college or university	10	16
Private university	11	14
Private teachers college or normal school	1	4
Other private college	2	11
State teachers college and other type of institution	10	2
Other combinations	3	–
	100%	100%

men's families is generally lower than that of the women's, a larger proportion of the men than the women attended private institutions and that nearly twice the proportion of the women as men principals had attended public institutions such as state teachers' colleges and normal schools. The cost of attending private institutions of higher learning, however, is much greater than that of attending public colleges or universities. What might account for this apparent inconsistency? One possibility is that when the principals were of college age, parents assigned greater importance to providing what they consider to be a "superior" college education for their sons than for their daughters, and hence were more willing to make the necessary financial sacrifice to send a son than a daughter to a private institution.[3] A second possibility is that the men more frequently attended private undergraduate institutions than the women because many more of the males than the females had careers other than teaching in mind when they were undergraduates, and thus fewer of the men than the women were attracted to state teachers' colleges. We return to this matter in Chapter 4. A third possibility is that the image of teaching as a woman's profession, and the general acceptance of teachers' colleges as a place to prepare for it, may account for the disproportionate attendance of the women at public institutions.

The number of semester hours of courses in education that the principals completed when they were undergraduate students can be viewed as one measure of their formal preparation for teaching. Table 3-4 shows that the women principals had taken more education courses as undergraduates than the men: over twice as many women as men (51% vs. 25%) had taken more than 40 semester hours of education courses. Furthermore, twice the proportion of men as women (28% vs. 13%) had taken less than 21 hours of courses of this kind. These findings are congruent with one reported earlier: twice the proportion of women as men attended state teachers' colleges or normal schools, institutions whose curricula consisted primarily of courses in education.

We noted earlier that the quality of the academic performance of the women principals was higher than that of the men when they attended

TABLE 3-4. Percentage Distribution of Semester Hours of Undergraduate Education Courses Taken by Women and Men Principals

Semester Hours	Women (N = 86)	Men (N = 97)
None	1%	5%
1 - 10	–	5
11 - 20	12	18
21 - 30	17	30
31 - 40	19	17
41 - 50	13	6
51 - 60	9	6
More than 60 hours	29	13
	100%	100%

TABLE   3-5.   Percentage Distribution of Quality of Undergraduate Academic Work of Women and Men Principals

Quality of Academic Work	Women (N = 91)	Men (N = 98)
Graduated with honors	20%	8%
Above average	63	59
Average	17	32
Somewhat below average	–	1
	100%	100%

secondary school. Did the women principals also outperform the men academically when they attended college? We found that the women's performance, on the average, was superior to the men's: 83% of the women as compared to 67% of the men reported that their academic work in college was "above average" or that they "graduated with honors." Furthermore, almost twice as many men as women (32% vs. 17%) indicated that their work in college was of only "average" quality (Table 3-5).[4]

Graduate Study

Professional study in education at the graduate level constitutes a certification requirement for the principalship in nearly all the states. This circumstance undoubtedly accounts, in large part, for the fact that 188 of the 189 principals reported that they had completed graduate courses in education. In attempting to identify those aspects of their graduate training in which the men and women had been exposed to similarities and differences in their professional socialization experiences, we focused on five aspects of their studies: (1) highest academic degree received, (2) type of institution attended, (3) education courses taken, (4) courses completed in educational administration, and (5) whether they pursued their studies on a part- or full-time basis.

There were only slight differences in the proportion of the men and women principals who had earned a Doctor's or a Master's degree. Only 5% of the men and 3% of the women had been awarded a doctorate. The great majority of both the men and women principals had obtained a Master's degree: 85% of the women and 86% of the men (Table 3-6). The study conducted by the Department of Elementary School Principals reported similar findings: 81% of the men and 76% of the women principals in its investigation held Master's degrees.[5] The fact that a somewhat larger proportion of both the men and women principals in our inquiry were recipients of a Master's degree than the male and female principals in the NEA study probably reflects the circumstance that our study included only principals in large city school systems. A Master's degree is generally a prerequisite for an appointment to the principalship in large urban communities. As Table 3-6 indicates, however, 9% of both the women and men administrators had only earned a bachelor's degree and 3% of the women held a teaching certificate. These findings undoubtedly reflect the low certification requirements for the principalship of certain states prior to World War II.

We have seen that there were important differences in the type of undergraduate institutions that the men and women principals attended. Did they also take their graduate studies at different kinds of institutions? The findings revealed two major differences between men and women in this respect (Table 3-7): first, over twice as many of the men as women principals (41% vs. 19%) pursued their graduate studies at state universities; and second, a larger proportion of women than

TABLE 3-6. Percentage Distribution of Highest Academic Degree Received by Women and Men Principals

Highest Academic Degree	Women (N = 91)	Men (N = 98)
Certificate	3%	0%
Bachelor	9	9
Master	85	86
Doctorate	3	5
	100%	100%

TABLE 3-7. Percentage Distribution of Type of Graduate Institution Attended by Women and Men Principals

Type of Graduate Institution	Women (N = 84)	Men (N = 96)
State university	19%	41%
State teachers college or normal school	9	4
Other public college or university	21	17
Private university	42	29
Private teachers college or normal school	4	5
Other private institution	5	4
	100%	100%

men principals (42% vs. 29%) attended private universities. As Table 3-7 indicates, the proportion of both the men and women who attended other types of institutions as graduate students was very similar.

In view of their career interests and state certification requirements, nearly all of the elementary school principals took their graduate studies in schools or departments of education. Is there a sex difference in the amount of formal training in graduate education that the principals received? The findings, reported in Table 3-8, indicate only minor differences in the total number of graduate education courses taken by the women and men administrators: 68% of the men and 64% of the women reported completing 31 hours or more of graduate education courses. However, one sex difference finding in Table 3-8 should be noted: 32% of the men as compared to 22% of the women took 51 or more hours of graduate courses in education. Since women generally took more education courses as undergraduates than men, this finding may reflect the men's efforts to compensate for their deficiency in this area. It also could indicate the men's stronger desire and preparation for upward mobility, an issue examined in detail in Chapter 14.

Did the men principals also take more work in educational administration during their graduate studies than the women? Table 3-9 shows

TABLE 3-8. Percentage Distribution of Semester Hours of Graduate Education Courses Taken by Women and Men Principals

Semester Hours	Women (N = 86)	Men (N = 96)
None	–	1%
1 – 10	6%	2
11 – 20	10	11
21 – 30	20	18
31 – 40	30	26
41 – 50	12	10
51 – 60	5	16
More than 60	17	16
	100%	100%

TABLE 3-9. Percentage Distribution of Semester Hours of Educational Administration Courses Taken by Women and Men Principals

Semester Hours	Women (N = 89)	Men (N = 97)
None	1%	2%
1 – 10	24	13
11 – 20	39	28
21 – 30	20	31
31 – 40	6	11
41 – 50	3	9
51 – 60	2	1
More than 60	5	5
	100%	100%

TABLE 3-10. Percentage Distribution of Mode of Graduate Study of Women and Men Principals

Mode of Graduate Study	Women (N = 88)	Men (N = 96)
Full-time	6%	20%
Part-time	94	80
	100%	100%

that they did: 57% of the men, but only 36% of the women, completed more than 20 semester hours in administration. This sex difference implies again that during their graduate studies the men were devoting greater efforts to preparing for advancement to administrative positions than the women. Individuals interested in the principalship could especially be expected to concentrate on courses of this kind.

Both the men and women pursued their graduate studies predominantly on a part-time basis. Only 20% of the men and 6% of the women reported that they had taken their graduate work as full-time students (Table 3-10). The sex difference in this connection cannot be explained by the financial support that was available to men from the GI Bill: only 6 of the 19 men involved were eligible for its benefits as veterans. Two reasons probably accounted for why the men undertook more concentrated study than the women. The first was the men's greater desire for occupational advancement. The second is that many of the men had wives who worked and thus they were in a better financial position than the women, most of whom were single, to study on a full-time basis.

CAREER EXPERIENCES

Teaching

Although experience as a teacher is one of the prerequisites for certification for the principalship in nearly all the states, 2 of the 189 principals reported no teaching experience in their occupational histories (see Ta-

ble 3-11). The two "deviants," both men, had obtained their principalships after holding relatively minor administrative positions in the
central office of their school systems. They had been granted permission to take the principal's examination in their school system,
scored high on it, and were later appointed principals.

We had predicted that women who served as elementary school principals would have a greater amount of teaching experience in general,
and also at the elementary level, than men who held this position. The
findings support the prediction that the total years of teaching
experience of the women would be greater than the men's: over half of
the women administrators (51%) but only 14% of the men had taught
16 or more years.[6] Furthermore, 30% of the men, in comparison to 8%
of the women, had less than six years of *total* teaching experience of any
kind. The mean total teaching experience of the women was 15.9 years
and 9.2 years for the men and the difference of 6.7 years is statistically
significant (Table 3-12).

The men and women administrators in our inquiry are responsible
for the management of elementary schools and they differ in many important respects from junior and senior high schools. Therefore, the
amount of prior experience they had as a teacher in elementary schools

TABLE   3-11.   Percentage Distribution of the Career Patterns of Women and
Men Principals Prior to First Principalship ($N = 185$)*

Career Patterns	Women (N = 87)	Men (N = 98)
Never a teacher	0%	2%
Teacher only	45	50
Teacher and in-school administrator	41	39
Teacher and system-wide administrator	10	5
Teacher, in-school administrator, and system-wide administrator	4	4
	100%	100%

*Data unavailable for four of the 189 principals.

TABLE 3-12.   Percentage Distribution of Total Years of Teaching Experience of Women and Men Principals ($N = 187$)*

Total Years of Teaching Experience	Women		Men	
	N	Percent	N	Percent
0 years	0	0%	2	2%
+[			+[	
1 - 5	7	8	27	28
6 - 10	16	18	37	38
11 - 15	21	23	18	18
16 - 20	18	20	9	9
21 - 25	13	15	4	4
26 or more	14	16	1	1
	89	100%	98	100%
Mean years	15.9		9.2	

*Data unavailable for two of the 189 principals.

+In computing chi-square, the first two rows were combined.

$\chi^2 = 40.60$, 5 <u>df</u>, p < .001.[a]

[a]One-tailed <u>p</u> value.

may have a more important influence on their behavior as an elementary principal than the length of their teaching experience in secondary schools. Did the women principals have more teaching experience at the elementary school level than the men? They definitely did: eight times the proportion of women as men (49% vs. 6%) had taught at the elementary school level for 16 years or longer. Furthermore, 34% of the men, as compared to only 3% of the women, had never taught in elementary school at all (Table 3-13). The mean years of elementary teaching experience for the women was 14.7 years and only 4.6 years for the men; the difference of 10.1 years is significant statistically.

Similar findings were reported in the inquiry conducted by the Department of Elementary School Principals of the National Education Association: the median years of experience as an elementary classroom teacher was 15 for women for supervising principals of elementary schools; it was only 5 years for men.[7] This striking difference in the teaching experience of the women and men principals enters into a number of analyses that are presented in later chapters.

Administration

Many administrative positions in school systems are viewed as stepping-stones to the principalship. To individuals who hope to be principals these positions offer them opportunities to become acquainted with the routines and realities of the principal's work. Before becoming prin-

TABLE 3-13. Percentage Distribution of Years of Elementary School Teaching Experience of Women and Men Principals $(N = 187)$*

Years of Elementary Teaching Experience	Women		Men	
	N	Percent	N	Percent
0 years	3	3%	33	34%
1 - 5	10	11	33	34
6 - 10	16	18	18	18
11 - 15	17	19	8	8
16 - 20	22	25	4	4
21 - 25	10	11	2	2
26 or more	11	13	-	-
	89	100%	98	100%
Mean Years	14.7		4.6	

*Data unavailable for two of the 189 principals.

$\chi^2 = 69.26$, 6 <u>df</u>, p < .001.[a]

[a]One-tailed <u>p</u> value.

TABLE 3-14. Percentage Distribution and Mean Years of Experience in In-school Administrative Positions Other Than the Principalship ($N = 187$)*

In-school Administrative Experience	Women (N = 89)		Men (N = 98)	
	Percent	Mean years	Percent	Mean years
Assistant and/or vice-principal	18%	5.6	18%	4.1
Teaching principal	16	4.9	26	5.4
Department head or chairman	–	–	2	4.5
Guidance and counseling	2	9.0	1	2.0
Other in-school administrative positions (junior principal, supervising teacher)	20	4.1	7	2.7
Mean years		5.8		4.9

*Data unavailable for two of the 189 principals.

cipals, 55% of the women and 48% of the men had obtained, in addition to their teaching experience, some form of exposure to administrative tasks. What types of jobs did they hold? How long did they occupy them? Were there any important differences in the experiences of the female and male principals during this phase of their careers?

The administrative positions that the principals had previously occupied in public school systems can be classified in terms of whether their work focused on *in-school* or *system-wide* problems. The data presented in Table 3-14 show that there is no appreciable difference in the proportion of the men and the women who had both teaching and in-school administrative experience (41% of the women and 39% of the men). Table 3-14 reports the in-school administrative positions previously held by the principals and reveals two sex differences of interest: a greater proportion of men than women (26% vs. 16%) had served formerly as teaching principals but almost three times as many women (20%) as men (7%) had served in other in-school administrative positions such as supervisor of teachers or head teacher of a school. The proportion of men and women who had been an assistant or vice-principal was identical—18%. Only a few of the men or women principals had served as department chairmen or had been involved in administrative activities related to guidance and counseling programs. There were only slight differences in the mean number of years that the male and female principals had spent in these administrative assignments and in the proportion of the men and women who had in-school administrative experience of any kind (Table 3-14).

Did the men and women principals differ with respect to the amount of their experience in system-wide positions such as supervisor or resource teacher? Approximately 15% of both the men and the women administrators reported that they had held jobs of this kind. The average length of time that the women were in such positions was 4.6 years; the average for men was 5.3 years (Table 3-15). The sex differences are again quite small in these comparisons.

Length of Time to Achieve the First Principalship

We reported earlier that the women principals on the average had been teachers for a considerably longer period of time than the men. In view

TABLE 3-15. Percentage Distribution of Men and Women Principals Who Had Held System-wide Administrative Positions ($N = 187$)*

System–wide Administrative Experience	Women (N = 89)	Men (N = 98)
Supervisor	7%	3%
Resource or helping teacher	7	3
Superintendent or assistant superintendent in small community	–	4
Supervisor of attendance	–	2
Other	2	1
Mean years	4.6	5.3

*Data unavailable for two of the 189 principals.

TABLE 3-16.   Percentage Distribution of Number of Years between First Educational Job and First Principalship of Women and Men Principals $(N = 187)$*

Years between First Educational Job and First Principalship	Women (N = 87)	Men (N = 98)
0 years	0%	0%
1 - 5	3	15
6 - 10	7	31
11 - 15	23	17
16 - 20	14	20
21 - 25	26	11
26 or more	27	6
	100%	100%

*Data unavailable for two of the 189 principals.

of this difference in their occupational histories, we would expect that the period of time that elapsed between the women's appointments to their first teaching job and their selection as a principal would be much greater than that for the men. This expectation is supported by the evidence presented in Table 3-16: over four times the proportion of men than women (46% vs. 10%) were appointed principals within 10 years after their initial appointment as a teacher. Furthermore, 63% of the men, in comparison with 33% of the women, became principals within 15 years after entering teaching. Even more striking is the finding that 27% of the women, as compared to 6% of the men, waited 26 years or more after obtaining their initial teaching position before being appointed to their first principalship.

Age at First Becoming Principal

In view of the findings just presented, we would expect that women on the average were considerably older than the men at the time they secured their first principalships. The women definitely were: over twice the proportion of women as men (39% vs. 15%) were 46 years old or older when they first became a principal (Table 3-17). Furthermore, over twice the proportion of men than women (42% vs. 20%) were 35 years of age or younger when they first became a principal. The same overall pattern of sex differences in the age at which principals received their initial appointment was noted in the study conducted by the Department of Elementary School Principals: "Among men supervising principals 67 in 100 were first appointed when they were less than 35 years of age; among women supervising principals 61 in 100 were first appointed when they were between 35 and 49 years of age."[8]

Experience in the Principalship

Is the gender of the administrators related to their length of service in the principalship or the number and types of these positions they held?

First, we consider the total number of years that the men and women

TABLE 3-17. Percentage Distribution of Age of Women and Men Principals on Assuming First Principalship ($N = 187$)*

Age on Assuming First Principalship	Women (N = 89)	Men (N = 98)
21 – 25	1%	3%
26 – 30	5	15
31 – 35	14	24
36 – 40	22	25
41 – 45	19	18
46 – 50	31	12
51 or older	8	3
	100%	100%

*Data unavailable for two of the 189 principals.

TABLE 3-18.   Percentage Distribution and Mean Number of Years the Women and Men Principals Had Served in the Principalship ($N = 187$)*

Total Years in All Principalships	Women (N = 89)	Men (N = 98)
1 - 5 years	24%	30%
6 - 10	26	26
11 - 15	20	21
16 - 20	19	9
21 - 25	5	8
26 or more	6	6
	100%	100%
Mean number of years in all principalships	11.9	11.0

*Data unavailable for two of the 189 principals.

administrators had served in any type of principalship (Table 3-18). The findings indicate that the women had served as principals slightly longer than the men: the mean years of service for the women was 11.9 and 11.0 for the men. Table 3-18 also reveals that a somewhat larger proportion of the men than the women (30% vs. 24%) had been principals for fewer than 6 years and that a greater proportion of women than men (19% vs. 9%) had served in this capacity for 16 to 20 years. In comparison to the sex difference in the teaching experience of the administrators, the difference in the length of service of the men and women in the principalship is relatively small.

What about their present principalships? Is there a sex difference in the length of time they had been in their present jobs? The findings show that the women had served in their present principalship somewhat longer than the men (Table 3-19). The women's length of service was 8.2 years; for the men, it was 6.9 years.[9] Fifteen percent of the women as compared to 8% of the men had been principal of their present school for 16 years or longer. However, 54% of the men in comparison with 40% of the women had held their present position for less than 6 years.

Are there sex differences in the number and types of principalships that the men and women held during their educational careers? Table 3-20 shows that 57% of the men and 54% of the women were serving in their first principalship. Forty-five percent of the female administrators and 33% of the males who had held a previous principalship reported that their earlier position was also at the elementary school level. Ten percent of the men, as compared to only 1% of the women, reported some type of former involvement with the administration of secondary schools. The findings also revealed that the men and women differed only slightly with respect to the number of years they had served as a school principal prior to assuming their present position. The prior

TABLE 3-19. Percentage Distribution and Mean Number of Years in Present Principalship of Women and Men Principals ($N = 187$)*

Number of Years in Present Principalship	Women (N = 89)	Men (N = 98)
1 – 5 years	40%	54%
6 – 10	32	26
11 – 15	12	12
16 – 20	13	2
21 – 25	–	2
26 or more	2	4
	100%	100%
Mean number of years in present principalship	8.2	6.9

*Data unavailable for two of the 189 principals.

TABLE 3-20.   Percentage Distribution and Mean Number of Years in Principal-ships Held Prior to Present Position by Women and Men Principals ($N = 187$)*

Type of Principalship	Women (N = 87)	Men (N = 98)
No previous principalship	54%	57%
Elementary	45	33
Junior High School	–	–
High School	–	1
Elementary and Junior High School	1	–
Elementary and High School	–	5
Junior High School and High School	–	–
Elementary, Junior High and High School	–	4
	100%	100%
Mean number of years served in other principalships prior to present position	3.9	4.0

*Data unavailable for two of the 189 principals.

experience of the men in the principalship was 4.0 years; for the women, it was 3.9 years.

NOTES AND REFERENCES

1.   Anne Anastasi, *Differential Psychology* (New York: The Macmillan Company, 1958), pp. 492–496.

2.   The difference between the proportion of men and women who attended private universities and private teachers' colleges was quite small; both of these categories include only a minority of the total sample.

3.   Our examination of the type of undergraduate institution attended by men according to their age revealed that the subsidization of college attendance by the GI Bill, which would have minimized the effect of the financial factor, does not account for this difference. The distribution of type of undergraduate school attended by men in the "young"

group, which would have been most affected by the GI Bill, showed that few had been in attendance at private institutions.

4.   In a study of the career plans and aspirations of a national sample of June 1961 college graduates, Davis reported that of the students planning to enter education, the women were more likely to get good grades. See James A. Davis, *Undergraduate Career Decisions,* NORC Monograph in Social Research No. 2 (Chicago: Aldine Publishing Co., 1964), p. 87.

5.   DESP study, *op. cit.,* Table 16, p. 24.

6.   In the DESP study, the median years of experience as a classroom teacher was not presented by sex. See *The Elementary School Principalship in 1968—A Research Study* (Washington, D.C.: National Education Association, 1968), p. 21.

7.   DESP study, Table 12, p. 20.

8.   DESP study, p. 13.

9.   In the DESP study, this was also the case: the median number of years the women had been in their present positions was eight years, the men, five years. See DESP study, *op. cit.,* Table 14, p. 22.

4

The Decision to
Become a Teacher

The career line in public education is structured so that those who serve as principals of elementary schools will have faced two key career decisions: the selection of teaching as a vocation and the decision to become a principal.[1] In this and the next chapter, we focus on sex differences in the timing, context, and motivation of choice with respect to these two career decisions. In this one, we consider the decision to enter teaching.

THE TIMING OF THE DECISION

During our interviews with the elementary men and women principals, we asked them when they had initially considered teaching as a possible career and when they had made their final decision to become a teacher. Because teaching is generally thought of as a woman's occupation and is more attractive in remuneration and prestige to women than to men,[2] we had predicted that the women would have both considered and chosen teaching as a career earlier than the men. Do the findings support these predictions?

They do: the data showed that on the average, the women administrators had thought of teaching as a vocation much earlier in their lives than the men. Almost two-thirds of the women (65%) stated that the idea of becoming a teacher first occurred to them while they were in elementary school; only one-tenth (11%) of the men said they had considered it at such an early time. Furthermore, 44% of the men, but only 10% of the women, informed us that they had not given consideration to teaching as a possible vocation until they were in, or had completed, college (Table 4-1).

56

Did the women principals generally also make the *final decision* to become a teacher earlier than men? Again, the answer is definitely "yes". Seventy-six percent of the women, but only 27% of the men, indicated that they had made a firm decision to become a teacher by the time they had completed high school. Furthermore, only 7% of the women, in contrast to 42% of the men, reported that they did not finally decide on teaching until their junior or senior year in college or later (Table 4-2).

It needs to be emphasized that these findings refer only to the considerations and decisions of the principals about a specific vocation—teaching—and not to their early deliberations about careers in general. Thus, while the men considered teaching much later on the average than did the women, the men may have considered *other* types of occupations earlier than the women.

TABLE 4-1. Time at Which Men and Women Principals Initially Considered Teaching as a Career ($N = 177$)*

Time of Initial Consideration	Women		Men	
	N	Percent	N	Percent
Grammar school	54	65%	10	11%
High school — freshman or sophomore year	4	5	10	11
High school — junior or senior year	17	20	26	28
Between high school and college	–	–	6	6
College — freshman or sophomore year	5	6	27	29
College — junior or senior year	2	2	8	9
After college	2	2	6	6
	84	100%	93	100%

*Data unavailable for 12 of the 189 principals.

$\chi^2 = 61.47$, 6 <u>df</u>, p < .001.[a]

[a]One-tailed <u>p</u> value.

TABLE 4-2.   Time at Which Men and Women Principals Made Final Decision to Become a Teacher ($N = 180$)*

	Women		Men	
Time of Final Decision	N	Percent	N	Percent
Grammar school	13	15%	3	3%
High school -- freshman or sophomore year	9	11	2	2
High school -- junior or senior year	43	50	21	22
Between high school and college	1	1	8	9
College -- freshman or sophomore year	14	16	21	22
College -- junior or senior year	1	1	23	25
After college	5	6	16	17
	86	100%	94	100%

*Data unavailable for nine of the 189 principals.

$\chi^2 = 34.21$, 6 df, $p < .001$.[a]

[a]One-tailed p value.

ATTRACTION TO TEACHING

Although teaching has been only one of a large number of professions open to men, it has been one of the few that has been readily accessible to women. Because of the relatively higher status of teaching as a vocation for women than for men, we predicted that the women principals would have been more strongly attracted to it than the men administrators. As indices of its attractiveness, we used two types of data. The first had reference to the strength of the appeal that teaching in comparison to other vocations had for the principals as indexed by whether teaching had been their first choice occupation. The second concerned the extent to which teaching had held little attraction for them when they decided to enter it. In short, we employed both positive and negative indicators of attractiveness.

The principals' responses to the question, "What really was your first choice occupation?" provided support for the prediction: 80% of the women, but only 46% of the men, replied that teaching had been their first choice occupation (Table 4-3). The men who gave a profession or occupation other than teaching as their first choice generally gave professions with a higher status than teaching: 21% mentioned medicine and 10% responded that they had wanted to be lawyers. The first choice preferences of women for whom teaching was not their initial choice covered a range of occupations. They most frequently mentioned law; 5% gave this response.[3]

We asked those principals who stated that they had preferred a vocation other than teaching, "Why did you enter teaching if it wasn't your first choice as an occupation?" Since only a small minority of the women responded that teaching was not their first choice occupation, we consider only the responses of the men to this question. The reason they most frequently gave was "lack of money" (63%) either to prepare for or to enter the preferred occupation (Table 4-4). The critical importance of financial considerations for their occupational decision is indicated by these typical responses:

M-88:   It was a depression and jobs were scarce in those days. I was trained for a draftsman and couldn't continue my education due to financial problems. I answered an ad for a teacher of industrial arts in

TABLE 4-3. Percentage of Women and Men Principals Who Reported That Teaching Was Their First-Choice Occupation ($N = 188$)*

Teaching Reported as First-choice Occupation	Women		Men	
	N	Percent	N	Percent
Teaching first-choice	73	80%	45	46%
Teaching not first-choice	18	20	52	54
	91	100%	97	100%

*Data unavailable for one of the 189 principals.

$\chi^2 = 23.04$, 1 df, $p < .001$.[a]

[a]One-tailed p value.

TABLE 4-4.   Reasons Reported by 51 Men Principals for Not Entering Their First-Choice Vocation

Reason Reported by Principal	Percent Who Mentioned
Lack of money to prepare for or to enter preferred occupation	63%
Lack of employment opportunities	10
Lack of requisite aptitudes or abilities	12
Limited opportunities for advancement in preferred occupation	6
Lack of adequate guidance	2
Other reasons	7

_____ and to my surprise I was accepted. I had no intention of becoming a teacher.

M-64: My mother was a six-day a week domestic. She literally scrubbed the way of her children through college. I wanted to be a surgeon but it was clear that I would not be able to become one because of lack of money. I had no father, and therefore no financial support. I thought the next best thing to do, since I liked to work with people, would be to become a teacher.

M-83: I would have gone into medicine, but I simply didn't have the money.

M-67: I wanted to become a lawyer or a writer but I didn't have the money for either of these activities so I decided to choose a temporary occupation until I could get through law school. And so I chose teaching.

M-79: I got out of college very young, and I was not old enough to start medical school which represented my first love. So I took a master's degree in the teaching of science and started to teach and then stayed in. It was necessary and important to keep my teaching job. Four years of medical school looked tough because it was so expensive, and the money that was already coming in was a considerable help to my family.

The men principals also cited other reasons, for example, lack of opportunities for advancement or employment in their first choice occupation and inadequacies in their aptitudes and skills. However, less than 10% mentioned circumstances of this kind.

Next, we turn to the second indicator of the principals' attraction to teaching: whether they mentioned that they had little motivation to enter teaching when discussing their decision to enter the field. Fifty-nine percent of the men but only 22% of the women gave responses of this kind during their interviews (Table 4-5). The findings, in short, clearly support our prediction that women principals were more strongly attracted to, and more highly motivated to, enter teaching than the men administrators.

TABLE 4-5. Percentage of Men and Women Principals Who Reported Not Being Highly Motivated to Enter Teaching ($N = 188$)*

Reported Not Being Highly Motivated	Women		Men	
	N	Per Cent	N	Per Cent
Yes	20	22%	57	59%
No	71	78	40	41
	91	100%	97	100%

* Data unavailable for one of the 189 principals.

$x^2 = 26.39$, 1 df, $p < .001$.[a]

[a]One-tailed p value.

PERSONAL INFLUENCES

The influence of "significant others" may constitute an important factor in the making of career and other important decisions. Again, because of the different evaluations of teaching as a vocation for men and for women, we predicted that the women principals would receive more encouragement to enter it than the men principals.

In exploring the social context of this career decision, we asked the principals, "Are there any persons who especially encouraged you in your decision?" Contrary to our expectation, only a slightly larger percentage of the women than the men administrators (80% vs. 73%) gave an affirmative reply to this question (Table 4-6). The difference in the proportion of female and male principals who replied "yes" is not significant statistically.

On the assumption that specific individuals, for example, parents or teachers, could have served as "significant others" for the principals in their early career deliberations, we also asked them to specify the particular types of persons who had encouraged them to enter teaching. Their responses to this question indicated that the types of encouragement that had been received by the female and male principals varied

TABLE 4-6. Percentage of Women and Men Principals Who Reported That They Had Received Special Encouragement to Enter Teaching ($N = 188$)*

Received Special Encouragement	Women		Men	
	N	Per Cent	N	Per Cent
Yes	73	80%	71	73%
No	18	20	26	27
	91	100%	97	100%

* Data unavailable for one of the 189 principals.

$x^2 = 1.29$, 1 df, $p > .05$.[a]

[a]One-tailed p value.

TABLE 4-7.   Percentage of Women and Men Principals Who Reported Specified
Sources of Encouragement for Their Decision to Become a Teacher ($N = 188$)*

Sources of Encouragement	Women (N=91)	Men (N=97)
Family	75%[a]	51%[a]
Mother	21	11
Father	6	9
Both parents	28	6
Wife/husband	--	7
Other relatives	15	16
Family in general	9	7
Professional	35%[a]	45%[a]
Teacher	25	18
Professor or college teacher	6	11
Principal	1	6
Superintendent	4	5
Other professionals	1	8
Friends	4%	10%

* Data unavailable for one of the 189 principals.

[a] Responses do not add to category total since some respondents mentioned
more than one source of encouragement.

in three major respects. First, over twice as many of the women as the
men (55% vs. 26%) reported that they had been encouraged to become
teachers by one or both parents (Table 4-7). Evidently the image that
their parents held of teaching predisposed them to view it as a more ac-
ceptable vocation for young women than young men. Second, the findings showed that a larger proportion of the men than the women (45%
vs. 35%) reported that they had received encouragement to enter teaching from one or more persons in the educational profession. Third, a
slightly larger proportion of the women than the men administrators
reported that they had been encouraged to enter teaching by school
teachers, while a greater proportion of the men than the women stated
that professors and other persons in higher education had urged them to

become teachers. The third finding probably reflects in part the fact that a substantially larger proportion of the men than the women made the decision to enter teaching during or following their undergraduate years.

We now turn to the other side of the coin: attempts that had been made to discourage the principals from entering teaching. On the basis of the assumption that teaching is generally viewed as a vocation that is more suitable for women than men, we predicted the men would have been discouraged from entering teaching more than the women. The findings supported the prediction: a significantly larger proportion of the men than the women reported being discouraged (31% vs. 14%) (Table 4-8).

Were the men and women principals discouraged from becoming teachers by the same types of individuals? Table 4-9 shows that they were. Both the men and the women mentioned the same three kinds of individuals in discussing attempts that had been made to dissuade them from entering teaching: family members, professional educators, and friends. Although the proportion of principals who mentioned any specific source of discouragement is relatively small, the findings show that a greater proportion of the men than the women reported exposure

TABLE 4-8. Percentage of Women and Men Principals Who Reported Being Discouraged from Entering Teaching.

Reported Being Discouraged	Women		Men	
	N	Per Cent	N	Per Cent
Yes	13	14%	30	31%
No	78	86	67	69
	91	100%	97	100%

* Data unavailable for one of the 189 principals.

$x^2 = 7.34$, 1 df, $p < .01$.[a]

[a]One-tailed p value.

TABLE 4-9.   Percentage of Women and Men Principals Who Reported Specified Sources of Discouragement for Their Decision to Become a Teacher ($N = 188$)*

Sources of Discouragement	Women (N=91)	Men (N=97)
Family	8%	15%
Professionals	3	9
Friends	2	10

* Data unavailable for one of the 189 principals.

to discouragement from family members, professional educators, and friends.

DISCUSSION

The findings revealed that (1) women in the principalship both considered and chose teaching as their vocation earlier than the men; (2) teaching as a career had been more attractive to the women than the men administrators; and (3) men were more frequently discouraged from entering teaching than the women. Contrary to our prediction, the findings did not indicate that the women received more encouragement than men to become teachers from members of their social networks. They did reveal, however, that the women received more encouragement from their parents to enter teaching than the men.

The striking differences between the men and women administrators in the timing of, and the motivation for, their decisions to enter teaching raise two interesting questions: first, did the men principals who were late deciders about becoming teachers possess less academic ability than the "early deciders"?; second, are there other circumstances, in addition to the different prestige of teaching as an occupation for females and males, that could account for its greater attractiveness to the women than the men?

There is an old questionable saying, "Those who can, do; those who can't, teach." Does this aphorism apply to the late deciders, particularly the men principals for whom teaching was a reluctant choice? More specifically, among the men principals were those who belatedly turned to teaching less academically able than the ones who indicated a relatively early interest in it? If this turned out to be the case, it would suggest that they lacked the academic talents required to engage in the occupation or profession that had been their first choice. Perhaps the reason they most frequently gave for not pursuing their first-choice vocation, financial limitations, was simply a rationalization for their academic limitations. To explore this matter, we compared the high school academic reports of those men who had evinced a relatively early interest in teaching with those who had considered it much later as a vocational possibility (Table 4-10). The findings indicate that among the men in our sample, those who considered teaching relatively late, that is, during college or after graduation from college, had better academic records on the average than those who had indicated an earlier interest in it. We conclude that among the late deciders, their belated consideration of teaching was probably not attributable to their inadequate scholastic achievement[1] and their academic abilities were not inferior to the early deciders.

TABLE 4-10.   Time at Which Men Principals Initially Considered Teaching as a Vocation by High School Grades ($N = 93$)*

| High School Grades | Time of Initial Consideration | | | |
| | Before College | | During/After College | |
	N	Per Cent	N	Per Cent
Above average	32	62%	32	78%
Average or below	20	38	9	22
	52	100%	41	100%

* Data unavailable for five of the 98 male principals.

$x^2 = 2.93$, 1 df, p > .05.[a]

[a]Two-tailed p value.

We now inquire about circumstances, in addition to the differential status of teaching as an occupational pursuit for females and males, that may have a bearing on the greater attractiveness of teaching as a vocation for the women than the men administrators.

One possible circumstance is suggested by Thielens' discussion of early identification with occupational roles.[5] He maintains that familiarity or contact with a professional or occupational role facilitates early commitment to it. He argues that one of the reasons that medical students generally have an earlier commitment to their profession than law school students is that students in medical school have contacts with doctors much earlier than law students have any relationships with lawyers. The socialization process in medical school, in short, is ". . . a matter of direct experience and knowledge to a greater extent . . ."[6] than in law school. On the basis of this reasoning, we would expect that the men and the women administrators would have made a commitment to teaching at approximately the same time since they had the same degree of contact and familiarity with teachers. But, as noted, this was not the case. We suggest that our findings imply that the way individuals *evaluate* the status of occupations or professions may be as important, or perhaps more important, than early contact with individuals associated with them in influencing the timing of vocational decisions.

A second circumstance that can be invoked to account for the different sentiments that the men and women principals held toward teaching is the gender of the role models they encountered when they attended school. Elementary schools have long been staffed primarily by women, whereas the sex ratio is more nearly equal in secondary schools. From our knowledge about the process of psychosocial development and identity-formation in children and adolescents,[7] we would expect that children would primarily identify with role models of the same sex as their own. The sex ratio among teachers in the elementary school undoubtedly results in an early interest in teaching on the part of girls. The fact that boys are exposed to relatively few male teachers results in their having few positive role models with which to identify. These conditions could largely explain why most of the women but so few of the men said that the idea of teaching first occurred to them in elementary school. Many women principals probably chose teaching as a "fantasy choice" in the primary grades, inspired by the example of numerous models of the same sex, and in time it developed into their actual choice. We might also speculate that the "compulsive" masculinity norm for boys of elementary school age may have led most of them to respond in a neutral or negative manner to their women teachers and to stereotype teaching as "women's work."

What accounts for the selection of teaching, rather than some other occupation or profession, as the option chosen by those principals, especially the men, who did not pursue their primary vocational interest? We offer the following explanation: Teaching is an easily accessible vocation for those individuals who enter college and later find it difficult or impossible either to pursue their initial objectives or to make decisions about their plans for the future. Education, in contrast to medicine or law, does not require a highly specialized course of preparation or training.

It deserves note that at the time many of the principals in our study were launching their careers, standards of licensing or certifying teachers were lax, and in some states they were nonexistent. A college degree or normal school certificate was the only formal requirement for a teaching position in some regions of the country. A college student could make the decision to become a teacher in his final undergraduate years or even after graduation with little difficulty due to the ease of entry into the educational profession. A belated decision to enter medicine or law, however, would have entailed greater difficulties because of the more stringent requirements for admission to medical and law school.[8] Thus education was, and still is, an easily entered profession. It constituted an especially attractive alternative for those principals who could not pursue their primary vocational interests, since it required little or no specialized training and permitted late deciders to enter its ranks with ease.

The findings suggest a multifaceted explanation of the differences between the men and women principals in the timing and mode of their decisions to enter teaching. The relatively low financial return and prestige of elementary school teaching, combined with its image as a preeminently woman's occupation and the relative scarcity of male models for boys in the elementary school, led most men principals initially to consider seriously professions and occupations commanding higher income and prestige. Then reality and situational circumstances, in part financial in nature, exerted a crucial influence on their vocational decisions. They were required to rethink their vocational plans and this process led to their belated consideration and choice of teaching as a vocation. Teaching was their occupational choice largely because it required no highly specialized prerequisites for study and training.

The situation was quite different for the women principals. In frequent contact, from elementary school on, with teachers of the same sex who could serve as role models, and influenced by the view that teaching is an excellent profession for a woman, they evaluated teaching more favorably than men as a vocation and identified themselves much earlier with it. The influence and persuasion of their parents and teachers reinforced their positive orientation to educational employment, and in consequence, they considered and then decided on teaching as their vocational choice much earlier than men.

NOTES AND REFERENCES

1.   It deserves note that principals do not invariably make their career decisions in this order. Mason et al., report that 51% of the men in their first year of teaching expected ". . . to continue in the field of education until retirement, but . . . move from classroom teaching into some other area of education eventually." (See Ward S. Mason et al., "Sex Role and the Career Orientations of Beginning Teachers," *Harvard Educational Review,* XXIX (1959), p. 374.) In addition, our own data indicate that 10% of the men considered the principalship before they were 21 and 43% before they were 26.

2.   For a discussion of the differential importance of careers to men and women in our society, see Talcott Parsons, "Age and Sex in the Social Structure of the United States," in *Essays in Sociological Theory* (Glencoe: The Free Press, 1954), pp. 89–103; and Talcott Parsons et al., *Family, Socialization and Interaction Process* (Glencoe: The Free Press, 1955), Chapter 1, especially pp. 12–15. Concerning probable differences between men and women in the prestige of teaching as a profession, see C. C. North and Paul K. Hatt, "Jobs and Occupations: A Popular Evaluation," in Reinhard Bendix and Seymour M. Lipset (Eds.), *Class, Status, and Power* (Glencoe: The Free Press, 1953), pp. 411–425; and Lucille Baudler and D. G. Paterson, "The Social Status of Women's Occupations," *Occupations,* XXVI (1948).

3.   Of the 54% of the men whose preferred occupation was not teaching, their first choices were engineering (4%), chemistry, physics, or related areas (2%), medicine (21%), law (10%), journalism (4%), business (6%), scholarly work (4%), and miscellaneous occupations (3%). Of the 20% of the women whose first choice of an occupation was not teaching, the preferred occupations were chemistry, physics, or related areas (1%), medicine (1%), law (5%), nursing (2%), business (3%), scholarly work (1%), and miscellaneous occupations (7%).

4.   It is interesting to note that if we had used the 10% rather than 5% level of statistical significance, we would have concluded that there was a significant difference between the two groups in favor of the late deciders.

5.   Wagner Thielens, Jr., "Some Comparisons of Entrants to Medical and Law School," in Merton et al., *op. cit.,* p. 136.

6. *Ibid.*

7. Talcott Parsons, "Family Structure and the Socialization of the Child," in Parsons et al., *op. cit.*, pp. 35–131; and Erik H. Erikson, *Childhood and Society* (New York: W. W. Norton Co., 1955), *et passim.*

8. For a more detailed discussion of the effect of entrance requirements on the timing of career decisions, see Thielens, *op. cit.*, pp. 139–143.

5

The Decision to
Become a Principal

We direct attention in this chapter to the phase of the career histories of the 189 male and female principals in which they deliberated about, and then made, the decision to become an elementary school principal. First, we inquire if there was a sex difference in terms of the age at which the administrators gave initial consideration to leaving teaching for the principalship. Then, we turn our attention to the circumstances that motivated the men and women to seek an administrative post and attempt to identify the major forces and factors that influenced their deliberations. Finally, we present findings about the type of individuals who encouraged and discouraged the administrators to become principals.

THE TIMING OF THE DECISION

We predicted that after the administrators made the decision to enter teaching and had secured positions as teachers, the men would give earlier consideration to the possibility of becoming a principal than the women on the assumption that the men would be more concerned about occupational advancement than would the women. Since a move from a teaching position to the principalship represents a step upward in both status and income in the pyramidal structure of school districts, we reasoned that the greater importance attached to occupational mobility and increased income by the males would have predisposed the men to give serious thought to becoming a principal sooner than the women.

The findings revealed support for the prediction: 43% of the men but

only 13% of the women reported that they had given serious consideration to the principalship by the time they were 25 years old. Furthermore, they indicated that over twice as many men as women (74% vs.
35%) reported that they had given serious thought to such a career
move by the age of 30 (Table 5-1). Moreover, the data show that 91% of
the men, but only 59% of the women, had entertained the idea by the
time they had reached the age of 35.[1]

In the case of the principalship, then, the situation is the opposite of
the one that we found for teaching: the women administrators gave

TABLE 5-1.   Age at Which Women and Men Principals Reported They First
Considered Becoming a Principal $(N = 172)$*

Age	Women		Men	
	N	Per Cent	N	Per Cent
20 or under	3	4%	9	10%
21 – 25	7	9	30	33
26 – 30	18	22	28	31
31 – 35	20	24	15	17
36 – 40	14	17	5	6
41 – 45	15	18	2	2
46 – 50	3	4	1	1
51 and over	+[2	2	+[--	--
	82	100%	90	100%

* Five women and one man responded that they never considered the
   principalship before they were asked to become a principal.
   Data were unavailable for four women and seven men.

+ In computing chi-square, these categories were combined.

x^2 = 36.40, 6 df, p < .001.[a]

[a]One-tailed p value.

serious consideration to teaching much earlier than did the men but the men administrators had evinced interest in the principalship much earlier than did the women. The earlier interest of the men in the administrative role is especially noteworthy in view of the finding, reported in Chapter 4, that the men generally decided to become teachers at a much later age than the women.

MOTIVATION

To determine whether there were sex differences in the administrators' motivations for seeking the principalship, we had asked them to tell us in their own words why they had wanted to become a principal. In responding to the question, most of the men and women administrators gave several reasons. An analysis of their replies indicated that they could be classified into eight categories: financial reasons, desire for upward mobility, greater service to education, possession of abilities "to do the job," influenced or persuaded by others, attractive aspects of the principal's role, disliked aspects of teaching, and accidental reasons or no clear motivation.

As noted earlier, our prediction that the men would give earlier consideration to the principalship than the women was based on two assumptions: that the men would have greater interest in both professional advancement and in increasing their income than would the women. In examining whether the motivations of men and women for seeking the principalship differed, we initially consider the findings bearing on these two assumptions.

The data required to test the first one, that the men had a greater interest in professional upward mobility than the women, are reported in Table 5-2. The findings support the assumption: a greater proportion of the men than the women (36% vs. 23%) reported that their interest in the principalship reflected their desire for professional advancement. The sex difference of 13% in their responses is significant statistically.

To illustrate how the men administrators described their concern for professional advancement, we present brief excerpts from two of the interviews:

M-216:   It was the only possible chance for advancement. I was as far as I could go.

TABLE 5-2.   Percentage of Women and Men Principals Who Reported Upward Mobility as a Reason for Wanting to Become a Principal ($N = 187$)*

| | Women | | Men | |
Mentioned Upward Mobility	N	Per Cent	N	Per Cent
Yes	21	23%	35	36%
No	69	77	62	64
	90	100%	97	100%

* Data unavailable for two of the 189 principals.

$x^2 = 3.59$, 1 <u>df</u>, p < .05.[a]

[a] One-tailed <u>p</u> value.

M-482:   This is the ultimate goal of any young man who goes into teaching. I started to prepare for it in my second year of teaching. I think I wanted to reach the highest point of achievement.

Our findings also offered support for the assumption that the men would place greater stress on increased income as a motivating condition for seeking the principalship than the women. Over twice as many men as women (51% vs. 23%) cited financial reasons (Table 5-3). The importance attributed by the men to the income factor is suggested by these representative responses:

M-196:   At that time it was money—there was more money [in administration] than in teaching.

M-350:   First and foremost [it was] a matter of economics.

To this point we have focused on the reasons that were disproportionately given by the men as motivating conditions for seeking the principalship. We have seen that the men administrators gave greater weight than did the women to the need for increased income and professional advancement as reasons for their desire to become a principal. What about the other side of the coin? Did the women place greater stress than the men on any of the motivating circumstances that were mentioned? The data presented in Table 5-3 indicate that the female administrators disproportionately gave two types of responses. First, they reported much more frequently than the men that other individuals had influenced their decision or persuaded them to become school principals: 54% of the women versus 26% of the men cited this motivating condition. We consider the specific types of individuals who influenced them later.

Second, a larger proportion of the women than the men (35% vs. 23%) stated that they never had felt a strong desire to become a principal or that they had become one due to "accidental circumstances." Three responses of women principals who gave this type of reply are

TABLE 5-3.   Percentage Distribution of the Responses of Women and Men Principals to the Question: Why Did You Want to Become a Principal? ($N = 187$)*

Reasons for Desiring a Principalship	Women (N=90)	Men (N=97)
Financial	23%[a]	51%[a]
Upward mobility	23	36
Greater service to education	19	21
Ability to do job	27	28
Influence or persuasion of others	54	26
Accidental reasons, no clear motivation	35	23
Enjoyment of administrative tasks	37	41
Negative aspects of teaching	11	6

[a] Responses do not add to 100% since respondents frequently mentioned more than one reason.

* Data unavailable for two of the 189 principals.

presented:

W-436:   I never thought of becoming a principal. In my second year of teaching the principal became ill. The superintendent and the supervisor asked me to take over as acting principal. I was kind of pushed into it. I did not want to be one. I accepted under strong encouragement from my aunt and school officials.

W-337:   The superintendent offered me the job. . . . If the offer hadn't come, I would still be teaching.

W-383:   My principal had a serious illness and I took over her office. She died during the year and I kept the office that year. I was pushed in by accident—and liked it.

Table 5-3 also shows that there were only slight sex differences with respect to these motivating conditions: desire to offer greater service to education, belief in ability to do the job, attractive aspects of the principal's work, and unattractive aspects of teaching.

Were the motivating conditions most frequently mentioned by the men the same as those most often reported by the women administrators? The reasons most frequently mentioned by the men for wanting to become a principal were financial considerations (51%), enjoyment of administrative tasks (41%), and a desire for professional advancement (36%). Those cited by the women were: other persons felt that they would make good principals (54%), enjoyment of administrative tasks (37%), and accidental circumstances (35%).

These findings also indicate that one of the highly important motivating circumstances for seeking the principalship of both the men and women was the gratification that they believed they would derive from performing the tasks of a principal. In addition, they disclose that two of the three motivating conditions that the male principals reported as being most salient to them—the desire for increased remuneration and for professional advancement—were of less importance to the women principals. Furthermore, the findings show that two of the three circumstances that the women most frequently described as influencing their desire to become principals—influence or persuasion by others and accidental reasons—were less frequently mentioned by men. We conclude from this set of findings that the motivations that prompted the men and women to seek the principalship were similar in certain respects, but different in others.

Personal Influences: Encouragement and Discouragement

We expected that the women administrators would report that they had received greater encouragement than the men to become principals because of their exposure to negative sentiments that generally prevailed, prior to the sixties, with respect to women assuming managerial positions. When the women administrators were deliberating about the principalship, the work of supervising subordinates, regardless of their level of skills, had been formally or informally reserved for men because of reasons related to the structure and content of sex roles in the family and occupational spheres.[2] There were, of course, some women in such positions but they were, as they still are today, a small minority of the women in the world of work. We further assumed that this condition would predispose the women to turn away from administrative positions, even if they felt that they had the capabilities to perform them and would enjoy that type of work. What circumstances would serve as countervailing forces to their assumed reservations about becoming an administrator? We reasoned that it most probably would be the support, encouragement, and urging of colleagues and superiors who had a high regard for their capabilities.[3] This possibility raises the question of whether the women were encouraged or persuaded more frequently than the men to seek the principalship. The findings indicate that they were. A significantly larger proportion of the women than the men (89% vs. 78%) reported encouragement (Table 5-4). Furthermore, as reported earlier in this chapter, twice as many women as men (54% vs. 26%) cited the influence or persuasion of others as an important factor in their decision to become a principal (Table 5-3). The study conducted by the Department of Elementary School Principals reported a similar type of finding: over three times as many women as of men (56% vs. 17%) mentioned the encouragement of the superintendent's office as their primary reason for becoming a principal.[4]

Were the kinds of persons who urged the men and women to become principals essentially similar? When the principals identified the "significant others" who influenced their decision to teach, both the men

TABLE 5-4. Percentage of Women and Men Principals Who Reported That They Had Been Encouraged to Become a Principal ($N = 188$)*

Reported Being Encouraged	Women		Men	
	N	Percent	N	Percent
Yes	81	89%	76	78%
No	10	11	21	22
	91	100%	97	100%

* Data unavailable for one of the 189 principals.

$x^2 = 3.87$, 1 df, p < .05.[a]

[a] One-tailed p value.

and women most frequently cited their parents as sources of encouragement. However, in making up their minds about whether to become a principal, both the male and the female administrators cited most frequently professional kinds of support and encouragement (Table 5-5). The findings also reveal differences in the frequency with which the men and women noted educators and their families as encouraging them to seek the principalship: 88% of the women in constrast to 71% of the men cited professional educators; 32% of the men, only 20% of the women, mentioned members of their family.

Table 5-5 indicates only slight differences in the proportion of men and women who reported encouragement by teaching colleagues, their school superintendent, or professors. However, 64% of the women in comparison with 51% of the men reported encouragement from their immediate superior, the principal of their school, and over five times as many women (32%) as men (6%) reported that "other higher administrators," generally curriculum supervisors or staff specialists, urged them to become a school principal. Both the women and men, then, were encouraged primarily by professionals; the men, however, were encouraged more frequently by their families than the women.

On the assumption that the exercise of authority by women was generally frowned on when the administrators were considering whether to seek a principalship, we predicted that the female principals would have been exposed to greater discouragement from their friends and associates about making such a career decision than the males. The evidence, however, did not support this expectation (Table 5-6). Although a greater proportion of the women than the men reported that they had been discouraged to become a principal (26% vs. 17%), the difference is not statistically significant.

Who had discouraged them? Twenty-one percent of the women and 14% of the men mentioned professional educators. The particular group within this category that they most frequently named as discouraging them from seeking the principalship was their fellow teachers (Table 5-7); 12% of the women and 5% of the men reported efforts by teachers to dissuade them from becoming a school principal.

TABLE 5-5. Percentage of Women and Men Principals Who Reported Specified Sources of Encouragement for Their Decision to Become a Principal ($N = 188$)*

Sources of Encouragement	Women (N=91)	Men (N=97)
Family	20%[a]	32%[a]
One or both parents	6	6
Wife/husband	3	24
Other relatives	6	3
Family in general	7	3
Professionals	88%[a]	71%[a]
Teachers	13	12
Principal	64	51
Superintendent	15	14
Other higher administrator	32	6
Professor or higher educator	8	11
Other professional	4	3
Friends	4%	4%

[a] Responses do not add to category total since some respondents mentioned more than one source of encouragement.

* Data unavailable for one of the 189 principals.

TABLE 5-6. Percentage of Women and Men Principals Who Reported Being Discouraged from Becoming a Principal ($N = 188$)*

	Women		Men	
Discouraged from Becoming a Principal	N	Per Cent	N	Per Cent
Yes	24	26%	16	17%
No	67	74	81	83
	91	100%	97	100%

* Data unavailable for one of the 189 principals.

$x^2 = 2.70$, 1 df, p > .05.[a]

[a]One-tailed p value.

TABLE 5-7. Percentage of Women and Men Principals Who Reported Specified Sources of Discouragement for Their Decision to Become a Principal ($N = 188$)*

Sources of Discouragement	Women (N=91)		Men (N=97)	
Family	3%		1%	
Professionals	21%		14%	
Teachers		12		5
Principal		4		3
Others		5		6
Friends	5%		1%	

* Data unavailable for one of the 189 principals.

NOTES AND REFERENCES

1. A similar pattern of sex difference findings is reported by Mason. See Ward S. Mason et al., "Sex Role and the Career Orientations of Beginning Teachers", *Harvard Educational Review,* XXIX (Fall 1959), pp. 370–383.

2. Theodore Caplow, *The Sociology of Work* (Minneapolis: University of Minnesota Press, 1954), pp. 238–246.

3. Margaret Cussler, *The Woman Executive* (New York: Harcourt Brace and Co., 1958), pp. 17–26.

4. DESP study, Table 7, p. 14.

6

Criteria for Evaluating
Schools and Teachers

In a provocative essay on organizational leadership, Selznick noted the widespread tendency for executives ". . . to divorce means and ends by overemphasizing one or the other."[1] He argues that formal leaders who focus on means and slight the more complex problems of defining ends place undue emphasis on efficiency or routine decisions. It is his contention that this type of orientation, administrative management, defines the major problem of leadership as linking existing means to *given* ends. Selznick maintains that the "true province of leadership involves critical decisions that influence the fundamental character and mission of an organization. Those who manage enterprises go beyond efficiency only when they establish their basic goals and then develop social arrangements to accomplish them."[2]

Selznick's observations suggest the importance of determining how executives in education define the missions of their organizations and the roles of their key subordinates. In this chapter we explore these issues by examining how women and men in the principalship assess different criteria that can be used in evaluating the performance of their schools and their teachers. The criteria used by principals in assessing their schools and teachers, we assume, reflect the way they define the missions of their schools and their expectations for the performance of their faculty, and thereby influence the functioning of their organizations.

CRITERIA FOR EVALUATING SCHOOLS

The strategy we used to ascertain the importance principals attributed to a number of possible criteria that could be used in evaluating their organizations was as follows: they were asked during their interviews to assume that they had been appointed to a committee to evaluate *a school such as their own* and that its members had prepared a list of 25 possible criteria to assess it. The principals were requested to specify for each criterion: "How much importance do you believe this criterion should be given?" The response categories were "great," "some," "little," or "no importance."

The twenty-five questions to which they responded were designed to tap four general types of criteria that could be used in evaluating a school: concern for individual differences among pupils, the academic performance of pupils, the proportion of pupils who engage in deviant behavior, and concern for the social and emotional development of pupils. When the responses of the administrators to the specific criteria were factor-analyzed, five factors emerged. Four of them reflected the assessment criteria noted above. The fifth contained items that reflected the ability of a school to maintain pupil discipline, and we gave it this designation. We computed factor scores for each principal on each of the five evaluation criteria on the basis of the weights derived from the loadings of items included in each individual factor. These summary measures are used to test our hypotheses about differences in the emphasis men and women principals give to the criteria in evaluating their schools.

Differences among Individual Pupils

As professional educators, principals and teachers are enjoined to disregard differences in their pupils' race, socioeconomic status, religion, and ethnicity. However, they are also urged to give special attention to the differences in the aptitudes and abilities of their pupils and to develop each child's potential to the full extent of his capacities. The effort made by schools to conform to these expectations varies enormously; some give them little more than lip service while others have adopted them as basic norms. Do the men and women principals differ in the importance they attribute to a school's concern for individual differences as a criterion for assessing its performance?

Our hypothesis was that women in the principalship would ascribe greater importance than would the men to the school's obligation to take into account individual differences. It was based on the assumption that women, more than men, tend to emphasize an expressive orientation in relating to others whereas men, more than women, tend to stress an instrumental orientation in their social relationships. We then reasoned that the diffuse and personal emphasis which defines the expressive orientation—analogous to the wife-mother mode of interaction with family members—would result in women in the principalship giving special recognition and emphasis to the school's obligation to take account of the individual differences among its pupils whereas men would attribute less importance to it.

To test this hypothesis we used the factor score, Concern with Individual Differences among Pupils. The data on which the factor score is based were obtained from the replies of the principals about the degree of importance they attributed to the four following evaluative standards:

1. The degree to which special provisions are made for the "slow learner."
2. The degree to which special provisions are made for the "gifted child."
3. The degree to which teaching materials, in addition to textbooks, are being used.
4. The degree to which students work up to their capacities.[3]

When we compared the mean scores of the female and male administrators on this index of Concern for Individual Differences, the findings supported the hypothesis: the mean factor score obtained by the women is higher than that of the men (10.10 vs. 9.91) and the difference in their scores is statistically significant (Table 6-1).

This sex difference finding holds up with a high degree of consistency under various subgroupings of the principals (Table 6-2). The findings show that in all regions and in schools of varying size, the women, on the average, place greater emphasis on concern with individual differences among pupils as a school assessment criterion than the men principals. When we compare the mean factor scores of the men and women administrators whose schools were composed of pupils with the same average socioeconomic backgrounds, the findings indicate that women consistently obtain higher scores than the men. When we subclassify the principals by age and marital status, we come to similar conclusions. Of the 18 subcomparisons reported in Table 6-2, 17 are in the predicted direction. The one exception arises in the comparison made in cities of 1,000,000 or over. The mean scores of the men and women in this instance are nearly the same. We conclude that women in

TABLE 6-1. Mean Scores of Women and Men Principals on Concern with Individual Differences among Pupils as a Criterion for Evaluating Schools ($N =$ 185)*

Sex	Mean Score	Standard Deviation	Number of Cases
Women	10.10	0.61	87
Men	9.91	0.82	98

* Date unavailable for four of the 189 principals.

t = 1.83; p < .05.

general attribute greater importance than do men to a school's concern for individual differences among its pupils as a criterion for assessing the "goodness" of a school.

Academic Performance of Pupils

Two widely accepted goals of schools are to prepare children ". . . to be motivationally and technically adequate to the performance of adult roles."[4] To achieve them, pupils must be exposed to and learn bodies of knowledge and skills in various subject matter fields. The academic success of pupils is a generally accepted standard for evaluating their performance and that of their schools. In view of the widespread belief in the legitimacy and validity of this assessment criterion,, the hypothesis we tested was that men and women principals would not differ in the importance they attribute to the academic performance of pupils as a basis for judging their schools.

To test this null hypothesis, we used a factor score that had been developed from the principals' responses to the degree of importance they assigned to the following four evaluative standards included in the School Assessment Criteria Instrument:

1. The success of former students in whatever educational institutions they go to next.

TABLE 6-2.   Mean Scores of Women and Men Principals on Concern with Differences among Individual Pupils by Six Specified Subclassifications of Schools.

Subclassifcation#	Women			Men			Direction Predicted Correctly (+) or Incorrectly (−)
	Mean	S.D.	N	Mean	S.D.	N	
Region							
West	9.83	0.73	13	9.58	0.81	20	+
Midwest	10.21	0.46	24	9.98	0.79	30	+
East	10.08	0.70	32	10.00	0.88	19	+
South	10.21	0.43	18	9.99	0.74	29	+
Size of City							
Small	10.14	0.52	43	9.91	0.86	49	+
Medium	10.05	0.76	32	9.77	0.82	30	+
Large	10.11	0.47	12	10.12	0.62	19	−
Size of School							
Small	10.04	0.68	33	9.98	0.63	30	+
Medium	10.11	0.53	35	10.04	0.88	27	+
Large	10.20	0.62	19	9.77	0.87	41	+

See Appendix A for the definition of the subclassification categories.

2.   The proportion of students who eventually go on to college.

3.   The degree of student mastery of subject matter fundamentals.

4.   The achievement test scores of students.[5]

The mean factor scores of the men and women principals are presented in Table 6-3. The findings indicate that the mean factor score of the men (10.16) was slightly lower than that of the women principals (10.27) (low factor score = high score on assessment of the academic achievement criterion); however, the difference of 0.11 is not significant statistically. We therefore conclude that there is no significant dif-

TABLE 6-2. (*Continued*)

Subclassification#	Women			Men			Direction Predicted Correctly (+) or Incorrectly (-)
	Mean	S.D.	N	Mean	S.D.	N	
Socio-economic Level							
Low	10.23	0.50	28	9.97	0.76	35	+
Middle	10.02	0.79	26	9.84	0.85	35	+
High	10.06	0.52	33	9.92	0.83	28	+
Age of Principal							
Young	10.13	0.57	11	9.96	0.74	37	+
Middle	10.07	0.48	36	9.82	0.90	32	+
Old	10.13	0.72	40	9.93	0.79	29	+
Marital Status of Principal							
Married	10.21	0.52	23	9.93	0.82	90	+
Single	10.07	0.63	55	9.45	0.71	5	+
Other	--	--	9	--	--	3	*

See Appendix A for the definition of the subclassification categories.

* No comparison made when number of cases in smaller category is less than five.

ference in the importance men and women principals assign to the academic achievement criterion.

It will be recalled that in responding to the School Assessment Criteria Instrument, the principals were asked to use as their frame of reference "a school such as their own." Although we found no sex difference in the importance principals on the average assign to the academic performance criterion, men and women could differ in this respect under certain conditions.

A characteristic of schools that is highly and positively associated with the academic attainment of their pupils is the socioeconomic status (SES) of their families. This relationship implies that children

TABLE 6-3.   Mean Scores of Women and Men Principals on Importance Attributed to Academic Performance of Pupils as a Criterion for Evaluating Schools ($N = 185$)*

(Low Score = High Importance)

Sex	Mean Score	Standard Deviation	Number of Cases
Women	10.27	0.80	87
Men	10.16	0.72	98

* Data unavailable for four of the 189 principals.

t = 1.04; p > .05.

who come from low SES families experience greater difficulties in learning than those from families of higher SES. We assumed that since the women principals had greater teaching experience than the men, they would be better equipped and more able to deal with the learning problems and disabilities of children than the men administrators. In view of this circumstance, we reasoned that the male principals would be more predisposed than the women to accept the lowering of academic standards for low SES schools. Thus we thought that the female administrators would emphasize academic achievement more than the men would when the average SES of the pupils in their schools was relatively low.

To explore this possibility, we examined the mean factor scores of the men and women who served as principals of schools in which the average SES backgrounds of their pupils were relatively low for the sample. The findings, presented in Table 6-4, did not support our reasoning. The men, not the women, obtained the lower mean score in low SES schools (10.27 vs. 10.50; a low score reflects a high assessment on the academic performance criterion). The difference in their scores, however, was not significant statistically. We also examined the mean scores of the men and women principals who were in charge of schools with pupils whose SES backgrounds were average or relatively high for our sample. In schools with an "average" SES rating, the men had lower scores than the women (10.26 vs. 10.51); however, the difference of 0.25 was again not statistically significant. In schools with a relatively high SES rating, the mean scores of the men and women were almost identical.[6] We conclude that female and male administrators in charge of schools with pupils from similar socioeconomic backgrounds do not differ in the importance they assign to academic performance as a criterion for assessing them.

Concern for the Social and Emotional Development of the Child

The extent to which schools should take responsibility for the social and emotional development of the child has become a controversial issue in recent years. The controversy does not center on whether the school

TABLE 6-4. Mean Scores of Women and Men Principals on Importance Attributed to Academic Performance of Pupils for Two Specified Subclassifications of Schools

(Low Score = High Importance)

Subclassification*	Women		Men			Probability Less than
	Mean	N	Mean	N	t	
Socio-economic Level						
Low	10.50	28	10.27	35	1.40	n.s.
Middle	10.51	26	10.26	35	1.25	n.s.
High	9.90	33	9.89	28	0.02	n.s.
Competence of Staff						
Low	10.62	23	10.26	27	1.68	n.s.
Medium	10.25	30	10.23	36	0.07	n.s.
High	10.01	32	10.00	35	0.02	n.s.

* See Appendix A for the definition of the subclassification categories.

should completely eliminate this objective from its tasks. Most educators and laymen would probably subscribe to the idea, for example, that an elementary school should be charged with the task of instilling "proper" attitudes in its pupils about their responsibilities as citizens of the school community. This embraces things such as ". . . respect for the teacher, consideration and cooperativeness in relation to fellow-pupils, and good work-habits as fundamentals, leading on to capacity for 'leadership' and 'initiative.'"[7] One point of contention is related to the circumstance that institutions other than the school, for example, the family and the church, have a deep interest in the child's social and emotional growth and development and the schools, on occasion, have trespassed on "their turf." A second is that many parents and educators believe that the schools have assumed too many "auxiliary" functions, and in consequence, are inadequately performing their academic tasks. Others argue that developments such as the large expansion in the number of working mothers with children of elementary school age, declining church membership, and the increase in juvenile delinquency require that the school assume greater responsibility for certain of the socialization functions formerly performed by the church and the family. Do women and men in the elementary principalship differ in the importance they attribute to the school's concern for the social and emotional development of pupils?

Our hypothesis was that women principals would place heavier weight on this criterion than would men. It was based on the same line of reasoning we used earlier in this chapter when we predicted a sex difference on the criterion, Concern for Individual Differences among Pupils. We anticipated that because of the expressive emphasis of the feminine role with its diffuse and personal orientation to social relationships and the instrumental orientation of the masculine role with its greater specificity and impersonalism, women on the average would give greater weight than the men to their school's obligation to promote their pupils' social and emotional development.

The factor score, Concern for Social and Emotional Development of Pupils, was derived from the beliefs of the principals about the importance they attributed to three evaluative criteria:

1. The degree to which students exhibit *emotional* maturity.
2. The degree to which students exhibit *social* maturity.
3. The degree of tolerance toward fellow students of differing social backgrounds exhibited by students.[8]

The findings of our investigation offer support for the hypothesis. The mean factor score of the women was 10.27 and that of the men 10.05, and the difference of 0.22 is significant statistically (Table 6-5). Women principals, on the average, place greater weight than do men principals on concern for the social and emotional needs of pupils as a criterion for assessing their schools.

This sex difference finding reappeared in most of the subclassifications of the data that we examined (Table 6-6). It was internally replicated when we classified the principals by size of their school, size of city, age, marital status, and by their evaluation of the competence of their staffs. The predicted sex difference in the mean factor scores of the male and female principals also occurs in three of the four regions and in schools with pupils of low and average SES. In 19 of the 21 subclassifications presented in Table 6-6, the mean score of the women on the factor, Concern for Social and Emotional Development of Pupils, was higher than the men's. The two exceptions occur in the East and in schools with pupils from relatively high SES families.

Discipline of Pupils

Teaching and learning in the elementary school primarily take place in group settings. If teachers cannot maintain order in their classrooms and exercise some degree of control over their young pupils, learning will suffer, classroom activities will be disrupted, and the work of others impaired. The maintenance of order, then, is a basic prerequisite for the

TABLE 6-5. Mean Scores of Women and Men Principals on Concern for the Social and Emotional Development of the Child as a Criterion for Evaluating Schools ($N = 185$)*

Sex	Mean Score	Standard Deviation	Number of Cases
Women	10.27	0.72	87
Men	10.05	0.89	98

* Data unavailable for four of the 189 principals.

t = 1.84; p < .05.

TABLE 6-6. Mean Scores of Women and Men Principals on Concern for the Social and Emotional Development of the Child for Seven Specified Subclassifications of Schools

Subclassification#	Women			Men			Direction Predicted Correctly (+) or Incorrectly (-)
	Mean	S.D.	N	Mean	S.D.	N	
Size of City							
Small	10.29	0.64	43	9.92	0.96	49	+
Medium	10.16	0.83	32	10.15	0.75	30	+
Large	10.48	0.62	12	10.22	0.87	19	+
Size of School							
Small	10.23	0.81	33	9.97	0.82	30	+
Medium	10.24	0.70	35	9.91	0.97	27	+
Large	10.41	0.57	19	10.20	0.86	41	+
Age of Principal							
Young	10.23	0.55	11	9.84	1.06	37	+
Middle	10.49	0.49	36	10.26	0.76	32	+
Old	10.09	0.87	40	10.08	0.72	29	+
Marital Status of Principal							
Married	10.41	0.59	23	10.06	0.92	90	+
Single	10.25	0.78	55	9.70	0.39	5	+
Other	--	--	9	--	--	3	*

See Appendix A for the definition of the subclassification categories.
* No comparison made when number of cases in smaller category is less than five.

TABLE 6-6.   *(Continued)*

Subclassification#	Women			Men			Direction Predicted Correctly (+) or Incorrectly (-)
	Mean	S.D.	N	Mean	S.D.	N	
Competence of Staff							
Low	10.08	0.89	23	9.92	1.13	27	+
Medium	10.23	0.70	30	9.94	0.79	36	+
High	10.50	0.52	32	10.26	0.73	35	+
Region							
West	10.17	0.97	13	9.97	0.70	20	+
Midwest	10.28	0.62	24	9.83	0.86	30	+
East	10.24	0.71	32	10.26	1.09	19	-
South	10.39	0.65	18	10.20	0.84	29	+
Socio-economic Level							
Low	10.29	0.76	28	9.95	1.06	35	+
Middle	10.38	0.64	26	10.01	0.75	35	+
High	10.17	0.74	33	10.22	0.79	28	-

See Appendix A for the definition of the subclassification categories.

enactment of the core activities of the school. Because of the critical importance of the maintenance of discipline for purposes of learning and teaching, we did not anticipate a sex difference on this assessment criterion for the entire sample. Therefore, we tested the null hypothesis.

We used the factor score, Ability to Maintain Pupil Discipline, to test it. The factor score was based on the importance the principals attributed to the following three items as assessment criteria:

1. The degree to which teachers are able to maintain discipline in their classes.
2. The degree to which students have respect for the teachers.
3. The degree to which students exercise self-discipline.[9]

The findings provide support for the null hypothesis. The mean score of the women administrators is only slightly higher than that of the men and the difference is not statistically significant (Table 6-7).

Although elementary men and women principals in general do not give different weight to the importance of discipline as a standard for judging their schools, male and female administrators who serve in schools located in low SES areas may differ in this respect since the maintenance of discipline in schools of this kind can create special difficulties for women principals. To explore this line of speculation we sorted out the men and women principals whose pupils on the average came from relatively low SES backgrounds and compared the mean factor scores of the men and women principals. The findings reveal that in these schools the difference between the mean scores of the men and women principals was relatively small and it was not significant statistically (Table 6-8). We then examined the mean factor scores of the male and female administrators whose schools contained pupils of average SES backgrounds; again, the difference in their mean factor scores was not significant statistically. We next turned our attention to the schools with pupils from the highest SES families. The findings revealed that for schools with this type of pupil population, the women principals placed greater emphasis than did the men on the school's ability to maintain discipline. The mean score for the female principals was 10.17 as compared to 9.73 for the male principals and the difference of 0.44 is significant statistically.[10] We conclude that for schools

TABLE 6-7.   Mean Scores of Women and Men Principals on Ability to Maintain Pupil Discipline as a Criterion for Evaluating Schools ($N = 185$)*

Sex	Mean Score	Standard Deviation	Number of Cases
Women	10.04	0.62	87
Men	9.91	0.81	98

* Data unavailable for four of the 189 principals.

t = 1.23; p > .05.

TABLE 6-8. Mean Scores of Women and Men Principals on Ability to Maintain Pupil Discipline by Socio-economic Level of School

Subclassification*	Women		Men		t	Probability Less than
	Mean	N	Mean	N		
Socio-economic Level						
Low	10.11	28	10.02	35	0.53	n.s.
Middle	9.81	26	9.95	35	0.75	n.s.
High	10.17	33	9.73	28	2.23	.05

* See Appendix A for the definition of the subclassification categories.

with pupils from families of relatively high SES, women principals attribute greater importance than do men to the maintenance of discipline as a criterion to assess schools.

Pupil Deviant Behavior

Some pupils in nearly every school exhibit behavior that is at marked variance with its norms. The forces or conditions that account for their deviant behavior are frequently complex and may include factors such as an unstable family environment, deviant norms of a peer group, physiological impairments, or psychological problems. Some principals hold the view that, regardless of their essential causes, the school still must accept some blame for the deviant and disruptive behavior of its pupils. They contend that if teaching in a school is dull or of poor quality or if its curriculum is "meaningless" to children, then the school itself is partly responsible for the behavioral problems of its pupils. Other school administrators do not share this view. They assert that the school should not be held accountable for such behavior, since the fundamental conditions contributing to and engendering deviance lie beyond its area of influence. Do men and women in the principalship differ in the importance they attribute to the criterion, the extent of deviant behavior in a school, as a basis for evaluating their school?

The factor, Extent of Frequency of Pupil Deviant Behavior, allows us to explore this question. It contains the following items:

1. The proportion of students engaging in vandalism.
2. The proportion of students who are constant discipline problems.
3. The amount of student truancy.
4. The proportion of students who cheat.[11]

The findings indicate that women in the principalship on the average place greater emphasis on this criterion for evaluating schools than men: the mean factor score for women was 9.88 and for men 10.13 (a low factor score equals high evaluation of the criterion), and the difference between the mean scores is significant statistically (Table 6-9).[12]

Does this sex difference hold up regardless of the socioeconomic composition of the pupils in their schools? The answer is *yes*; when we subclassified the men and women principals into three groups according to the socioeconomic backgrounds of their pupils, the finding for the total sample is internally replicated in each category (Table 6-10). A similar conclusions is reached when we sorted the principals by their marital status and age. The findings persist in three of the four regions, the one exception being the West. Another exception occurred in medium-sized cities: in this instance, too, men had higher scores on this assessment criterion than women (Table 6-10). We conclude that

TABLE 6-9.   Mean Scores of Women and Men Principals on Extent of Pupil Deviant Behavior as a Criterion for Evaluating Schools ($N = 185$)*

(Low Score = High Emphasis)

Sex	Mean Score	Standard Deviation	Number of Cases
Women	9.88	0.77	87
Men	10.13	0.84	98

* Data unavailable for four of the 189 principals.

t = 2.07; p < .05.

TABLE 6-10. Mean Scores of Women and Men Principals on Emphasis They Place on Extent of Pupil Deviant Behavior for Six Specified Subclassifications of Schools

(Low Score = High Emphasis)

Subclassification#	Women			Men			Direction Predicted Correctly (+) or Incorrectly (−)
	Mean	S.D.	N	Mean	S.D.	N	
Region							
West	10.06	0.65	13	9.79	0.82	20	−
Midwest	9.84	0.71	24	10.29	0.84	30	+
East	9.96	0.85	32	10.39	0.76	19	+
South	9.69	0.76	18	10.04	0.81	29	+
Size of City							
Small	9.75	0.80	43	10.28	0.84	49	+
Medium	9.97	0.68	32	9.84	0.81	30	−
Large	10.14	0.81	12	10.22	0.78	19	+
Socio-economic Level							
Low	9.72	0.66	28	9.99	0.60	35	+
Middle	10.08	0.69	26	10.09	0.88	35	+
High	9.87	0.88	33	10.37	0.98	28	+

#See Appendix A for the definition of the subclassification categories.

TABLE 6-10.   *(Continued)*

Subclassification#	Women			Men			Direction Predicted Correctly (+) or Incorrectly (-)
	Mean	S.D.	N	Mean	S.D.	N	
Competence of Staff							
Low	10.05	0.75	23	10.13	0.72	27	+
Medium	9.76	0.62	30	10.13	0.74	36	+
High	9.95	0.88	32	10.13	1.01	35	+
Marital Status of Principal							
Married	9.65	0.62	23	10.13	0.84	90	+
Single	9.94	0.81	55	10.24	0.93	5	+
Other	--	--	9	--	--	3	*
Age of Principal							
Young	9.77	0.58	11	10.09	0.77	37	+
Middle	9.92	0.82	36	9.96	0.77	32	+
Old	9.89	0.78	40	10.38	0.94	29	+

See Appendix A for the definition of the subclassification categories.

* No test made when number of cases in smaller category is less than five.

women in the principalship generally attribute greater importance than do men to the extent of deviant pupil behavior as an assessment criterion for evaluating their schools.

CRITERIA FOR THE EVALUATION OF TEACHERS

Most large city school systems require that the performance of their teachers be assessed periodically. The responsibility for conducting these evaluations is usually assigned to principals since they are the immediate administrative superiors of teachers. These evaluations are designed to accomplish several purposes, including obtaining information to determine if a teacher on probation or one new to the system should be granted tenure, and encouraging or stimulating high standards of practice by experienced teachers.

We now turn to the views of men and women principals about two criteria for assessing teachers' performance: their technical skills and their conduct with reference to their nonteaching obligations to their schools.[13] The first criterion focuses on the teachers' professional capabilities with special reference to the way they perform in their classrooms; the second focuses on the nonclassroom responsibilities of teachers as members of a school faculty.

Technical Skills of Teachers

Do women and men principals differ in the importance they attribute to the technical skills of teachers in their evaluation of them? Our hypothesis was that the women principals would stress this criterion more than the men. We assumed that the women administrators had greater teaching experience at the elementary level than the men,[14] and therefore the women, more than the men, would be more aware of, and have more knowledge about, the instructional skills of their teachers and how these competencies can influence pupil learning. Hence, we expected that the women would attribute greater importance to the technical skills of teachers as an assessment criterion than would the men.

A factor analysis of the responses of the principals to the items in a Criteria for Evaluating Teachers Instrument yielded a three-item factor, Technical Skills of Teachers. The items in this criterion were as follows:

1. Ability to make subject matter interesting to students.
2. Comprehensiveness of lesson plans.
3. Knowledge of subject matter.[15]

A comparison of the mean factor scores of the men and women principals supports the hypothesis: the mean score of the women was higher than that obtained by the men (10.22 vs. 9.94), and the difference of 0.28 is statistically significant (Table 6-11).

This sex difference is internally replicated in nearly all of the

TABLE 6-11. Mean Scores of Women and Men Principals on Importance Attributed to the Technical Skills of Teachers as a Criterion for Evaluating Teachers ($N = 189$)

Sex	Mean Score	Standard Deviation	Number of Cases
Women	10.22	0.69	91
Men	9.94	0.87	98

$t = 2.37$; $p < .01$.

subclassifications of the data we examined (Table 6-12). When we classified the principals by the size of their schools, the SES backgrounds of their pupils, and the size of the city in which their school was located and examined the mean factor score of the men and women on the "technical skills" assessment criterion, the women's score was greater than the men's in every comparison. The finding also holds up when the principals are classified by age and in three of the four geographical areas. The only two deviations from the general pattern occurred in the Eastern region of the nation and among single principals: in these cases the mean factor score of the men was higher than that of the women. In view of the sex difference finding for the total sample and its internal replication in most of the subgroupings of the data, we conclude that women on the average attribute greater importance than men to the technical skills of teachers as a criterion in evaluating their performance.

Organizational Responsibility

Elementary school teachers are expected to arrive in their classrooms on time, submit reports promptly, deal with parents and their colleagues in a professional manner, serve on committees of the school, and cooperate with their administrators. The degree to which teachers conform to these obligations can influence the operations of a school in many ways and can have a major impact on the efficiency and effectiveness of the school as a total enterprise. Principals, however, vary in the importance they assign to this aspect of the behavior of teachers in assessing their performance.

Do men or women principals place greater stress on this criterion for evaluating teachers? The hypothesis we tested was that men would attribute more importance to it than women. We reasoned that the male principals would feel less confident than the female administrators in judging the classroom performance of teachers in view of their more limited knowledge about teaching, and thus would be more likely to place the greater emphasis on the extent to which teachers fulfill their non-classroom responsibilities. To test this hypothesis, we used the factor, Or-

TABLE 6-12.   Mean Scores of Women and Men Principals on Importance Attributed to the Technical Skills of Teachers for Six Specified Subclassifications of Schools

| Subclassification# | Women | | | Men | | | Direction Predicted Correctly (+) or Incorrectly (-) |
	Mean	S.D.	N	Mean	S.D.	N	
Region							
West	10.27	0.77	13	9.92	0.86	20	+
Midwest	10.26	0.61	26	9.64	0.90	30	+
East	10.03	0.65	33	10.43	0.50	19	-
South	10.44	0.70	19	9.96	0.89	29	+
Size of City							
Small	10.09	0.62	45	9.88	0.95	49	+
Medium	10.29	0.68	33	9.94	0.85	30	+
Large	10.49	0.80	13	10.12	0.63	19	+
Size of School							
Small	10.24	0.58	33	9.93	0.83	30	+
Medium	10.06	0.62	37	9.97	0.95	27	+
Large	10.45	0.85	21	9.94	0.85	41	+

See Appendix A for the definition of the subclassification categories.

TABLE 6-12. (*Continued*)

Subclassification#	Women			Men			Direction Predicted Correctly (+) or Incorrectly (-)
	Mean	S.D.	N	Mean	S.D.	N	
Socio-economic Level							
Low	10.32	0.69	29	10.12	0.72	35	+
Middle	10.18	0.68	27	9.90	0.88	35	+
High	10.16	0.68	35	9.78	1.00	28	+
Age of Principal							
Young	10.32	0.38	11	9.94	0.85	37	+
Middle	10.22	0.71	37	10.01	0.81	32	+
Old	10.19	0.72	43	9.87	0.95	29	+
Marital Status of Principal							
Married	10.18	0.69	25	9.93	0.87	90	+
Single	10.23	0.67	57	10.33	0.49	5	-
Other	--	--	9	--	--	3	*

See Appendix A for the definition of the subclassification categories.

* No comparison made when number of cases in smaller category is less than five.

ganizational Responsibility of Teachers, which was based on the principals' responses to the following items:

1. Cooperation with school administration.
2. Degree of promptness in submitting reports.
3. Degree of promptness in getting to classes.
4. Loyalty to the school administration.
5. Dress and general appearance.
6. Willingness to serve on committees of the school.
7. Ability to maintain good relations with fellow teachers.
8. Ability to maintain classroom discipline.[16]

The findings show a sex difference but it is opposite to the prediction specified in the hypothesis. The mean score of the women was higher than that obtained by the men (10.20 vs. 9.84) and the difference of 0.36 is significant statistically, using a two-tailed test (Table 6-13).

This unanticipated finding for the entire sample also occurred in 15 out of 16 subclassifications of the data that were examined (Table 6-14). Women consistently had higher scores than the men on this teacher assessment criterion when we subclassified the principals by region, by size of city, by size of school, and by the average socioeconomic status of the pupils in their schools. The single exception was in the case of the youngest principals; the factor scores of the men and women in this case were similar. These findings lead us to conclude that women generally place greater emphasis on the organizational responsibility of teachers as a criterion for evaluating their performance than do men principals.

TABLE 6-13. Mean Scores of Women and Men Principals on Importance Attributed to the Organizational Responsibility of Teachers as a Criterion for Evaluating Teachers ($N = 189$)

Sex	Mean Score	Standard Deviation	Number of Cases
Women	10.20	0.80	91
Men	9.84	0.91	98

$t = 2.82$; $p < .01$.

TABLE 6-14.   Mean Scores of Women and Men Principals on Importance Attributed to the Organizational Responsibility of Teachers for Five Specified Subclassifications of Schools

Subclassification*	Women			Men			Direction Predicted Correctly (+) or Incorrectly (−)
	Mean	S.D.	N	Mean	S.D.	N	
Region							
West	10.26	0.71	13	9.60	1.01	20	−
Midwest	10.30	0.80	26	9.77	0.89	30	−
East	10.11	0.81	33	9.84	0.80	19	−
South	10.18	0.83	19	10.09	0.87	29	−
Size of City							
Small	10.12	0.78	45	9.76	0.94	49	−
Medium	10.32	0.81	33	9.90	0.87	30	−
Large	10.18	0.81	13	9.96	0.87	19	−
Size of School							
Small	10.21	0.78	33	9.56	0.90	30	−
Medium	10.21	0.80	37	10.16	0.82	27	−
Large	10.16	0.82	21	9.85	0.91	41	−
Socio-economic Level							
Low	10.13	0.80	29	9.98	0.79	35	−
Middle	10.28	0.94	27	9.99	0.88	35	−
High	10.20	0.67	35	9.49	0.98	28	−
Age of Principal							
Young	9.62	0.93	11	9.65	0.98	37	+
Middle	10.18	0.74	37	9.78	0.96	32	−
Old	10.36	0.74	43	10.16	0.63	29	−

*See Appendix A for the definition of the subclassification categories.

NOTES AND REFERENCES

1.   Philip Selznick, *Leadership in Administration* (Evanston, Ill.: Row, Peterson and Co., 1957), p. 135.

2.   *Ibid.,* pp. 135–136.

3.   See Appendix C, Table C-3, for item means, standard deviations, and weights used

in computing the principals' scores on importance assigned the criterion, Concern with Individual Differences among Pupils.

4. Talcott Parsons, "The School Class as a Social System: Some of Its Functions in American Society, *Harvard Educational Review,* XXIX (Fall 1959), p. 297.

5. See Appendix C, Table C-4, for item means, standard deviations, and weights used in computing the principals' scores on importance assigned the criterion, Academic Performance of Pupils.

6. All statements about the probability levels under the three socioeconomic level categories in Table 6-4 are based on a two-tailed test of significance.

7. Parsons, *op. cit.,* pp. 303–304.

8. See Appendix C, Table C-5, for the item means, standard deviations, and weights used in computing the principals' scores on importance assigned to the criterion, Concern for the Social and Emotional Development of the Child.

9. See Appendix C, Table C-6, for the item means, standard deviations, and weights used in computing the principals' scores on importance assigned to the criterion, Ability to Maintain Pupil Discipline.

10. All statements about the probability levels under the three socioeconomic level categories in Table 6-8 are based on a two-tailed test of significance.

11. See Appendix C, Table C-7, for the item means, standard deviations, and weights used in computing the principals' scores on importance assigned to the criterion, Extent of Pupil Deviant Behavior.

12. The test of statistical significance involving the relationship of sex and the emphasis on the extent of pupil deviant behavior was two-tailed.

13. The other four factors that emerged from the factor analysis may be designated as identification with teaching profession, interest in parent and community affairs, commitment to teaching, and display of extra effort.

14. Evidence presented in Chapter 3, Tables 3-12 and 3-13, offers empirical support for this assumption.

15. See Appendix C, Table C-8, for the item means, standard deviations, and weights used in computing the principals' scores on the teacher assessment criterion, Technical Skills of Teachers.

16. See Appendix C, Table C-9, for item means, standard deviations, and weights used in computing the principals' scores on the teacher assessment criterion, Organizational Responsibility of Teachers.

7

Orientations and Reactions
to Major Responsibilities

Most, although not all, of the many duties of school principals de-
lineated in the official manuals of school systems can be grouped under
one or the other of their two most important general functions: supervision of the school's instructional program and management of its
administrative affairs. In this chapter, we focus on these two task areas
of the principalship and examine them from three perspectives. The
first has reference to the *importance* the men and women school
administrators attribute to the two functions. The second perspective
raises the question of how women and men in the principalship *evaluate*
their performance of the two functions. The third is concerned with the
gratification they derive from performing them. The opinion is
frequently expressed that women and men in the principalship have different orientations and reactions to their major responsibilities. Does
the evidence indicate that this view reflects reality or that it is a myth?

IMPORTANCE ASSIGNED TO MAJOR FUNCTIONS

Management of the Instructional Program

Teachers are, of course, more immediately and directly involved than
their administrators in the teaching and learning activities of schools.
However, principals are expected to be in overall charge of the educational program of their schools and they are charged with the responsibility of maintaining an instructional program of high quality. They are
expected to serve as catalysts for needed innovations, to develop and
implement in-service training programs, to advise teachers who are hav-

ing difficulties, to coordinate the work of teachers, and in general to offer the type of leadership required to improve the instructional program. During the course of their professional training and in their in-service training programs, principals are exhorted to serve as "instructional leaders" of their schools. This role conception implies that they have an obligation to give top priority to this aspect of their work. Do men and women in the principalship differ with respect to the importance they assign to the function, supervision of the instructional program?

Our hypothesis was that the women school administrators place greater stress on the importance of supervising instruction than do the men. It was based on the following reasoning: we assumed that the women principals would have had greater teaching experience in elementary schools than the men,[1] and therefore would more highly assess their capabilities to oversee the instructional program of their schools than would the men.[2] We further assumed that among a set of individuals who serve in the same managerial capacity, their evaluation of their own capabilities to perform one of its central functions is positively related to their assessment of its importance. From these assumptions it follows that women principals would attribute greater importance to supervising instruction than would men.

To test this hypothesis, we used a factor score to measure the importance a principal assigns to the function of supervising instruction. The data on which the factor score is based were secured from replies of the principals to eight questions with reference to the importance they attributed to instructional activities. We asked the principals: How important ("extremely important," "very important," "of moderate importance," "of little importance," "of no importance") do you view the following activities in carrying out your job as principal of your school:

1. Working on the improvement of the curriculum.
2. Introducing new teaching ideas.
3. Counselling pupils.
4. Carrying on in-service training programs for teachers.
5. Dealing with classroom problems of teachers.
6. Evaluating the performance of students.
7. Coordinating the work of teachers.
8. Conferring with individual teachers.

A factor score was computed for each principal based on weights derived from the loading of the items in the factor.[3] This measure was used to test the hypothesis that women in the principalship attribute greater importance than men to the supervision of instruction.

A *low* score on the factor, Importance Attributed to the Supervision of Instruction, reflects a *high* assessment of this function; therefore, if the findings support the hypothesis, the mean factor score of the women will need to be lower than that of the men. The mean score of the women was, indeed, lower than that obtained by the men (9.75 vs. 9.90), but the difference of 0.15 units is not statistically significant (Table 7-1).

We next considered possible circumstances that might have a bearing on the relationship between the gender of principals and the importance they assign to the management of instruction in their schools. One condition of this kind is the principals' evaluation of the competence of their faculties. We reasoned that men and women principals who had a high opinion of the competence of their staffs would differ little in the importance they attribute to supervising instructional affairs because they would feel that their subordinates required little assistance from them. But in those cases in which women and men principals held a relatively low opinion of their staffs' competence, although they both would recognize that their teachers needed assistance, the women would attach greater importance to supervision of instruction than the men

TABLE 7-1.   Mean Scores of Women and Men Principals on Importance Attributed to the Supervision of Instruction ($N = 186$)*

(Low Score = High Importance)

Sex	Mean Score	Standard Deviation	Number of Cases
Women	9.75	0.72	88
Men	9.90	0.59	98

*Data unavailable for three of the 189 principals.

$t = 1.60$; $p > .05$.

would because the females would feel that they could be of greater service to their teachers than the male administrators.

To explore this possibility, we classified the principals into three groups on the basis of the proportion of their teachers whom they regarded as "competent to carry out their teaching assignments." We next computed mean factor scores for the women and men principals who fell into each of the three categories. Table 7-2 reveals that for the male and female principals with low evaluations of their faculty, there is a statistically significant difference in the mean scores of the women and the men (9.50 vs. 9.93) and that it is the direction anticipated. The differences in the mean factor scores of the men and women administrators in the medium and high staff competency categories, however, were not statistically significant. Women, on the average, do attribute greater importance than men principals do to the management of instructional activities when they hold a relatively low opinion of the teaching competence of their staffs. We conclude, therefore, that for the total sample, there was no sex difference in the importance principals attribute to supervising instruction. When principals have a low assessment of the competency of their teachers, women assess the supervision of instruction as more important than the men.

Administrative Tasks

The school office and the custodians must be supervised; reports must be written and correspondence must be answered; attendance and grade sheets must be promptly checked; budget proposals need to be prepared; records must be kept; supplies must be ordered and distributed. Is there a difference in the importance that male and female principals attribute to such administrative duties?

The hypothesis that we tested was that men principals attribute greater importance than women do to the administrative aspect of the principal's role. It was based on the same argument we used in developing our hypothesis about sex differences in the importance principals attribute to supervision of instruction. In developing that hypothesis, we assumed that women evaluate themselves as more competent than men as supervisors of instruction. With respect to the hypothesis under consideration, we assumed that men would see themselves as better managers of the school's administrative routine.[4]

TABLE 7-2. Mean Scores of Women and Men Principals on Importance Attributed to the Supervision of Instruction by Principals' Assessment of Competency of Their Staffs

(Low Score = High Importance)

Subclassification*	Women		Men			Probability Less than
	Mean	N	Mean	N	t	
Competence of Staff						
Low	9.50	23	9.93	27	2.35	.05
Medium	9.89	32	10.03	36	0.95	n.s.
High	9.79	31	9.76	35	0.16	n.s.

*See Appendix A for the definition of the subclassification categories.

To test this hypothesis we used a factor score to measure the importance each principal assigned to administrative tasks. This measure was based on the same type of scoring procedure employed in gauging the importance principals attribute to the management of instruction. We asked the principals: How important do you view the following activity in carrying out your job as principal of your school:

1. Keeping school records.
2. Checking school attendance.
3. Taking inventory of equipment.
4. Ordering or distributing supplies.
5. Preparing reports for the higher administration of the school system.
6. Checking grade sheets or report cards.
7. Planning students' schedules or class plans.
8. Dealing with correspondence.
9. Keeping a watch on the school budget.
10. Managing the school office.
11. Supervising the custodial staff.

Since a low score on the factor, Importance Assigned to Administrative Tasks, represents a high assessment of the importance of these kinds of activities, the men should receive a lower mean factor score than the women if the evidence supports the hypothesis.[5] However, the findings show that, contrary to our expectation, the women on the average attribute greater importance to administrative tasks than the men: the mean factor score of the females is 9.58 as compared to 9.76 for the males (Table 7-3). The difference, however, of 0.18 between their mean scores is not significant statistically.[6] We conclude, therefore, that men and women in the elementary principalship do not differ in the importance they assign to the management of the administrative affairs of the school.

SELF-EVALUATION

The hypotheses that specified sex differences in the importance principals assign to their major functions were based on the assumption that women and men on the average differ in their assessments of their capabilities to perform them. Do women and men in fact differ in their self-evaluation of their ability to offer leadership to the instructional

TABLE 7-3. Mean Scores of Women and Men Principals on Importance Assigned to Administrative Tasks ($N = 186$)*

(Low Score = High Importance)

Sex	Mean Score	Standard Deviation	Number of Cases
Women	9.58	0.72	88
Men	9.76	0.75	98

*Data unavailable for three of the 189 principals.

$t = 1.64$; $p > .05$.

programs of their schools? Is there a sex difference in their self-assessment of their ability to perform the principal's administrative tasks in an efficient and effective manner? These are the issues we now examine.

Supervision of the Instructional Program

The hypothesis we tested was that women principals evaluate their performance in supervising the instructional programs of their schools more positively than men do. Our reasoning is based on the assumption that women administrators had served as elementary school teachers for a longer period of time than men, and therefore would have accumulated a larger body of knowledge and more technical skills about instructional activities than the men at the time they first became school principals. If we further assume that individuals who are better equipped and more qualified to carry out a function in an effective manner will have a more positive assessment of their performance of it, then it follows that women will assess their performance in supervising the instructional programs of their schools in a more positive manner than men.

To test this hypothesis we employed a factor score to measure self-evaluation of ability to supervise the instructional program. The data from which the factor score was derived were secured from the replies of the principals to eight questions about how they evaluated their ability to supervise instructional affairs in their school. We asked the principals: How would you evaluate your ability ("outstanding," "excellent," "good," "fair," "poor," "very poor") to perform the following activities:

1. Getting *experienced* teachers to upgrade their performance.
2. Improving the performance of *inexperienced* teachers.
3. Getting teachers to use new educational methods.
4. Giving leadership to the instructional program.
5. Communicating the objectives of the school program to the faculty.
6. Getting teachers to coordinate their activities.
7. Knowing about the strengths and weaknesses of teachers.
8. Maximizing the different skills found in a faculty.[7]

When we compared the mean scores of the men and women principals on the factor, Self-Evaluation of Ability to Supervise the Instructional Program, the findings supported the hypothesis (Table 7-4): the women's mean score was higher than the men's (10.28 vs. 9.85) and the difference of 0.43 is significant statistically.

When we grouped the principals on the basis of size of their schools and cities, the sex difference finding for the total sample was internally replicated. Similar findings resulted when we examined the mean scores of the female and male principals on Self-Evaluation of Ability to Supervise the Instructional Program in subgroups of the following variables: the socioeconomic status of the principals' schools, the principals' assessment of the competence of their staffs, the proportion of men teachers in their schools, and the variation and the average age of their staffs (Table 7-5). The findings for the total sample are internally validated in 24 of the 25 subclassifications of the data we examined. The single deviation was principals in the Eastern region of the country where the men's mean score was higher than that of the women. The high degree of consistency in these subsidiary findings increases our confidence in the conclusion that women principals generally evaluate their performance in supervising the instructional programs of their schools more favorably than do men.

Administrative Tasks

Do men and women also differ in their self-assessments of their ability to manage the administrative affairs of their schools? Our hypothesis

TABLE 7-4. Mean Scores of Women and Men Principals on Self-evaluation of Ability to Supervise the Instructional Program ($N = 189$)

Sex	Mean Score	Standard Deviation	Number of Cases
Women	10.28	0.75	91
Men	9.85	0.91	98

$t = 3.47; \ p < .001.$

TABLE 7-5. Mean Scores of Women and Men Principals on Self-evaluation of Ability to Supervise the Instructional Program for Eight Specified Subclassifications of Schools

Subclassification*	Women			Men			Direction Predicted Correctly (+) or Incorrectly (−)
	Mean	S.D.	N	Mean	S.D.	N	
Region							
West	10.52	0.59	13	9.92	0.91	20	+
Midwest	10.43	0.60	26	9.65	0.78	30	+
East	9.95	0.86	33	10.19	1.04	19	−
South	10.48	0.65	19	9.80	0.88	29	+
Size of City							
Small	10.18	0.83	45	9.66	0.89	49	+
Medium	10.30	0.63	33	9.85	0.71	30	+
Large	10.57	0.68	13	10.34	1.05	19	+
Size of School							
Small	10.33	0.86	33	9.88	0.90	30	+
Medium	10.07	0.56	37	9.64	0.91	27	+
Large	10.55	0.78	21	9.97	0.89	41	+
Socio-economic Level							
Low	10.27	0.71	29	9.93	0.98	35	+
Middle	10.23	0.97	27	9.84	0.82	35	+
High	10.32	0.59	35	9.77	0.92	28	+

*See Appendix A for the definition of the subclassification categories.

TABLE 7-5.   (*Continued*)

Subclassification*	Women			Men			Direction Predicted Correctly (+) or Incorrectly (−)
	Mean	S.D.	N	Mean	S.D.	N	
Competence of Staff							
Low	10.12	0.93	24	9.96	1.12	27	+
Medium	10.28	0.65	33	9.71	0.72	36	+
High	10.42	0.69	32	9.91	0.89	35	+
Proportion of Men Teachers							
Low	10.41	0.62	30	9.85	0.98	28	+
Medium	10.17	0.88	32	9.78	0.85	36	+
High	10.27	0.72	29	9.93	0.91	34	+
Mean Age of Teachers							
Young	10.45	0.74	33	10.12	0.90	32	+
Middle	10.24	0.66	31	9.55	0.85	29	+
Old	10.12	0.83	26	9.85	0.90	37	+
Variance in Teachers' Ages							
Low	10.50	0.69	25	10.04	0.97	37	+
Medium	10.28	0.52	30	9.61	0.90	33	+
High	10.13	0.93	34	9.88	0.78	28	+

*See Appendix A for the definition of the subclassification categories.

was that the men principals would rate themselves more highly than the women on this self-assessment dimension. It was linked to the assumption that the male administrators would probably devote more time and effort to the administrative component of their work than the females. To examine the hypothesis, we used a factor score, Self-Assessment of Administrative Abilities, that was based on data obtained from the administrators' responses to five questions about how they assessed their competency to deal with administrative tasks. We asked the principals: How would you evaluate your ability ("outstanding," "excellent," "good," "fair," "poor," "very poor") to perform the following tasks:

1. Keeping the school office running smoothly.
2. General planning for the school.
3. Directing the work of administrative assistants.
4. Cutting "red tape" when fast action is needed.
5. Publicizing the work of the school.[8]

Table 7-6 shows that the men's mean score on the factor, Self-Assessment of Administrative Abilities, is slightly higher than the women's (9.83 vs. 9.71); however, the difference of 0.12 is not significant statistically. We conclude, therefore, that the men and women principals do not differ in their self-evaluation of their ability to manage the administrative affairs of their schools.

TABLE 7-6.   Mean Scores of Women and Men Principals on Self-assessment of Administrative Abilities ($N = 189$)

Sex	Mean Score	Standard Deviation	Number of Cases
Women	9.71	0.79	91
Men	9.83	0.75	98

$t = 1.05$; $p > .05$.

SATISFACTIONS

Supervision of the Instructional Program

Now we inquire whether men and women in the principalship differ in the gratification they derive from carrying out these important role responsibilities. Our hypothesis was that women derive greater satisfaction from supervising instruction than men do. We anticipated this outcome for two reasons: first, because we expected that the women would have a greater interest in teaching than would the men principals in view of the women's much earlier choice of it as a vocation and the greater frequency with which they made it their first career choice;[9] and second, because we anticipated that female administrators would feel more comfortable in working with teachers on instructional activities than would the men on the assumption that the women had greater classroom experience and knowledge about teaching in the elementary school than men had.

To test this hypothesis, we used a factor score to measure satisfaction derived from supervision of the instructional program. The data on which the factor score is based were secured from the responses of the principals to the following seven questions: To what extent ("a great deal," "very much," "somewhat," "very little," "not at all") do you enjoy:

1.   Working with "exceptionally able" teachers.
2.   Working with "average" teachers.
3.   Working with new teachers.
4.   Supervising the instructional program.
5.   Working with curriculum specialists.
6.   Having the freedom to schedule one's own time.
7.   Having a vacation from work periodically during the school year.[10]

In examining the findings, it is important to know that in interpreting the factor score, Satisfaction Derived from Supervising the Instructional Program, a *low* score reflects a *high* degree of satisfaction with instructional activities. Therefore, if the hypothesis that women obtain greater satisfaction in supervising instructional activities than men receives support, the findings will reveal that the mean score obtained by the women is lower than the men's. The results do in fact offer support for the hypothesis: the mean factor score for the women is lower than the men's mean score (9.88 vs. 10.21) and the difference of 0.33 is statistically significant (Table 7-7).

When we examined the mean factor scores of the men and women administrators under different subclassifications of the data, the findings were internally replicated with a high degree of regularity (Table 7-8). In small, medium, and large cities the mean factor scores of the women were consistently lower than those of the men. The same sex dif-

TABLE 7-7.   Mean Scores of Women and Men Principals on Satisfaction Derived from Supervising the Instructional Program ($N = 189$)

(Low Score = High Satisfaction)

Sex	Mean Score	Standard Deviation	Number of Cases
Women	9.88	0.84	91
Men	10.21	0.85	98

$t = 2.74$; $p < .01$.

ference finding emerged when we examined the mean scores of the men and women principals in subgroupings of the following variables: age, marital status, average age of the principal's faculty, variation in its teaching experience, the principals' assessment of the competence of their staffs, and the socioeconomic status of pupils in their schools. The one exception to the pattern in the 24 comparisons we made occurred in cities located in the Eastern region of the nation; in this area the mean score of the women principals was somewhat higher than that of the men. The high degree of internal consistency in the findings increases our confidence in the sex difference found for the entire sample.

Administrative Duties

If, as our findings indicate, females in the principalship derive greater gratification on the average than males do from performing tasks associated with teaching and learning activities of their schools, do the men find the greater satisfaction from carrying out duties that are essentially administrative in nature? Our hypothesis was that they would. We anticipated this sex difference because we assumed that men in the principalship feel less comfortable than women in dealing with the schools' instructional problems, and therefore that the men would allocate more of their time and energies to, and hence derive greater

TABLE 7-8. Mean Scores of Women and Men Principals on Satisfaction Derived from Supervising the Instructional Program for Eight Specified Subclassifications of Schools

(Low Score = High Satisfaction)

Subclassification#	Women			Men			Direction Predicted Correctly (+) or Incorrectly (−)
	Mean	S.D.	N	Mean	S.D.	N	
Region							
West	9.54	0.81	13	10.34	1.02	20	+
Midwest	9.85	0.87	26	10.13	0.64	30	+
East	10.10	0.88	33	9.83	0.87	19	−
South	9.76	0.63	19	10.47	0.78	29	+
Size of City							
Small	10.07	0.84	45	10.30	0.82	49	+
Medium	9.76	0.80	33	10.39	0.73	30	+
Large	9.47	0.77	13	9.71	0.90	19	+
Mean Age of Teachers							
Young	9.72	0.87	33	10.19	0.87	32	+
Middle	9.92	0.82	31	10.42	0.83	29	+
Old	10.01	0.83	26	10.08	0.81	37	+
Mean Experience of Teachers							
Short	9.54	0.90	30	10.24	0.85	33	+
Medium	10.09	0.71	28	10.41	0.83	33	+
Long	9.97	0.83	31	9.98	0.80	32	+

#See Appendix A for the definition of the subclassification categories.

TABLE 7-8. *(Continued)*

Subclassification#	Women			Men			Direction Predicted Correctly (+) or Incorrectly (−)
	Mean	S.D.	N	Mean	S.D.	N	
Competence of Staff							
Low	9.78	0.97	24	10.17	0.84	27	+
Medium	10.01	0.72	33	10.46	0.79	36	+
High	9.81	0.88	32	10.00	0.85	35	+
Socio-economic Level							
Low	9.71	0.88	29	10.13	0.73	35	+
Middle	9.93	0.85	27	10.42	0.81	35	+
High	9.97	0.79	35	10.06	0.97	28	+
Marital Status of Principal							
Married	9.87	0.88	25	10.24	0.84	90	+
Single	9.90	0.85	57	9.93	1.08	5	+
Other	--	--	9	--	--	3	*
Age of Principal							
Young	9.84	0.92	11	10.36	0.81	37	+
Middle	9.84	0.93	37	10.17	0.97	32	+
Old	9.91	0.74	43	10.08	0.71	29	+

#See Appendix A for the definition of the subclassification categories.

*No test made when number of cases in smaller category is less than five.

pleasure from, this aspect of their managerial duties than the women would.

To test the hypothesis we used the factor score, Satisfaction Derived from Performing Administrative Tasks, which was derived from the principals' responses to the following set of questions: To what extent ("a great deal," "very much," "somewhat," "very little," "not at all") do you enjoy:

1. Supervising office personnel.
2. Supervising custodial personnel.
3. Preparing reports to the higher administration.
4. Preparing staff bulletins or announcements.
5. Handling administrative routine.
6. Allocating the school budget.
7. Evaluating teacher performance.[11]

A *low* score on the factor, Satisfaction Derived from Performing Administrative Tasks, once again represents a *high* degree of satisfaction. Therefore, if our hypothesis is tenable, men will receive a lower score than women on the factor. The findings indicate that men do derive greater gratification from these kinds of activities than women: the mean satisfaction score of the men principals was lower than the

TABLE 7-9.   Mean Scores of Women and Men Principals on Satisfaction Derived from Performing Administrative Tasks ($N = 189$)

(Low Score = High Satisfaction)

Sex	Mean Score	Standard Deviation	Number of Cases
Women	10.39	0.70	91
Men	10.07	0.86	98

$t = 2.80$; $p < .01$.

women's (10.07 vs. 10.39) and the difference of 0.32 is significant statistically (Table 7-9). As in the case of the finding reported earlier about the sex difference in satisfaction derived from instructional activities, there was a high degree of internal consistency in the findings when the mean factor scores of the men and women were compared under various subgroupings of the data (Table 7-10). In 23 of the 24 comparisons we made the sex difference found for the entire sample was internally replicated. In only one instance, in the largest cities, did the women obtain a lower satisfaction score (that is, express greater satisfaction) with the administrative aspect of their work than the men. These findings in combination with those presented earlier lead us to conclude that men in the elementary principalship generally derive greater satisfaction than women do from the administrative component of their work and that the women obtain more gratification than do the men from supervising the instructional activities of their schools.

TABLE 7-10. Mean Scores of Women and Men Principals on Satisfaction Derived from Performing Administrative Tasks for Eight Specified Subclassifications of Schools

(Low Score = High Satisfaction)

Subclassification#	Women			Men			Direction Predicted Correctly (+) or Incorrectly (−)
	Mean	S.D.	N	Mean	S.D.	N	
Region							
West	10.39	0.66	13	10.27	0.65	20	+
Midwest	10.39	0.57	26	10.08	0.89	30	+
East	10.48	0.77	33	10.27	1.08	19	+
South	10.25	0.74	19	9.80	0.70	29	+
Size of City							
Small	10.49	0.72	45	10.01	0.91	49	+
Medium	10.28	0.70	33	9.93	0.71	30	+
Large	10.36	0.54	13	10.46	0.85	19	−
Mean Age of Teachers							
Young	10.24	0.51	33	9.88	0.81	32	+
Middle	10.43	0.71	31	10.27	0.95	29	+
Old	10.52	0.83	26	10.08	0.79	37	+
Mean Experience of Teachers							
Short	10.30	0.65	30	10.02	0.75	33	+
Medium	10.36	0.64	28	10.16	0.91	33	+
Long	10.50	0.76	31	10.03	0.91	32	+

#See Appendix A for the definition of the subclassification categories.

TABLE 7-10.   *(Continued)*

Subclassification#	Women			Men			Direction Predicted Correctly (+) or Incorrectly (−)
	Mean	S.D.	N	Mean	S.D.	N	
Competence of Staff							
Low	10.65	0.61	24	10.02	0.86	27	+
Medium	10.27	0.72	33	10.01	0.89	36	+
High	10.36	0.68	32	10.17	0.83	35	+
Socio-economic Level							
Low	10.38	0.68	29	10.20	0.83	35	+
Middle	10.44	0.66	27	9.87	0.79	35	+
High	10.37	0.74	35	10.16	0.93	28	+
Marital Status of Principal							
Married	10.26	0.62	25	10.08	0.83	90	+
Single	10.44	0.71	57	9.71	0.57	5	+
Other	--	--	9	--	--	3	*
Age of Principal							
Young	10.69	0.66	11	10.11	0.67	37	+
Middle	10.38	0.71	37	10.14	0.97	32	+
Old	10.33	0.67	43	9.94	0.94	29	+

#See Appendix A for the definition of the subclassification categories.
*No comparison ma.e when number of cases in smaller category is less than five.

NOTES AND REFERENCES

1.   Evidence presented in Chapter 3 revealed support for this assumption: the mean years of elementary teaching experience of the women principals was 14.7 years and that of the men was 4.6 years.

2.   Evidence indicating that this assumption is valid is presented later in the chapter.

3.   For the item means, standard deviations, and weights used in computing the score, Importance Attributed to the Supervision of Instruction, see Appendix C, Table C-10.

4.   Evidence presented later in the chapter with respect to this assumption reveals that it receives no empirical support.

5. For the item means, standard deviations, and weights used in computing the score, Importance Assigned to Administrative Tasks, see Appendix C, Table C-11.

6. This interpretation is based on the use of a two-tailed test since the empirical findings were contrary to our prediction.

7. For the item means, standard deviations, and weights used in computing the score, Self-evaluation of Ability to Supervise the Instructional Program, see Appendix C, Table C-12.

8. For the item means, standard deviations, and weights used in computing the score, Self-assessment of Administrative Abilities, see Appendix C, Table C-13.

9. Evidence in support of this assumption was presented in Chapter 3: teaching was a first choice of 80% of the women but of only 46% of the men.

10. For the item means, standard deviations, and weights used in computing the score, Satisfaction Derived from Supervising the Instructional Program, see Appendix C, Table C-14.

11. For the item means, standard deviations, and weights used in computing the score, Satisfaction Derived from Performing Administrative Tasks, see Appendix C, Table C-15.

8

Control over Teachers

In the authority structure of public school systems principals occupy positions at the level of middle-management. They are superordinate to their teachers but subordinate to senior administrators in the central administration. One of the important responsibilities of top officials of a school system is to evaluate the performance of principals and the efficiency and effectiveness of their schools. The central administration expects principals to correct deficiencies in their organizations, to improve their performance, and to take the initiative in introducing promising innovations into their schools. It holds principals accountable not only for the overall operation of their schools, but also for the classroom performance of teachers. In short, it expects principals to intervene in school affairs whenever they deem it necessary and to exhibit professional leadership in coping with identified problems.

The expectation that principals should influence and exert control over the quality of teaching and learning that takes place in their schools is also specified in the rules and regulations of most school boards. They generally state that one of the primary responsibilities of a principal is "to supervise" teachers. Furthermore, in graduate programs for the preparation of principals and in their professional literature, their obligation to offer "instructional leadership" to their faculty is stressed. As a consequence of these circumstances, most principals feel that one of their primary obligations is to give leadership to the instructional program of their school.

To conform to this image of their role, principals must be able to influence, and exert control over, the performance of their teachers. However, a basic organizational characteristic of schools may restrict or even preclude their efforts to exercise control over their subordinates: teachers, because they perceive themselves as professionals, feel that principals should recognize and respect their right to autonomy in carrying out their professional responsibilities.[1] Members of a profession claim the right to know what the problems and interests of their clients are and what courses of action will be of maximum benefit for them, with no direction or interference from fellow practitioners, or if they are employed by an organization, from their superordinates. In the case of the school, the norm of teacher autonomy directly collides with the norm that a principal should exert influence over the instructional activities of his school, and therefore, over the performance of teachers.[2]

Most principals, partly because of their previous experience as teachers, are acutely aware of this role conflict. They recognize that their efforts to exercise control over the performance of members of their faculty can be resented, resisted, or even rejected by their teachers because they can interpret initiatives of this nature as an encroachment on "their domain" and as a violation of their professional rights.

The possibility that teacher resistance may occur when a principal attempts to exercise control over the behavior of staff members raises the issue of the rewards and punishments available to both parties in the relationship. Principals appear to have four types of sanctions at their disposal. The first, general and diffuse in nature, derives from their responsibility to prepare periodic teacher assessment reports for the personnel office of the school district. The second relates to their power to assign "easy" or "tough" classes to teachers. The third stems from their right to offer rewards and punishments in dispensing odious and enjoyable assignments, for example, corridor and recess duty versus serving as the school representative at an out-of-town conference. The fourth sanction is the power of principals to lend or withhold support to teachers who become involved in conflicts with parents or pupils.

Teachers also have various protective mechanisms and punitive devices at their disposal. Experienced teachers are protected by tenure and efforts to discharge a teacher are rare occurrences in the public schools, reserved only for very extreme instances of unprofessional behavior. Furthermore, in most school systems, teachers have the right to apply to the central office for transfer to another school, and principals know that an informal index used by the central administration for evaluating their performance is the number of teacher requests for transfer that emanate from their school. In addition, teachers can employ the technique of passive resistance, thereby largely ignoring the suggestions and pronouncements of their principal.

In determining how much control to exercise over their subordinates principals, like other functionaries with supervisory responsibilities, are generally aware that although they possess power over their subordinates, their subordinates also possess power over them. In view of these circumstances, it can be anticipated that the degree of control a principal exercises over his teachers will reflect his perceptions of the norms and feelings of his teachers about the "supervision issue." If he ignores their views, he exposes himself to the risk of having his directives and proposals rejected or circumvented.

Control over professional activities, then, is an important and sensitive area for both teachers and principals. We now turn to the question, Do men or women in the principalship exert greater control over the professional activities of teachers?

THE HYPOTHESIS

The hypothesis to be tested is that women principals exercise more control over their teachers than men principals do. It was based on the following three lines of reasoning. We started with the assumption that the longer a superordinate had served in the same role occupied by the subordinates under his jurisdiction, the greater will be the superordinate's efforts to influence their behavior and the more willing they will be to accept it. Among principals, those with greater teaching experience and knowledge of classroom problems of teachers could therefore be expected to attempt to exercise greater control over their teachers. If we assume that women principals have had greater experience as elementary school teachers than men, and as a consequence possess greater technical competence as elementary educators, then it follows that women would exercise greater control over their staffs than would men principals.[3]

A second line of reasoning is based on the assumption that professional administrators who have a more positive evaluation of their competence to advise their professional subordinates will attempt to exercise more control over their performance than administrators with a less positive assessment of their ability to be of service to their subordinates. If we further assume that women principals, because of their greater experience in the classroom and their greater enjoyment of tasks directly related to the instructional program, will place a higher value on their own professional capabilities,[4] it follows that women will exercise more control over their teachers than will men principals.

A third idea relevant to the hypothesis is that among a group of professional administrators, those who give the greater primacy to their work can be expected to be more concerned about the functioning of their organizations and therefore attempt to exercise greater control over what takes place in them. We noted earlier that women are more frequently confronted with obstacles than are men in achieving responsible managerial and supervisory positions such as the principalship, and this circumstance, we assume, will lead women to give more time and effort to their managerial role than men. And if, as we assumed, the time and effort devoted by superordinates to their work is positively related to the control they attempt to exercise over their subordinates' activities, then it follows that women principals will exert more control over their subordinates than men.

Each of these three lines of reasoning leads to the hypothesis that women principals exercise more control over the professional activities of their teachers than do men principals.

TESTING THE HYPOTHESIS

To test this hypothesis we used a factor score to measure the principal's control over teachers' professional activities. The data on which the factor score is based were obtained from the responses of the teacher-observers to the following eight questions: How frequently ("always," "almost always," "occasionally," "almost never," "never") does your principal engage in the following kinds of activities:

1. Require that teachers discuss their major classroom problems with the principal.
2. Ask teachers to report all major conferences with parents to the principal.
3. Require teachers to keep the principal informed about "problem" children in their classrooms.
4. Closely direct the work of teachers who are likely to experience difficulty.
5. Require that teachers' classroom behavior conform to the principal's standards.
6. Check to see that teachers prepare written lesson plans.
7. Know what is taking place in most classrooms during most of the day.

8.   Determine what the objectives of the guidance program should be in the school.[5]

The first seven questions deal with different ways that a principal can maintain control over the professional activities of teachers. The eighth question, "How frequently does your principal determine what the objectives of the guidance program should be in the school?" is not directly related to the principal's control of the teachers' professional tasks; however, the guidance program in an elementary school can impinge on the teacher-pupil relationship in a number of ways—hence its relevance.

To obtain the best estimate of the extent to which principals exercised control over teachers' professional performance, we computed, on the basis of the teachers' responses to the eight questions, a score for each teacher based on the weights derived from the loadings of items included in the factor. The teacher-observer factor scores in each school were then averaged to obtain the best estimate of the degree to which principals Control Teachers' Professional Activities.[6] A comparison of the mean scores obtained by the women and men principals on this index of the control principals exercise over the professional activities of their teachers reveals that the hypothesis is supported: the mean score of the women is higher than the men's (8.94 vs. 7.67) and the difference of 1.27 is significant statistically (Table 8-1). We conclude that women principals in elementary schools do exercise more control over the professional activities of their teachers than do men.

It is important to inquire if the sex difference in the principals' con-

TABLE 8-1.   Mean Scores of Women and Men Principals on Control over Teachers' Professional Activities ($N = 175$)*

Sex	Mean Score	Standard Deviation	Number of Cases
Women	8.94	1.88	86
Men	7.67	1.93	89

*Data unavailable for 14 of the 189 principals.

$t = 4.37; \ p < .001.$

trol of their subordinates could be an artifact of other variables such as staff size, the experience or competence of the faculty, the principal's age, or marital status. These variables deserve consideration as "confounding" variables for the following reasons: the fewer the teachers in his school, the more time a principal will have for supervision; the less competent or experienced the staff, the more effort a principal could be expected to expend in attempting to exercise control over their performance. If the women, on the average, were administrators of smaller schools or had less competent or experienced staffs than the men, then the sex difference in control of staff might be "explained away" by these confounding variables. In addition, we reported earlier that the women principals were older than the men and that most of the women, but only 10% of the men, were single. It could be argued that older principals attempt to exert greater control over teachers than younger ones and that single principals, having more time to devote to their work than the married, exhibit greater control over the performance of their teachers than married principals.

To explore these possibilities, we re-examined the relationship between the sex factor and the principal's control of his staff, holding constant each of these five variables *in seriatim*.

The findings reveal that for each of the 13 subclassifications on which we were able to make comparisons, the mean factor score of the women principals is higher than that of the men (Table 8-2). The magnitude of the differences varies, but not their direction. We conclude that the finding that female principals exercise greater control over the professional performance of teachers than do male principals cannot be viewed as an artifact of any of these "third" variables.

Four additional categorizations of schools were used to determine the degree of internal consistency of this sex difference finding for our sample of principals: region, socioeconomic level of school, size of city, and the proportion of men teachers on the faculty. When the mean scores for the principal's control of teachers' professional behavior were computed for the female and male principals whose schools were located in different regions, in different socioeconomic areas, and in subclassifications of the other two categorizations of schools, the findings revealed that in 12 of the 13 subgroupings the women principals scored higher than the men (Table 8-3). The one exception is the principals of schools in the largest cities. The overall high degree of consistency of these analyses increases our confidence in the finding for the total sample of principals.

TABLE 8-2. Mean Scores of Women and Men Principals on Control over Teachers' Professional Activities for Five Specified Subclassifications of Schools

Subclassification#	Women			Men			Direction Predicted Correctly (+) or Incorrectly (-)
	Mean	S.D.	N	Mean	S.D.	N	
Size of School							
Small	9.21	1.46	30	8.01	1.95	26	+
Medium	8.71	2.06	35	7.53	1.84	25	+
Large	8.93	2.06	21	7.53	1.94	38	+
Mean Teacher Experience							
Short	8.98	1.82	29	8.23	1.97	29	+
Medium	9.39	1.73	27	7.55	1.90	30	+
Long	8.51	2.01	29	7.25	1.77	30	+
Competence of Staff							
Low	9.30	1.59	23	8.16	1.95	26	+
Middle	8.55	1.99	30	7.83	1.97	32	+
High	9.06	1.96	31	7.09	1.70	31	+
Age of Principal							
Young	9.06	1.80	11	8.04	2.01	32	+
Middle	8.73	2.28	34	7.72	1.85	30	+
Old	9.07	1.48	41	7.18	1.79	27	+
Marital Status of Principal							
Married	8.02	1.76	23	7.63	1.89	82	+
Single	--	--	55	--	--	4	*
Other	--	--	8	--	--	3	*

\# See Appendix A for the definition of the subclassification categories.

* No comparison made when number of cases in smaller category is less than five.

TESTING THE REASONING

We have maintained that three variables might account for the relationship between the sex of principals and their control over their teachers' activities: professional experience, self-evaluation, and primacy assigned to work. To test the reasoning underlying the hypothesis, we use now the logic and procedures presented in Chapter 1, pages 15–16. We

TABLE 8-3. Mean Scores of Women and Men Principals on Control over Teachers' Professional Activities for Four Specified Subclassifications of Schools

Subclassification*	Mean	S.D.	N	Mean	S.D.	N	Direction Predicted Correctly (+) or Incorrectly (−)
Region							
West	8.28	1.74	10	6.59	1.49	17	+
Midwest	8.84	1.78	26	7.15	2.15	27	+
East	9.67	1.69	32	8.88	1.39	17	+
South	8.13	1.94	18	8.09	1.67	28	+
Socio-economic Level							
Low	8.38	1.83	26	8.11	2.03	32	+
Middle	9.74	1.50	25	7.62	1.85	30	+
High	8.78	1.98	35	7.21	1.77	27	+
Size of City							
Small	9.02	1.98	45	7.65	2.07	46	+
Medium	9.24	1.53	29	6.94	1.56	27	+
Large	7.91	1.93	12	8.99	1.26	16	−
Proportion of Men Teachers							
Low	8.86	1.76	27	7.80	1.90	26	+
Middle	9.06	2.07	31	7.15	1.81	30	+
High	8.88	1.76	28	8.04	1.94	33	+

* See Appendix A for the definition of the subclassification categories.

initially determine if each "presumed explanatory" or intervening variable is related to both the independent variable (sex) and the dependent
variable (control) in the manner assumed. If the postulated relationships
do not exist, then the assumptions underlying the hypothesis are not
tenable. If they do, then we can proceed to the next step.

The findings with reference to the assumed relationships between the
intervening and the independent and dependent variables are presented
in Table 8-4. They show the following:

1. Experience as indexed by number of years in elementary teaching
   is greater for the women than the men, and it is positively correlated with control.
2. The women have a higher self-evaluation of their ability to direct
   the instructional program than the men have, and self-evaluation
   is positively related to control over professional staff.
3. Women devote greater time and effort to their work, as indexed
   by the nights spent on school business, than do men; it is also
   positively correlated with control.

Each of these three variables, then, is related to both the independent
and dependent variables. Now we examine if the evidence supports the

TABLE 8-4. Correlation Coefficients for the Relationships Between Three
Assumed Intervening Variables and the Independent Variable (Sex) and Dependent Variable (Control over Teachers' Professional Activities) ($N = 175$)

Assumed Intervening Variable	Sex[#] (Point-biserial r)	Control over Teachers' Professional Activities (Pearsonian r)
Years of elementary school teaching experience	.60*	.29*
Self-evaluation of ability to direct instructional program	.25*	.14*
Nights spent on school business	.20*	.22*

[#] Female = 1; male = 0.

* $p < .05$.

final condition required for them to be considered as intervening variables: the zero-order relationship between sex and control should decrease when they are held constant (Table 8-5).

The zero-order point-biserial correlation coefficient between sex and control over professional staff is .32. When the number of years of elementary teaching experience is held constant, the relationship drops to .19. It diminishes only slightly to .29 when self-evaluation is held constant, and only to .28 when primacy of work role is held constant. When each of the intervening variables is held constant, the relationship between the independent and dependent variables does decrease,

TABLE 8-5. Zero-order, First-order, and Higher-order Partial Correlation Coefficients between Sex and Control over Teachers' Professional Activities ($N = 175$)

	Zero-order r	First-order Partial r	Higher-order Partial r
Sex and Control over Teachers' Professional Activities	.32		
Holding Constant:			
Years of elementary school teaching experience		.19	
Self-evaluation of ability to direct instructional program		.29	
Nights spent on school business		.28	
Years of elementary school teaching experience and self-evaluation of ability to direct instructional program			.16
Years of elementary school teaching experience, self-evaluation of ability to direct instructional program, and nights spent on school business			.12

but the "third variables" vary considerably in the extent to which they influence the original zero-order correlation coefficient: years of elementary teaching experience results in the sharpest drop, while removing self-evaluation and primacy of work role have only a minor effect.

When both years of elementary teaching experience and self-evaluation in combination are held constant, the correlation coefficient of .32 (zero-order) drops to .16 (second-order partial correlation). When the linear effect of time and effort devoted to work role is removed in addition, the coefficient decreases further to .12 (third-order partial correlation). These findings suggest that among the three variables, years of elementary teaching experience has the greatest single impact on the relationship between sex and control over professional staff, but that all three of them in combination have the greatest influence on it. We interpret these findings as supporting the *possibility* that the three variables posited as intervening between the principal's sex and control over the professional staff may be operating in this manner.

FURTHER ANALYSES

We now turn to a brief examination of the mean scores obtained by the men and women principals on the individual items included in the control measure (Table 8-6).[7]

In which areas do both women and men exert the greatest and least control? The data indicate that determining "what the objectives of the guidance program should be in the school" evokes the highest degree of control by both men and women principals. The guidance program is an ancillary service that can and often does have important implications for teacher-pupil relationships and teacher-principal relationships. In the elementary school, problems of learning or discipline requiring counselling and guidance are usually referred to guidance personnel by teachers with the consent of their principal. Although guidance services are generally viewed as supplementary to, rather than an integral part of, the instructional program, principals apparently feel it essential to exercise control over them.

Both men and women principals exert least control over checking on their teachers' written lesson plans; this is usually done "occasionally" by women and slightly less frequently by men. Generally speaking, principals believe that written lesson plans are important for beginning

TABLE 8-6. Mean Scores of Women and Men Principals on Items Included in the Factor Score, Control over Teachers' Professional Activities

	Women			Men		
Items and Response Weights	Mean	S.D.	N	Mean	S.D.	N

How frequently [always (5), almost always (4), occasionally (3), almost never (2), never (1)] does your principal:

1. Require that teachers discuss their major classroom problems with the principal.	3.43	0.57	86	3.18	0.50	89
2. Ask teachers to report all major conferences with parents to the principal.	3.67	0.67	86	3.21	0.60	89
3. Require teachers to keep the principal informed about "problem" children in their classrooms.	3.62	0.54	86	3.37	0.56	89
4. Closely direct the work of teachers who are likely to experience difficulty.	3.61	0.53	86	3.40	0.58	89
5. Require that teachers' classroom behavior conform to the principal's standards.	3.74	0.51	86	3.39	0.57	89
6. Check to see that teachers prepare written lesson plans.	2.89	1.04	86	2.56	1.13	89
7. Know what is taking place in most classrooms during most of the day.	3.61	0.51	86	3.53	0.44	89
8. Determine what the objectives of the guidance program should be in the school.	3.86	0.54	86	3.61	0.51	89

*Items ordered in terms of decreasing magnitude of factor weight.

teachers; without specific planning, lessons may be disorganized and attention and rapport with the class lost. For the experienced teacher, their feeling probably is that "she knows what she's doing," and detailed outlines are not necessary. The fact that experienced teachers greatly outnumber beginning teachers in most schools may explain to some extent the principals' responses.

On what aspects of control do men and women especially *differ*? The sharpest differences occur on these two items: "require that teachers' classroom behavior conform to the principal's standards" and "ask teachers to report all major conferences with parents to the principal." In both instances, the women principals' mean is closer to the "almost always" response, while the men principals' mean is closer to the "occasionally" category. In line with the reasoning of the control hypothesis, we might speculate that women principals are more likely than men to require their teachers to conform to their standards, because due to their greater experience, women are more confident than men that their standards are sound and legitimate.

The item on which the men and women principals differ least is "know what is taking place in most classrooms during most of the day." According to their teachers, both men and women principals usually have some awareness about what is going on in their classrooms. Our informal observations in schools indicate that this is generally accomplished by walking around the building or stopping for brief informal visits in classrooms. Our findings, however, also suggest that women are more likely to request that teacher-parent conferences be reported to them. This is not only an indirect means of control; it also serves as a device for gaining a more complete picture of the actual or potential problems of their staffs.

Table 8-6 also reveals that women principals on the average are more likely than men to exercise control over their teachers in the following areas: in closely directing the work of teachers who are likely to experience difficulty, in requiring teachers to discuss their major classroom problems with them, in having teachers inform the principal about "problem" children in their rooms, and in determining the objectives of the school's guidance program. For every item in the control measure, the data show that the female principals exercised a greater degree of control over the professional activities of their teachers than did the male administrators.

NOTES AND REFERENCES

1. A. M. Carr-Saunders and P. A. Wilson, *The Professions* (Oxford: Clarendon Press, 1933) and Edward Gross, *Work and Society* (New York: Thomas Y. Crowell Co., 1958), pp. 77–83.

2. For a discussion of similarities and differences in professional and bureaucratic standards see Peter M. Blau and W. Richard Scott, *Formal Organizations* (San Francisco: Chandler Publishing Co., 1962), pp. 60–63.

3. For evidence to support this assumption about sex differences in teaching experience, see Chapter 3, Table 3-13.

4. For evidence supporting this assumption, see Chapter 7, Table 7-4.

5. See Appendix C, Table C-16 for item means, standard deviations, and weights used in computing the principals' scores on Control over Teachers' Professional Activities.

6. See Chapter 1, pp. 14–15 for a consideration of the factor analysis procedures used in the study and other issues related to measuring the performance of principals.

7. The scores are based on the weights specified in Table 8-6 and represent the means of the average scores obtained by the men and the women principals on the basis of the reports of the teacher-observers in each school.

9

Teacher Responsibilities to Pupils

An administrator of an organization staffed by professionals who is committed to maximizing its human and material resources for the benefit of its clients can at times be exposed to vexing situations. He could find himself in such a situation if his staff were reluctant or unwilling to expend the time and effort needed to meet client needs. A school principal, for example, may believe that pupils with serious learning difficulties have a right to receive extra help from their teachers and that they have a professional obligation to provide it after regular school hours. His teachers, however, may not share this view. They may believe that their principal has no right to expect them to extend their work day or saddle them with additional problems and responsibilities.

Another troublesome problem for a principal arises when a serious conflict erupts between a teacher and pupil in his school and the teacher is clearly in the wrong. In this case, the obligation of a principal as a professional educator to support the child may clash with the expectation of the staff that their administrator should support the teacher, right or wrong.

It is issues of this kind that concern us in this chapter, and our special interest in them is whether they evoke different responses from men and women principals. More specifically, we focus on two questions: (1) Is there a sex difference in the extent to which principals encourage teachers to offer maximum service to their pupils? (2) Do men and women principals differ in backing teachers in cases of conflict between teacher and pupil?

LEVEL OF TEACHER EFFORT

Practitioners of medicine, law, and education vary in their beliefs about the scope of the services their clients have a right to expect of them. For example, in education some teachers define their professional function as requiring them to be responsible only for the intellectual growth of their pupils; other teachers, however, subscribe to a definition of their role that includes concern for their social-emotional development. How teachers allocate their time and effort in the classroom reflects in part their conception of the scope of their role.

The regulations of school systems specify the time when teachers must arrive at school each morning and the time at which they may leave in the afternoon. In effect, these time specifications establish the *minimum* hours they are expected to devote to their teaching and related school activities. In some schools teachers devote additional time and effort to their pupils, but in others, they do not. The stress administrators place on the responsibility of their teachers to be of maximum service to their pupils undoubtedly influences the quantity and quality of additional services the children in their school receive. Do men or women in the principalship exhibit the greater concern for maximizing the services of teachers for the benefit of pupils? This is the question we now examine.

The Hypothesis

The hypothesis we tested, that women principals place greater emphasis than men on the teacher's obligation to offer maximum service to pupils, was based on two lines of reasoning.

The first begins with the assumption that in professional organizations the amount of effort and time superordinates devote to their own tasks will be positively related to the amount of time and effort they expect their subordinates to give to theirs. We further assumed that women devote more time and effort than men to their managerial tasks.[1] From these assumptions it follows that women principals will place greater stress than men on a teacher's obligation to give maximum service to its pupils.

The second line of reasoning is based on the assumption of a sex difference in the emphasis principals place on individual differences among pupils. Those who make much of individual differences are in effect demanding that teachers take into account the special as well as common needs and problems of their pupils. This conception of the teachers' role demands more of their time and effort. Therefore, the more principals stress the differences among individual pupils, the more they could be expected to emphasize the importance of teachers offering greater service to their pupils. Since we assumed that women principals are more concerned about individual differences than men,[2] we anticipated that the women would stress teacher service to pupils more than the men.

Testing the Hypothesis

To test this hypothesis we used a factor score to measure the principals' emphasis on the teacher's obligation to offer maximum service to pupils. The data on which the factor score is based were secured from the responses of the teacher-observers in each school to three questions about how frequently principals exhibit behavior of this kind. We had asked the teachers: How frequently ("always," "almost always," "occasionally," "almost never," "never") does your principal:

1. Encourage worthwhile student activities that would require additional work by teachers.
2. Encourage teachers to give extra help in their "free" periods to students needing that help.
3. Put the student's welfare above that of the teacher's when the two are opposed.[3]

To secure the best estimate of how frequently the principals exhibited concern for maximizing teachers' service to pupils, we averaged the factor scores of the teacher-observers in each school.

When we compared the mean factor scores of the women and men principals on this index, the findings did not support the hypothesis (Table 9-1): although the mean score of the women is higher than that of the men (9.24 vs. 9.13), the difference of 0.11 is not significant statistically.

Although the hypothesis did not receive support with reference to our total sample of large city elementary principals, a sex difference may occur under certain conditions. One condition of this kind is when the pupils of a school come from poor or deprived families. If, as it is generally assumed, teachers must devote greater time and effort to children from low SES than high SES families to obtain equivalent learning outcomes, then in schools located in the lowest socioeconomic areas, women principals might be more insistent than men on the teacher's obligation to be of maximum service to pupils.

To ascertain if the data offered support for this speculation, we sorted the principals in our sample into three categories that reflected the dif-

TABLE 9-1. Mean Scores of Women and Men Principals on Concern for Maximizing Teachers' Service to Pupils ($N = 175$)*

Sex	Mean Score	Standard Deviation	Number of Cases
Women	9.24	0.45	86
Men	9.13	0.51	89

* Data unavailable for 14 of the 189 principals.

t = 1.56; p > .05.

ferent average SES of pupils in their schools. We then computed mean scores for the men and for the women principals whose schools were located in neighborhoods where the families were of relatively low socioeconomic status (Table 9-2). The findings provide evidence in support of a conditional relationship. The women principals had a higher mean factor score than the men (9.30 vs. 9.04) on maximizing teacher

TABLE 9-2. Mean Scores of Women and Men Principals on Concern for Maximizing Teachers' Service to Pupils for Two Specified Subclassifications of Schools

Subclassification*	Women Mean	N	Men Mean	N	t	Probability Less than
Socio-economic Level						
Low	9.30	26	9.04	32	2.06	.05
Middle	9.23	25	9.17	30	0.41	n.s.
High	9.21	35	9.18	27	0.22	n.s.
Mean Teacher Experience						
Short	9.32	29	9.07	29	2.07	.05
Medium	9.18	27	9.05	30	1.02	n.s.
Long	9.21	29	9.26	30	0.40	n.s.

* See Appendix A for the definition of the subclassification categories.

services to pupils, and the difference of 0.26 is significant statistically. Are there differences in the mean factor scores of the men and women whose schools were located in the other two socioeconomic areas? In schools situated in relatively high and intermediate socioeconomic areas, the mean factor scores of the women were slightly higher than the men's, but in both cases the differences were small and not significant statistically (Table 9-2)[4]. We conclude that women principals place greater emphasis on a teacher's obligation to offer maximum services to pupils than men when they administer schools in relatively low SES areas but that their performance in this respect is not significantly different when they administer schools in higher SES areas.

A second condition that might result in men and women principals placing different emphasis on the faculty's obligation to give maximum service to pupils is the teaching experience of the staff. It could be argued that among principals whose staffs have had relatively little teaching experience women administrators will be more insistent than men on the school's obligation to provide the services their pupils need because inexperienced teachers have greater respect for, and hence take more seriously, the professional views of women than men principals.

When we examined the mean factor scores of the women and men principals who were responsible for schools whose faculties had little teaching experience on the index of the teacher's obligation to offer maximum service to pupils, we found support for a second conditional relationship: the women obtained a higher mean score than the men (9.32 vs. 9.07) and the difference of 0.25 was significant statistically (Table 9-2). When we compared the mean index scores of the men and women who were principals of schools in which the teachers' average experience was of medium length and of longer duration, the findings showed that the difference in their mean scores was not significant statistically in both comparisons (Table 9-2).[5]

CONFLICT BETWEEN TEACHER AND PUPIL

Hughes has observed that "in many of the things which people do for one another, the *for* can be changed to *to* by a slight overdoing or by a shift of mood. . . . The danger of major distortion of relationship and function within the framework of a formal office lurks wherever people go or are sent for help or correction. . . . "[6] Most principals recognize that conditions of this kind can occur when they find it necessary to intervene in conflicts between teacher and pupil.

Elementary principals, as former teachers, know that pupils may easily misinterpret what the teacher says or does. Children may think that what is being done *for* them is being done *to* them. In telling their parents about "what happened in school today," they may give a distorted account of what the teacher did and fail to understand why it was done. Principals are also aware, however, that teachers on occasion can become exasperated, flustered, or lose their tempers and that during such episodes may treat their pupils in an unprofessional or even irresponsible manner. Then too, principals are usually aware that teachers and parents frequently bring different perspectives to the same situation. Thus, a teacher may severely reprimand a child for disregarding her instructions because she believes that unless the pupil is firmly dealt with, other children will also engage in the behavior. The parents of the sanctioned child, however, will probably view the teacher's action as indefensible. In view of a principal's obligations to protect the rights of both teachers and pupils, maintaining the delicate balance between their interests is never simple or easy. The question we now examine is whether men and women principals differ in supporting teachers when conflicts arise between teacher and pupil.

The Hypothesis

We tested the hypothesis that there would be no difference between female and male principals in their support of teachers in case of conflict between teacher and pupil. We reasoned that teachers cannot carry out their responsibilities to pupils without their cooperation. In addition to involving themselves actively in learning, children must accept almost without question the authority of the teacher. What should be learned, how and when it should be learned, conferring rewards, imposing punishments, and such things as determining seating arrangements are prerogatives of the teacher. A child or parent who objects to a teacher's decision is in effect challenging her authority. A principal who does not side with a teacher when such challenges erupt into disputes places her in a difficult, even untenable situation. This is the case since the teacher, in contrast to the physician who sees his patients separately and for short periods of time, must confront all of her pupils simultaneously and must work continuously with them every day, month after month.[7] If, because of the principal's failure to give her unqualified support, pupils begin to oppose or scorn her authority, the consequences for her and her work can be catastrophic. Her judgments may be open to continuous questioning by her pupils and her ability to control the class may be materially impaired. If the principal fails to take her side against a pupil, it will appear to the teacher as if she has been betrayed.

It could be argued that female principals might be inclined to support pupils when there is trouble between teacher and pupil more frequently than males because women show greater concern for the social-emotional development of the child. We reasoned, however, that the principals' concern about undercutting the authority of their teachers and the negative consequences of their failing to back them, even when the teacher is definitely in the wrong, would predispose both women and men to back up teachers in cases of conflict between teacher and pupil. In short, the null hypothesis was based on the idea that both men and women administrators as former teachers would be strongly inclined to support the teachers because of their fear of undermining their authority and of jeopardizing their relations with teachers by failing to support them. We reasoned that although women principals might be somewhat more inclined to support pupils than the men principals, the detrimental effects of their "abandoning" their teachers would be so great that both the women and the men principals would engage in essentially the same type of behavior.

Testing the Hypothesis

To test the hypothesis we used a factor score based on the responses of the teacher-observers in each school to four questions. We asked the teachers: How frequently ("always," "almost always," "occasionally," "almost never," "never") does your principal engage in the following kinds of activities:

1. Side with the teacher when a student complains about the teacher's behavior, even if the student's complaint is legitimate.
2. Support a teacher's discipline decision that the principal believes is grossly unfair to the child.
3. Back the teacher in any public controversy between teacher and student.
4. Insist that students obey teacher's instructions first, and complain about them later.[8]

To obtain the best estimate of the principals' support of teachers in cases of conflict between teachers and pupils, we once again averaged the teacher-observers' factor scores in each school to secure a summary measure of the principals' behavior.

When the mean factor scores of the men and women on this measure were compared, we found that although the score of the women was higher than that of the men (10.36 vs. 10.23), the difference of 0.13 was not significant statistically (Table 9-3).[9] The hypothesis that female and male principals do not differ in their support of teachers in cases of conflict between teachers and pupils is supported.

Men and women principals, however, might differ in their support of teachers under certain conditions. One possible condition of this kind is when their faculty, on the average, has relatively little teaching experience. Since men principals generally have less teaching experience and familiarity with the classroom than women administrators, the men principals might be expected to identify more with teachers and hence give greater support to their teachers than the women.

To put this speculation to the test, we sorted the principals into three groups on the basis of the average teaching experience of their staffs and then computed the mean scores of the men and women principals on our index of support of teachers for those who fell into each of the three categories. The findings revealed that the men principals obtained a higher mean score on the index than the women (10.49 vs. 10.22) in

TABLE 9-3.   Mean Scores of Women and Men Principals on Support of Teachers in Cases of Conflict between Teacher and Pupils ($N = 175$)*

Sex	Mean Score	Standard Deviation	Number of Cases
Women	10.36	0.72	86
Men	10.23	0.89	89

* Data unavailable for 14 of the 189 principals.

$t = 1.08$; $p > .05$.

schools whose teachers had relatively little experience as teachers; however, the difference of 0.27 was not significant statistically (Table 9-4). When we examined the mean scores of the men and women principals on the index of support of teachers for schools whose teachers had an intermediate amount or a relatively large amount of teaching experience, the findings indicated that, although the women's mean score was higher than the men's in both cases, the differences were not significant statistically (Table 9-4).[10]

A second condition that might influence the support that men and women principals offer their teachers in cases of teacher-pupil conflicts is the average socioeconomic level of the families of pupils in their schools. If, as is frequently asserted, parents of high SES are, generally speaking, more interested in school affairs and the progress of their children than those of lower SES, and hence are more likely to question how teachers behave, then, in high SES schools, women principals might be more disposed to support their teachers than the men in cases of teacher conflict with pupils because their greater knowledge of, and

TABLE 9-4.   Mean Scores of Women and Mean Principals on Support of Teachers in Cases of Conflict between Teacher and Pupils for Two Specified Subclassifications of Schools

Subclassification*	Women		Men			Probability Less than
	Mean	N	Mean	N	t	
Mean Teacher Experience						
Short	10.22	29	10.49	29	1.18	n.s.
Medium	10.41	27	10.22	30	1.03	n.s.
Long	10.41	29	9.98	30	1.95	n.s.
Socio-economic Level						
Low	10.24	26	10.25	32	0.05	n.s.
Middle	10.27	25	10.32	30	0.22	n.s.
High	10.52	35	10.09	27	2.47	.05

* See Appendix A for the definition of the subclassification categories.

skills in, teaching permit them to withstand pressure from parents and to deal with their arguments in a more efficacious manner than men principals.

To find out if there was support for this contention, we sorted the principals into three groups on the basis of the socioeconomic backgrounds of pupils in their schools and then calculated the mean scores of men and women principals whose schools were in each of the three socioeconomic categories. The findings revealed that women principals do give greater backing to teachers in cases of conflict between pupils and teachers in schools with the highest socioeconomic rating. The mean score for women was 10.52 and for men it was 10.09; the difference of 0.43 is significant statistically (Table 9-4). In schools with pupils whose parents had relatively low SES, the mean scores of the men and women on the index were almost identical (10.25 vs. 10.24); in those schools with pupils from families in the middle range of SES, the men's scores were slightly higher than the women's (10.32 vs. 10.27), but the difference in this case, too, was not significant statistically (Table 9-4).[11]

NOTES AND REFERENCES

1.   See Chapter 8, Table 8-4, for evidence supporting this assumption.

2.   See Chapter 6, Table 6-1, for evidence in support of this assumption.

3.   See Appendix C, Table C-17, for the item means, standard deviations, and weights used in computing scores on Concern for Maximizing Teachers' Service to Pupils.

4.   All statements about the probability levels under the three socioeconomic level categories in Table 9-2 are based on a two-tailed test of significance.

5.   All statements about the probability levels under the three mean teacher experience categories in Table 9-2 are based on a two-tailed test of significance.

6.   Everett C. Hughes, *Men and Their Work* (Glencoe, Ill.: The Free Press, 1958), p. 70.

7.   Talcott Parsons, *The Social System* (Glencoe, Ill.: The Free Press, 1951), p. 464.

8.   See Appendix C, Table C-18, for the item means, standard deviations, and weights used in computing the principals' scores on Support of Teachers in Conflict with Pupils.

9.   A high score on this factor represents a high degree of support for teachers in cases of conflict with pupils.

10.   All statements about the probability levels under the three mean teacher experience categories in Table 9-4 are based on a two-tailed test of significance.

11.   All statements about the probability levels under the three socioeconomic level categories in Table 9-4 are based on a two-tailed test of significance.

10

Social Distance in
Relationships with Teachers

In his classic treatment of bureaucracy Weber stressed the necessity and importance of formal distinctions of status and social distance among members of an organization to assure impartiality and efficiency in their conduct.[1] However, in work establishments where superordinates and their subordinates are members of the same profession, for example, in schools or institutions of higher learning, such a view of organizations is not compatible with the idea that members of the same profession are expected to associate with each other on a collegial basis or as a "company of equals."[2] In the case of the relationship between a principal and a teacher, the principal occupies the position of greater authority and prestige; following Weber's conception of a bureaucracy, it would be anticipated that the relationships between a principal and a teacher would be characterized more by social distance than social nearness.[3] Yet, since principals and teachers are colleagues in the same professional endeavor, one looks for closeness and a considerable measure of equality in their relationships. How do school administrators respond to this apparent dilemma? We consider in the first part of this chapter whether male or female principals maintain the greater social distance with their teachers inside their schools.

Parsons has noted that "the concept of 'closeness' of social relationship is not a simple one"[4] and one of its complexities may be that the social distance between a superordinate and his subordinates may vary according to context. In the case of schools, it may be of one magnitude inside the school building and another on the outside. Hence, later in the chapter, we examine the social distance separating men and women school principals from their teachers in their out-of-school relationships.

SOCIAL DISTANCE IN THE SCHOOL

In considering the concept of social distance, Simmel noted:

> ... it is hard to reconcile personal relations, which are the very life principle of small groups, with the distance and coolness of objective and abstract norms without which the large group cannot exist.[5]
>
> This dualism of nearness and distance is necessary for our behavior to be consistently correct. It inheres, so to speak, in the fundamental forms and problems of our life.[6]

Simmel maintained that social nearness leads to knowledge and understanding; social distance to objectivity and detachment—all qualities of direct relevance to the interaction of principal and teacher. Although they are subordinates, teachers, as professionals who have passed through much the same educational experiences as the principals and who share with them the norms and values of their calling, look to the principal for a sympathetic understanding of their problems in the classroom. On the other hand, the principals occupy a different and higher place in the hierarchical structure and from time to time may have to exercise their formal authority over the teachers under them, for example, by sanctioning them. They must also evaluate teachers for purposes of recommending tenure or promotion. Studies of leadership show as Kadushin puts it, that "too high a felt social proximity between leader and follower leads to too high an emotional involvement with the group and a reduced efficiency."[7] He attributes the decline in efficiency as being a result of the leader's unwillingness or inability to exert his power.[8] This type of relationship is not uncommon in some elementary schools.

In their relationships with teachers, principals have innumerable opportunities to convey whether they prefer a principal-teacher social climate that is characterized by distance or nearness. They can stress or deemphasize gradations of rank. At informal gatherings administrators may discourage or encourage teachers to show them deference. They can also display their pleasure or displeasure when teachers call them by their given names.

The Hypothesis

Do the men or the women administrators maintain the greater social distance between themselves and their teachers inside the school? Our hypothesis was that the men would be more distant in their bearing towards teachers than women. We arrived at it by way of three lines of reasoning.

First, we assumed that the greater an individual's interest in occupational advancement, the more he will insist on recognition of the status accruing to his present position and, at the same time, on distinctions of status between himself and subordinates, from whom he is apt to keep at a distance. If we assume further that the men among the principals generally aspire higher than the women, then it follows that they will maintain the greater social distance between themselves and their teachers.

Second, for a principal to maintain relationships of social nearness to his teachers while at the same time serving as the official responsible for sanctioning them on occasion and for assessing their professional performance, implies a high degree of self-confidence in his professional skills. In a relationship of this kind familiarity may breed respect or contempt. We assumed that among a group of principals, those with a relatively low degree of self-confidence in their professional abilities would be more likely to maintain a high degree of social distance in relating to their subordinates than those who had a higher assessment of their competencies. If we further assume that men principals in general set a lower value on their professional abilities than women,[9] then it follows that they should be more likely than women administrators to keep their staffs at a greater social distance.

The third line of reasoning concerned the differential effect on social distance of interactions that involve members of the same or the opposite sex. It has been observed that ". . . in most strata men and women in each other's presence talk conventionally, act more formally, than in groups of one's sex, and the conventions influence the style as well as the amount and content of expression."[10] This will also occur, we assumed, when the interaction occurs between individuals on different levels in a hierarchical structure.[11] The great majority of elementary school teachers are women; therefore, in elementary schools, women principals associate primarily with members of their own sex while men principals generally must relate to members of the opposite sex. These considerations also led us to expect that men principals would maintain more social distance between themselves and their subordinates inside the schools than would women administrators.

TESTING THE HYPOTHESIS

To test the hypothesis we used a factor score as an index of the social distance a principal maintained with his teachers inside the school. Each score was based on data obtained from responses of the teacher-observers to four questions about the frequency with which principals stress distinctions of status. The teachers were asked: How frequently ("always," "almost always," "occasionally," "almost never," "never") does your principal engage in the following kinds of activities:

1. Discourage teachers from treating him as "one of the gang" at informal gatherings of teachers.
2. Encourage all teachers to call him by his first name when students are not present.
3. Make it a practice to have lunch frequently with the teachers in his school.
4. Insist, tactfully, that teachers show due respect for his position as principal.[12]

The factor scores of the teacher-observers in each principal's school were averaged to secure the best estimate of the social distance the principals maintained with their teachers *inside* the school. When the mean scores of the men and women principals on this measure of social distance were compared, the findings indicated that the hypothesis was not supported. The mean scores of the men and women, 9.15 versus 9.16 respectively, were almost identical (Table 10-1). We conclude, therefore,

TABLE 10-1. Mean Scores of Women and Men Principals on Social Distance in the School ($N = 175$)*

Sex	Mean Score	Standard Deviation	Number of Cases
Women	9.16	1.00	86
Men	9.15	0.88	89

* Data unavailable for 14 of the 189 principals.

  $t = 0.06$; $p > .05$.

that men and women in the elementary principalship do not differ in the social distance they maintain with their teachers inside their schools.

To explore whether the average age of the teachers in a school might have a bearing on the social distance that men and women principals maintain with them in school, we classified the administrators into three groups on the basis of the average age of their teachers and then computed the mean social distance scores for the male and female principals (Table 10-2). For schools in which the faculties were relatively young or intermediate in average age, the mean factor scores of the men principals were higher than those of women, but in neither case was the difference significant statistically. In schools where the teachers were relatively old, the women principals had higher social distance scores than the men, but the difference in their scores in this case was also not significant statistically.[13]

TABLE 10-2. Mean Scores of Women and Men Principals on Social Distance in the School by Mean Teacher Age

Subclassification*	Women		Men			Proba-bility Less than
	Mean	N	Mean	N	t	
Mean Age of Teachers						
Young	9.00	31	9.05	27	0.23	n.s.
Middle	9.26	31	9.44	27	0.74	n.s.
Old	9.24	24	9.00	35	1.01	n.s.

* See Appendix A for the definition of the subclassification categories.

SOCIAL DISTANCE OUTSIDE THE SCHOOL

It could be argued that whether, and the extent to which, principals relate to their teachers outside the school should be determined solely by their personal inclinations. However, it also must be recognized that the contacts principals maintain with their teachers *outside* the school can affect their relationships within it. As Hughes points out. "If some group of people continues to act together, even with regard to a secular matter, claims are likely to develop."[14] Even in relationships that are not characterized by strong bonds, moral and personal claims may grow up among individuals. Extramural interaction between principals and members of their faculty, then, can give rise to claims by one party on the other with the consequence that particularistic criteria could supercede universalistic considerations. The principal's impartiality in school affairs could be jeopardized.

Do men and women principals differ as to the social distance they maintain between themselves and their staffs *outside* the school? This is the question we now examine.

The Hypothesis

The hypothesis tested, that men administrators will maintain greater social distance in their out-of-school relationships with their teachers than will women administrators, was based on the following arguments.

The first focuses on the principals' assessment of their own skills in interpersonal relationships and how this circumstance will influence their extramural relationships with their staff members. Association with teachers outside of the school can create a delicate situation for principals. Although they may come to know and understand their teachers better, they may in the process lose the objectivity and detachment that are necessary if they are to serve as impartial administrators. The contacts principals have with teachers outside of school may tempt their subordinates to make claims on their principal intramurally. We reasoned that the more confidence a principal had in his skill in dealing with people, the less likely he would be to insist on a high degree of social distance in his out-of-school relationships with teachers. If we also assume that men principals have a lower evaluation of their interpersonal skills than women principals,[15] it follows that the men would maintain greater social distance between themselves and their teachers in extramural situations than would the women.

The second argument starts with the assumption that ambitious individuals are more likely to restrict their social contacts with work associates to their formal work relationships than those with more modest aspirations. Therefore, the more ambitious principals could be expected to maintain extramural contracts with teachers at a more distant and formal level than those whose aspirations were lower

Assuming that the career aspirations of men principals are generally higher than those of women,[16] it follows that the male administrators would maintain greater social distance between themselves and their teachers in their associations outside the school than will the women administrators.

The third argument was based on the difference in the marital status of the men and women principals. As noted in Chapter 2, 92% of the male principals in our sample are married; in contrast, 63% of the women are single. Unmarried principals will generally have more time and a greater inclination to socialize with teachers after school hours than married ones; moreover, the unmarried also probably have more money to spend on diversions. This line of reasoning also leads to the conclusion that men administrators would maintain greater distance between themselves and their staffs outside the school than would the women.

The fourth argument focuses on the customary modes and conditions of interaction between men and women in American society. More specifically, there is usually greater social distance in cross-sex interaction than when individuals are of the same sex. Furthermore, "complications" are more likely to arise when male superordinates relate to women subordinates during after school hours than when female superordinates associate with them. To avoid these complications, we assume that men generally observe the convention of greater distance in cross-sex than in same-sex encounters. Since most elementary school teachers are women, it follows than men principals would tend to maintain greater social distance toward their teachers outside the school than would women principals.

Testing the Hypothesis

To test the hypothesis, we developed a factor score based on the teacher-observers' reports to five questions. We asked the teachers: How frequently ("always," "almost always," "occasionally," "almost never," "never") does your principal engage in the following kinds of activities:

1. Discourage social invitations from faculty members.
2. Avoid social involvement with groups of teachers.

3. Refrain from joining a social club to which a number of his teachers belong.
4. Follow the policy of not having members of the faculty as close personal friends.
5. Spend an occasional evening with faculty members.[17]

To obtain the best estimate of the amount of social distance principals maintain with their teachers in their out-of-school relationships, the factor scores of the teacher-observers were again averaged. When the mean scores for the male and female principals were calculated on the index of "external" social distance, the findings supported the hypothesis: the score for the men is higher than that of the women's (10.34 vs. 9.87) and the difference of 0.47 is significant statistically (Table 10-3). Men in the principalship on the average do in fact maintain greater social distance with their staffs outside of school than do the women.

When the findings have previously supported a hypothesis in earlier analyses, we have inquired whether the relationship might simply be an artifact of one or more "confounding" variables; marital status has been introduced into the analysis on several occasions in this connection. In the reasoning leading to the development of the social distance hypothesis, however, marital status was employed as a possible explanatory variable. Whether marital status does in fact account in part for sex differences in the principals' social distance with their teachers in their out-of-school relationships is considered later.

TABLE 10-3. Mean Scores of Women and Men Principals on Social Distance outside the School ($N = 175$)*

Sex	Mean Score	Standard Deviation	Number of Cases
Women	9.87	1.29	86
Men	10.34	1.15	89

* Data unavailable for 14 of the 189 principals.

$t = 2.56$; $p < .01$.

To determine whether the relationship holds up under different conditions we subclassified the principals in terms of both the region and size of city in which their schools were located, the socioeconomic level and size of their school, and the mean age of their teachers. When we examined the relationship between the sex of the principals and social distance outside the school under each of these five conditions, the findings show that in each of the 16 subgroupings of the data the men, without exception, had higher social distance scores than the women (Table 10-4). The relationship reported for the total sample is internally replicated under each of these conditions.

Testing the Reasoning

The "external" social distance hypothesis was based on the following arguments. (1) We assumed that male principals would assess their interpersonal skills less favorably than female administrators and that self-evaluation in this respect is negatively related to social distance; therefore, men principals will maintain greater distance from their teachers than women. (2) We assumed that men administrators would hold higher career aspirations than women and that the desire for upward mobility is positively related to social distance with subordinates; hence, men principals will display greater social distance in relations with their teachers than women administrators. (3) We assumed that men principals would generally be married and that women principals would not and that "being married" tends to increase social distance between principals and their teachers outside the school whereas "being single" tends to decrease it; hence, in the principalship men will maintain greater social distance in their relationships with the faculty than the women. (4) We assumed that sex norms require greater social distance in cross-sex than in same-sex encounters; since elementary school principals deal with predominantly female staffs, the men among them will tend to maintain greater social distance from their teachers than will the women.

To determine the explanatory value of the variables that we assumed "intervene" between the sex of principals and the social distance they maintain with their teachers, we use the procedures described in detail in Chapter 1, pages 15–16. The data necessary to test the association between the intervening and the independent and the dependent varia-

TABLE 10-4.   Mean Scores of Women and Men Principals on Social Distance outside the School for Five Specified Subclassifications of Schools

Subclassification	Women			Men			Direction Predicted Correctly (+) or Incorrectly (−)
	Mean	S.D.	N	Mean	S.D.	N	
Region							
West	9.28	0.67	10	9.72	0.92	17	+
Midwest	10.16	1.73	26	10.58	0.97	27	+
East	10.00	1.13	32	10.77	1.28	17	+
South	9.53	0.82	18	10.24	1.16	28	+
Size of City							
Small	9.70	1.08	45	10.11	1.12	46	+
Medium	9.99	1.25	29	10.60	1.18	27	+
Large	10.21	1.89	12	10.59	0.99	16	+
Socio-economic Level							
Low	10.07	1.51	26	10.70	1.11	32	+
Middle	9.76	1.07	25	10.07	1.19	30	+
High	9.80	1.25	35	10.24	1.03	27	+
Mean Age of Teachers							
Low	9.89	1.42	31	10.48	0.99	27	+
Middle	9.82	1.20	31	10.07	1.13	27	+
High	9.91	1.23	24	10.46	1.23	35	+
Size of School							
Small	9.84	1.19	30	10.17	1.28	20	+
Medium	9.57	1.05	35	10.17	1.04	25	+
Large	10.40	1.60	21	10.58	1.08	38	+

bles are presented in Table 10-5.[18] The findings reveal (1) that the principals' self-assessment of their interpersonal skills is not related to their gender or social distance; (2) that although career aspiration is associated with the sex of principals, its relationship with their social distance is not statistically significant; and (3) that marital status is associated with the social distance and sex of principals, as we assumed.

TABLE 10-5. Correlation Coefficients for the Relationships Between the Assumed Intervening Variables and the Independent Variable (Sex) and Dependent Variable (Social Distance outside the School) ($N = 175$)

Assumed Intervening Variable	Sex[#] (Point-biserial $\underline{r}$)	Social Distance outside School (Pearsonian $\underline{r}$)
Self-evaluation of interpersonal skills	.11	-.06
Level of aspiration	-.38*	.11
Marital status (marriedness)	-.66*	.20*

[#] Female = 1; male = 0.

*p < .05.

In short, neither self-assessment in interpersonal skills nor career aspiration meets the initial specifications required if they were to serve as intervening variables. Only one of the variables, marital status, fulfills the requisite criteria.

Does the relationship between the sex of principals and their social distance decline when marital status is held constant? The zero-order point-biserial correlation between sex and social distance is -.19. When marital status is held constant, the relationship drops to -.10 (Table 10-6). This finding points to the possibility that marital status may

TABLE 10-6. Zero-order and First-order Partial Correlation Coefficients of Sex and Social Distance outside the School ($N = 175$)

	Zero-order $\underline{r}$	First-order Partial $\underline{r}$
Sex and Social Distance outside the School	-.19	
Holding constant:		
Marital status (marriedness)		-.10

operate as an explanatory variable that accounts in part for the difference in social distance exhibited by men and women in the principalship in their out-of-school relationships with teachers who serve on their faculties.

NOTES AND REFERENCES

1. Max Weber, *The Theory of Social and Economic Organization*, Talcott Parsons (Ed.), translated by A. M. Henderson and Talcott Parsons (New York: Oxford University Press, 1947), pp. 329–334.

2. For an analysis of four dimensions subsumed under the concept of social distance, see Charles Kadushin, "Social Distance between Client and Professional," *American Journal of Sociology*, LXVII (1962), pp. 517–531. For an examination of the relationship between status distance and personal distance in a different type of situation, see Leonard I. Pearlin and Morris Rosenberg, "Nurse-Patient Social Distance and the Structural Context of a Mental Hospital," *American Sociological Review*, XXVII (1962), pp. 56–65.

3. See Weber, *op. cit.*

4. Talcott Parsons, *The Social System* (Glencoe, Ill.: The Free Press, 1951), p. 279.

5. Kurt H. Wolff (Ed.), *The Sociology of Georg Simmel* (Glencoe, Ill.: The Free Press, 1950), p. 97.

6. *Ibid.*, p. 97 fn.

7. Fred E. Fiedler, "A Note on Leadership Theory: The Effect of Social Barriers between Leaders and Followers," *Sociometry* (1957), pp. 87–94; cited in Kadushin, *op. cit.*

8. Kadushin, *op. cit.*, p. 529.

9. For evidence supporting this assumption, see Chapter 7, Table 7-4.

10. Mark Benney, David Riesman, and Shirley A. Star, "Age and Sex in the Interview," *American Journal of Sociology*, LXII (1956), p. 144.

11. *Ibid.*

12. See Appendix C, Table C-19, for item means, standard deviations, and weights used in computing the principals' scores on Social Distance in the School.

13. All tests of significance used in Table 10-2 are based on two-tailed tests.

14. Everett C. Hughes, "Institutions," in Alfred M. Lee (Ed.), *Principles of Sociology* (New York: Barnes and Noble, Inc., 1951), p. 232.

15. Evidence presented later in the chapter, Table 10-6, indicates that this is a tenuous assumption.

16. For evidence supporting this assumption, see Chapter 14, Table 14-1.

17. See Appendix C, Table C-20, for item means, standard deviations, and weights used in computing principals' scores on Social Distance outside the School.

18. Since out data provide no evidence to examine the fourth line of reasoning about the sex norms, the intervening variable analyses deal with only three of the assumed intervening variables.

11

Involvement of Parents in School Affairs

The extent to which parents should be involved in school affairs has long constituted a very controversial issue both within and outside of public education circles. One aspect of this matter that especially perplexes school administrators is whether parents, in addition to pupils, should be viewed as clients of the school. Part of their difficulty in dealing with this question stems from the varying postures that parents adopt toward the schools their children attend. Some relate to them primarily as adults concerned about the overall educational progress of their children. Others, however, assert that since their taxes pay the bills for the operation of the public schools and it is their own children who are being educated,[1] their views should be taken into account in determining the policies and programs of the schools and in assessing their performance.

Another facet of the problem is linked to the ages of the children served by elementary schools. Their ages may range from 6 to 14. They generally are not aware of their own rights and interests and hence, it is difficult for them to judge the professional services they receive.[2] The law recognizes these and other age-related circumstances in viewing children as minors and in establishing procedures to protect certain of their interests. Doctors, for example, must obtain the written approval of parents before performing surgical operations on children. In schools, parental permission must be secured before children can be taken on school trips or placed in experimental programs.

The Parent Teacher Association (P.T.A.) or similar organizations associated with most elementary schools attest to the school's recognition of the importance of maintaining some form of communication with parents. The scope of the activities of the P.T.A. varies greatly and appears to reflect primarily the vigor of their leadership and the principal's view of its legitimate functions.

The "parent involvement" issue arises not only in the schools, but in nearly all institutions that deal with children. The stereotype of pediatrics held by medical students, for example, is one that ". . . contains a strong suggestion that the patient relationships will be unsatisfactory because of the difficulty of communicating with children and dealing with their parents."[3] To practitioners of medicine who have children as patients, parents are apparently seen as necessary, but not always helpful, participants in the professional-child client relationship.

In the elementary school the issue, as we noted, is not whether parents have a right to be concerned about the progress and well-being of their children, but over the extent and the nature of their participation. Why should the degree of involvement of parents in school affairs be treated as a problem by teachers and administrators? The reason is that like other professionals, educational practitioners claim a mandate to define public values in their area of specialized training that also constitutes an area vital to the welfare of society. Furthermore, in regard to the education of children, they believe they should have the right to specify the conduct appropriate for laymen in matters connected with their work.[4] "Improper" participation of parents in deliberations about school objectives or methods of teaching could lead to their challenging the mandate of their profession.

Lay interference in the more established professions such as medicine or law is largely precluded by the esoteric nature of the knowledge and skills of their practitioners: the layman usually has neither the technical knowledge nor the experience to judge the services he receives. For the educational practitioner in the elementary school the situation is different. Teachers in the primary grades claim a mandate to transmit knowledge and skills that are more in the realm of the familiar than the esoteric. Parents, therefore, can more readily pass judgment on their performance. Furthermore, the circumstance that parents themselves are products of the schools and that so many of them are high school and college graduates results in their feeling that they have the knowledge base required to question or challenge the work of the schools.

A unique characteristic of the elementary school exacerbates the problem of parental participation at this educational level: unlike the junior or senior high school, the elementary school is geographically and sociologically a neighborhood institution.[5] Neighborhood tensions are likely to be felt within the school and information and gossip about its activities can be expected to be widely and rapidly circulated among parents.

Conditions of this kind make the issue of parent involvement in activities of the school an especially troublesome area for principals in their capacity as its organizational representative. In addition, while teachers usually deal with parents primarily as the mother or father of a particular child in their classes, a principal must also deal with parents when they are assembled in larger groups, for example, at meetings of the P.T.A.

Elementary principals, then, must come to terms with the question, To what extent should the parents of pupils in their school be involved in its affairs? As we have seen, the issue is complex: on the one hand, because their organizations educate young children, principals must accept the fact that parents have a right to be concerned about the welfare of their children; on the other hand, principals and their teachers generally view themselves as professionals whose training has equipped them to be experts in imparting skills and knowledge to young children. If principals encourage parents to participate actively in school affairs, they could embark on activities that trespass on the professional domain of teachers and that constitute an invasion of their rights as professionals.

Given this situation, principals vary in the choices among the available options. Some severely restrict the participation of parents in school activities. Others strongly encourage it in nearly all of its forms. And still others approve of it with respect to selected aspects of the school's operations and discourage it in other areas of its functioning. If principals choose the second or third alternatives, they may attempt to co-opt parents by appointing them to advisory committees or by inviting them to serve as part-time school aides.[6] If parents involved in these types of participation find them meaningful and gratifying, their involvement with the school may result in their achieving a greater understanding of what it is attempting to accomplish and the rationale underlying its educational strategies and programs. Strategies of this kind tend to reduce disputes and relieve tensions between parents and teachers. There are dangers, too, in this type of approach, but the range of "safe" activities in most schools is fairly wide. It also deserves note that involvements of these kinds can also exacerbate latent tensions if parents come to perceive that their ideas are not taken seriously and that the effort they have devoted to school activities has been largely a waste of their time.

With this background we turn to our special interest in the issue of parent participation in school affairs. Is there a sex difference among elementary school principals in the extent to which they involve parents in school affairs?

THE HYPOTHESIS

We tested the hypothesis that women principals involve parents more in school affairs than men. It was based on three arguments.

The first argument starts with the assumption that principals who hold a relatively high assessment of their ability to direct the instructional program would feel more comfortable in working with parents, answering their questions, explaining, and, if necessary, defending school programs than those with a lower self-evaluation in this respect. We further assumed that those principals who felt more at ease in working with parents would be more predisposed to involve them in school affairs than those who felt less comfortable in their relationships with them. If we further assume that women judge themselves more favorably than men in the evaluation of their own ability to manage the instructional program,[7] then we would expect women principals to encourage the parents to involve themselves in school activities more than would men.

The second argument is rooted in the assumption that individuals who work with clients vary in their self-evaluation of their interpersonal skills. In any profession, be it medicine, law, or education, there are practitioners who possess outstanding technical skills but who recognize that they are unable to make the best use of them due to their inadequate skills in human relations. We assumed that those principals with a relatively low regard for their skills in social relations would be predisposed to avoid potentially disruptive or threatening situations, such as working with parent committees, more than those with a higher opinion of their own ability in this respect. And, if it is assumed that female school executives evaluate their skills in dealing with people more favorably than the males, then it would follow that schools administered by women would be characterized by greater involvement of parents than those supervised by men.

The reasoning on which the final argument is based may be stated elliptically: the more stress principals place on the social and emotional development of pupils, the more important they will feel that their school should work closely with parents in view of the vital role they play in the growth and development of their children. If we assume that women place greater emphasis on this aspect of their pupils' development than men,[8] we would anticipate that women principals encourage greater participation of the parents than the men.

TESTING THE HYPOTHESIS

We used a factor score to measure the principals' involvement of parents in school affairs in testing the hypothesis. The data on which the factor score is based were secured from the responses of the teacher-observers to six questions about the frequency with which their principal involves parents in affairs of the school. We asked them: How frequently ("always," "almost always," "occasionally," "almost never," "never") does your principal engage in the following kinds of activities:

1. Encourage a group of parents to discuss and help formulate the educational philosophy to be used in the school.
2. Use interested parents as volunteer part-time "teacher helpers."
3. Encourage parents to help during school hours on school or class trips or projects.
4. Use interested parents as an advisory group when making out the course of study.
5. Encourage interested parent groups to evaluate how well the school is achieving its curricular objectives.
6. Encourage parental attendance at school assemblies.[9]

To obtain the best estimate of the degree to which principals involve parents in the schools' activities, we averaged the factor scores of the teacher-observers in each principal's school.

When the mean scores of women and men principals on this Index of Parental Involvement were computed, the findings did not support the hypothesis: the men, not the women as we had predicted, had the higher mean score (7.69 vs. 7.63). However, the relatively small difference of 0.06 in their scores was not significant statistically (Table 11-1).[10] We conclude that on the average, women and men in the prin-

TABLE 11-1. Mean Scores of Women and Men Principals on Parental Involvement ($N = 175$)*

Sex	Mean	S.D.	N
Women	7.63	1.40	86
Men	7.69	1.26	89

* Data unavailable for 14 of the 189 principals.

$t = 0.30$; $p > .05$.

cipalship do not differ significantly in their involvement of parents in school activities.

In our further exploration of this issue, we considered several conditions that might lead men and women principals to assign differential importance to the involvement of parents in school activities. We concluded that the condition that would most likely have such an effect was the circumstance that the pupils of a school came from deprived backgrounds. We assumed that the women administrators would generally place somewhat greater emphasis than the men on the social and emotional development of the child and generally would also be more aware than men of the importance of a supportive family environment for the child's school performance. On the basis of this reasoning, we anticipated that the women would hold a more positive orientation than the men to parent participation when they served in low SES schools.

To determine whether the data supported this line of reasoning, we sorted out those principals who administered schools in which the pupils came from families of relatively low SES and then calculated the mean Parental Involvement scores for the men and women principals of these schools. The findings revealed that women did obtain a higher score than the men (7.57 vs. 7.12) in these schools; however, the difference of 0.45 is not significant statistically (Table 11-2). We also computed the mean Parental Involvement scores of the men and women principals whose pupils were members of families of relatively high and of medium SES. The data showed that in those schools with pupils from relatively high socioeconomic backgrounds, the mean score of the men on Parental Involvement was greater than that of the women (8.34 vs. 7.75); however, the difference of 0.59 is not significant statistically (Table 11-2). The male principals of schools with children from middle socioeconomic backgrounds also obtained a higher mean score on Parental Involvement than the female administrators of schools with this type of student population (7.70 vs. 7.51); however, in this case, too, the difference in the mean scores of the male and female principals is not significant statistically.

When we re-examined the Parental Involvement scores of the men and women administrators separately in terms of the SES levels of the families of the pupils in their schools, an interesting finding emerged. Table 11-2 shows that for the male principals, the higher the SES of the families served by the school, the higher the Parental Involvement score of the principal. The mean Parental Involvement score of male administrators was 7.12 in low SES schools, 7.70 in middle SES schools, and 8.34 in high SES schools. In the case of the women principals, those with pupils from families with the highest SES also had the highest mean Parental Involvement score (7.75). However, there was only a slight difference in the mean scores of those who were in charge of low and middle SES schools (7.57 vs. 7.51). These findings imply that principals of both sexes who administer high SES schools involve parents in school affairs more frequently than those in charge of schools whose pupils come from lower SES backgrounds. They also suggest that women administrators, in contrast to the men, tend to involve parents in school activities to approximately the same degree when they are in charge of low or middle SES schools.

TABLE 11-2.   Mean Scores of Women and Men Principals on Parental Involvement by Socio-economic Level of their School

Subclassification*	Women		Men			Probability Less than
	Mean	N	Mean	N	t	
Socio-economic Level						
Low	7.57	26	7.12	32	1.19	n.s.
Middle	7.51	25	7.70	30	0.57	n.s.
High	7.75	35	8.34	27	1.94	n.s.

* See Appendix A for the definition of the subclassification categories.

FURTHER ANALYSES

We now turn to an examination of the manner in which the men and women principals behaved with respect to each of the different types of parent participation included in the Index of Parental Involvement (Table 11-3). The first question to be considered is, In what school activities do *both* men and women principals most frequently welcome parent participation? The data indicate that they most frequently encourage a quite passive type of involvement: attendance at school assemblies (item 6, Table 11-3). Next in frequency is drawing on the services of parents in connection with school trips or class projects (item 3). This, too, is a fairly restricted form of participation, and like attending school assemblies, one that is highly limited in scope and that can be tightly controlled.

What kinds of parent participation do both men and women principals almost always discourage? The two types of involvement least frequently encouraged, according to the teachers' reports, are the use of "interested parents as an advisory group when making out the course of study" and the use of parents as part-time teacher helpers (items 4 and 2). Principals also call on parents infrequently to consider the educational philosophy of the school or to judge how well it is achieving its curricular objectives (items 1 and 5).

This set of findings can be interpreted as revealing that principals welcome the participation of parents in activities that they and their staffs can carefully delimit and control and that do not impinge on the professional prerogatives of teachers. They also indicate that principals do not encourage parent activities that will involve them in an examination of the objectives of their school or its performance. Parent attendance at school assemblies or their offering assistance to teachers on class trips have little or no bearing on teaching or learning. The participation of parents in discussions of educational philosophy, curriculum, or how well the school is achieving its objectives, however, could readily result in their exercising a direct influence on the school program and the staff.

The principals' disinclination to use parents as part-time helpers to teachers is of special interest. One reason for their lack of enthusiasm for this type of parent participation is that, if permitted, it would bring parents directly into the teachers' place of work and permit them to become witnesses and possibly critics of the teachers' performance. Another is that the elementary school pupil is supposed to be judged by

TABLE 11-3. Mean Scores of Women and Men Principals on Items Included in the Parental Involvement Factor Score

Item*	Women			Men		
	Mean	S.D.	N	Mean	S.D.	N
How frequently [always (5), almost always (4), occasionally (3), almost never (2), never (1)] does your principal:						
1. Encourage a group of parents to discuss and help formulate the educational philosophy to be used in the school.	2.21	0.64	86	2.26	0.48	89
2. Use interested parents as volunteer part-time "teacher helpers."	1.95	0.70	86	2.02	0.67	89
3. Encourage parents to help during school hours on school or class trips or projects.	3.47	0.65	86	3.46	0.65	89
4. Use interested parents as an advisory group when making out the course of study.	1.88	0.75	86	2.12	0.93	89
5. Encourage interested parent groups to evaluate how well the school is achieving its curricular objectives.	2.29	0.59	86	2.33	0.52	89
6. Encourage parental attendance at school assemblies.	3.93	0.56	86	3.83	0.56	89

* Items ordered in terms of decreasing magnitude of factor weight.

norms of universalistic achievement and not the particularistic criteria used by his family. Mothers serving as part-time helpers can be expected to face difficulties in applying the school's standards to their children. A third difficulty is that parents serving in the classroom would also observe and react to the behavior of other children in the local neighborhood. A fourth problem arises because the child often inadvertently conveys private information about members of his family to adults at school. Professionals know that they have an obligation to treat such information as confidential, bound as they are to respect confidences about client affairs; but not so the parents of other children. A fifth difficulty relates to a matter we noted earlier, the familiar nature of the subject matter in the primary grades. This circumstance makes it relatively easy for a parent to raise questions about teaching methods and the content of the curriculum. But teachers frequently cannot offer a rigorous justification of why they do what they do; hence a "questioning" parent in the classroom may create tensions. And finally, if, as many contend, elementary school teaching is a vocation involving little esoteric knowledge, then what little mystique it contains may be further reduced if outsiders become observers.

To sum up: the findings indicate that the women and men did not differ in any important respect in regard to their use of specific kinds of parent involvement in school affairs. Of the six types of parental participation considered, the only sex difference worthy of any mention occurs in the principals' use of parents as an advisory group in making out the course of study: the men involve parents in it somewhat more often than do the women.

NOTES AND REFERENCES

1. Neal Gross, *Who Runs Our Schools?* (New York: John Wiley and Sons, 1958).

2. A lay person is seldom able to evaluate the competence of a professional in any technical way, but in the medical instance, he can assess whether he feels "better" or in the case of the law, whether he is winning or losing his case. The point we wish to emphasize is that a child is less able than an adult to make even an approximate assessment of the services he receives.

3. Howard S. Becker et al., *Boys in White* (Chicago: University of Chicago Press, 1961), p. 410.

4. Everett C. Hughes, *Men and Their Work* (Glencoe, Ill.: The Free Press, 1958), p. 79.

5. Burton R. Clark, *Educating the Expert Society* (San Francisco: Chandler Publishing Co., 1962), p. 159.

6. Selznick defines cooptation as "the process of absorbing new elements into the leadership or policy-determining structure of an organization as a means of averting threats to its stability or existence." See his *TVA and the Grassroots* (Berkeley: University of California Press, 1949), pp. 259–264.

7. For evidence in support of this assumption, see Chapter 7, Table 7-4.

8. For evidence supporting this assumption, see Chapter 6, Table 6-5.

9. See Appendix C, Table C-21, for the item means, standard deviations, and weights used in computing the Index of Parental Involvement.

10. Since the finding was opposite to the prediction, a two-tailed test of statistical significance was employed.

12

Organizational Performance

An aphorism of school superintendents is: "As the principal, so the school." Does it follow that: "As the sex of the principal, so the performance of the school"?

As noted in Chapter 1, the steady decline in the proportion of women appointed to the elementary principalship in recent decades suggests that the officials and committees assigned the responsibility of selecting elementary school administrators have approached their tasks with a sex bias in favor of men. They apparently have assumed that greater educational benefits will accrue from placing a man rather than a woman in the principal's office. Is there any basis for the assumption that schools administered by male principals will outperform those in which women are at the helm? More specifically, does the quality of teachers' performance, their morale, and pupil learning tend to be higher in schools administered by men than women?

These questions are not only of interest to sociologists concerned with the impact of sex roles on the functioning of organizations. They deal with matters of importance to individuals in and outside of education perplexed or concerned about the implications of the sharp decline in the proportion of women in the elementary principalship during the last four decades.[1] If schools managed by men and women do not differ in their educational "productivity," teacher performance, or morale, or if schools managed by men outperform those administered by women, then the present trend, while it can be attacked on grounds of sex discrimination in employment, cannot be viewed as having any detrimental consequences for pupils or their teachers. However, if schools with women principals perform more effectively than those with men, then the tilting of the sex ratio in favor of men and the practice of reserving vacancies in the elementary principalship for them can be challenged as being indefensible on educational grounds.

THE PERFORMANCE OF TEACHERS

In both their formal and informal relationships with teachers, principals have many opportunities to influence their subordinates' performance. They can, for example, encourage their staffs to try out new instructional methods and materials; they can offer advice and suggestions to teachers encountering difficulty in motivating children, in maintaining order, or in using new curriculum materials. They may welcome or look with disfavor on innovations that teachers introduce into their classes. Principals, then, can influence the performance of their teachers in innumerable ways.

The hypothesis we tested was that teachers would perform in accord with professional standards with greater frequency in schools administered by women than in those managed by men. It was based on the assumption that the women, in comparison with men principals, bring longer teaching experience to their work, have greater self-confidence in their ability to direct instructional activities, and have a deeper commitment to the principalship. We further assumed that teachers working in schools whose principals had considerable practical experience in teaching, a high degree of self-confidence in their ability to be of service to the instructional program, and a strong commitment to their own professional role would find their work environments more conducive to maintaining or striving for high standards of performance than teachers whose administrators had less teaching experience, less self-confidence in their capability to be of service to the instructional program, and were less committed to their administrative role. From these assumptions it follows that teachers would conform to professional standards with greater frequency in schools that were administered by women than by men principals.

To test this hypothesis we used a factor score to measure the professional performance of the teachers in each school. The data on which the factor score is based were obtained from the responses of the teacher-observers to the following questions: Of the teachers in your school what per cent:

1. Are committed to doing the best job of which they are capable.
2. Maintain a professional attitude towards their work.
3. Maintain an interest in improving the educational program of the school.
4. Maintain effective discipline in their classes.

5. Usually "drag their feet" when new ideas are introduced into the school program.
6. Try new teaching methods in their classrooms.
7. Do "textbook" teaching only.
8. Waste a lot of time in their classroom activities.[2]

The factor scores of the teacher-observers in each school were averaged to obtain the best estimate of teachers' professional performance in each of the principals' schools, and it is these school scores that we used in testing the hypothesis.

When the mean scores of the schools administered by the women and the men are compared on the Index of the Professional Performance of Teachers, the findings support the hypothesis: schools with women principals have a higher mean score than those administered by men (13.29 vs. 12.24), and the difference of 1.05 is statistically significant at below the .05 level (Table 12-1).

To determine whether the relationship between sex of principal and professional performance of teachers might simply be an artifact of confounding variables, we undertook two additional analyses. The first explored the possibility that the relationship might be a function of the age difference between the women and men (the women, as we reported in Chapter 2, were on the average five years older than the men[3]). The second analysis examined whether it might be attributed to the circumstance that the women principals' staffs had greater teaching experience than the men's. Table 12-2 reveals that neither of these circumstances

TABLE 12-1.   Mean Scores of Schools Administered by Women and Men Principals on Professional Performance of Their Teachers ($N = 166$)*

Sex	Mean Score	Standard Deviation	Number of Cases
Women	13.29	3.22	84
Men	12.24	3.66	82

* Data unavailable for 23 of the 189 principals.

t = 1.95; p < .05.

TABLE 12-2. Mean Scores of Schools Administered by Women and Men Principals on Professional Performance of Their Teachers for Two Specified Subclassifications of Schools

Subclassification*	Women			Men			Direction Predicted Correctly (+) or Incorrectly (−)
	Mean	S.D.	N	Mean	S.D.	N	
Age of Principal							
Young	13.35	1.77	11	12.61	3.33	30	+
Middle	13.24	2.72	32	11.16	3.86	26	+
Old	13.31	3.82	41	12.89	3.57	26	+
Mean Experience of Teachers							
Short	12.24	3.65	29	11.60	4.25	27	+
Medium	13.12	2.98	27	12.76	2.94	28	+
Long	14.39	2.38	27	12.33	3.58	27	+

*See Appendix A for the definition of the subclassification categories.

can account for the relationship. The sex difference finding obtained for the entire sample of principals on the Index of Teacher Professional Performance occurs repeatedly when the men and the women administrators are subclassified into three age categories and into three subcategories on the basis of the average teaching experience of their faculties.

To find out the extent to which the finding obtained for the total sample of female and male principals would be internally replicated, we recomputed the mean Index of Teacher Professional Performance scores for schools administered by female principals and those managed by men principals under the following subclassifications of the data: region, city size, size of school, socioeconomic background of the pupils, and sex ratio of the staff. The mean score on Teacher Professional Performance was higher in schools administered by women principals in 14 of the 16 subcomparisons. The two exceptions occurred in the smallest schools and in those whose pupils came from middle socioeconomic backgrounds (Table 12-3).

TABLE 12-3. Mean Scores of Schools Administered by Women and Men Principals on Professional Performance of Teachers for Five Specified Subclassifications of Schools

Subclassification*	Women			Men			Direction Predicted Correctly (+) or Incorrectly (−)
	Mean	S.D.	N	Mean	S.D.	N	
Region							
West	12.55	4.50	10	12.08	2.80	17	+
Midwest	13.00	2.49	26	12.17	2.91	27	+
East	12.64	3.23	30	9.56	4.77	10	+
South	15.21	2.44	18	13.36	3.78	28	+
Size of City							
Small	13.68	2.68	45	12.67	3.12	46	+
Medium	13.11	3.80	29	12.13	3.77	27	+
Large	12.01	3.24	10	10.38	5.00	9	+
Size of School							
Small	13.41	3.65	30	13.93	3.01	26	--
Medium	13.72	2.86	35	12.45	3.87	25	+
Large	12.30	2.90	19	10.65	3.28	31	+
Socio-economic Level							
Low	12.81	3.82	26	10.64	4.24	30	+
Middle	12.99	3.10	25	13.02	2.87	29	−
High	13.89	2.65	33	13.34	2.91	23	+
Proportion of Men Teachers							
Low	14.80	1.83	26	13.83	3.05	22	+
Medium	13.21	3.15	30	11.67	3.46	29	+
High	11.96	3.67	28	11.64	3.89	31	+

*See Appendix A for the definition of the subclassification categories.

To determine whether there is empirical support for the reasoning on which the hypothesis is based, we first ask, as we have done in previous analyses of this type, whether each assumed intervening variable is related to both the independent variable (sex) and the dependent variable (professional performance of teachers) in the manner assumed. For those that are, we then will ascertain whether the magnitude of the zero-order relationship between the independent and dependent variables decreases when the intervening variable is held constant through partial correlational analysis.

As noted, the hypothesis was based on the three following assumptions: (a) women principals have more elementary teaching experience than the men; (b) women in the principalship have greater self-confidence in their ability to direct instructional affairs than the men; and (c) women in the principalship are more deeply committed to their work and role than the men.

The empirical evidence from the study that bears on these assumptions is presented in Table 12-4. The findings show that:

1. The women have more years of elementary teaching experience than the men and that teaching experience is positively related to the professional performance of teachers.
2. Women principals assess their own ability to direct instruction more favorably than the men, but that this self-assessment variable is not related to the professional performance of teachers.
3. The women are more deeply committed to the principalship than the men, but commitment is not related to the professional performance of teachers.[4]

In short, only one of the variables that we posited as linking the

TABLE 12-4. Correlation Coefficients for the Relationships Between Three Assumed Intervening Variables and the Independent Variable (Sex) and Dependent Variable (Professional Performance of Teachers) ($N = 164$)

Assumed Intervening Variable	Sex# (Point-biserial r)	Professional Performance of Teachers (Pearsonian r)
Years of elementary school teaching experience	.60*	.15*
Self-evaluation of ability to direct instructional program	.30*	-.01
Commitment to the principalship	.20*	.10

#Female = 1; male = 0.

*p < .05.

gender of principals and the professional performance of their teachers, the teaching experience of the principal, meets the required specifications for further consideration as an intervening variable.

Next, we examine whether the zero-order relationship between sex and teachers' performance drops when the variable, the principals' experience as an elementary teacher, is held constant. Table 12-5 shows that the zero-order point-biserial correlation between sex and the teachers' professional performance is .15; it drops to .07 when we hold constant the teaching experience of the principal. Although the size of the zero-order correlation between sex and teachers' professional performance is relatively low (.15), it nevertheless drops somewhat when the third variable is taken into account. We interpret these findings as supporting the *possibility* that the principal's experience as a teacher may act as an intervening variable, but that the other two posited intervening variables, self-assessment of ability to direct instruction and commitment to the principalship, do not (Table 12-5).

PUPILS' PERFORMANCE

Do schools administered by women surpass those managed by men in terms of the academic performance of pupils? Our hypothesis was that schools under the management of women would generally outperform the

TABLE 12-5. Zero-order and First-order Partial Correlation Coefficients for the Relationships Between Sex and Professional Performance of Teachers $(N = 164)$

	Zero-order r	First-order Partial r
Sex and Professional Performance of Teachers	.15	
Holding constant:		
Years of elementary school teaching experience		.07

men's schools. We assumed that the basic way principals influence the performance of pupils in their schools is not through direct association with them, but rather through the type of relationship they establish with their teachers. If we further assume that the performance of teachers will be of higher quality when they work under women than men administrators, an assumption supported by our findings, then it follows that pupils' learning will be greater in schools administered by women than in those supervised by men.

We used a factor score to measure pupils' academic performance in each of the principals' schools. The data on which the factor score is based were obtained from the responses of the teacher-observers in each school to five questions about the performance of the pupils in their classes. We asked the teachers: Of the pupils you teach, what per cent:

1. Are one or more years behind grade level in reading ability.
2. Are not mastering the subject matter or skills you teach at the minimum level of satisfactory performance.
3. Are not interested in academic achievement.
4. Were not adequately prepared to do the grade level work you expected of them when they entered your class.
5. Work up to their intellectual capacities.

We recognized and took account of two possible limitations of the responses of the teacher-observers to this set of questions. The first was that first-year pupils would not have been in school long enough to have been influenced very much by their teachers. The second was that the replies of beginning teachers would be open to question because of their limited experience. We therefore eliminated the reports of all teacher-observers who were first-grade teachers or who were in their first year of teaching, and thereby reduced our sample of observers to 964 teachers in 155 schools.

To secure a summary measure of the indices of pupils' performance, a principal components factor analysis was performed. The factor scores of the teachers in each principal's school were then averaged to obtain a school measure of Pupils' Academic Performance for each of the 155 schools.

When we computed the mean scores on pupils' academic performance for the schools administered by men principals and for those in which women served as principals, the findings supported the hypothesis: the mean score on pupils' academic performance of the schools administered by women was higher than that of the schools with men principals (12.20 vs. 10.89), and the difference of 1.31 between the mean scores of the two sets of schools is significant statistically (Table 12-6).

This finding could be an artifact of the circumstance that there is considerable variation in the average SES of pupils in different schools. If it turned out that women principals serve with greater frequency in schools with pupils of relatively high SES than do men, and if the SES of pupils is strongly and positively related to their academic performance,[7] then the relationship between the sex of principals and pupils' performance in their school could be accounted for by the differences in the SES of their pupils. To explore this possibility, we subclassified the principals into three groups on the basis of the average SES of their pupils. For each SES category, we then computed the mean Pupils' Academic Performance score for the schools administered by the men and the women principals (Table 12-7). The findings reveal that in each SES category of schools, the mean Pupils' Academic Performance scores were higher in the schools with women principals than in those with men administrators. The relationship between gender of principals and the academic performance of pupils in their schools cannot be viewed as an artifact of the SES backgrounds of their pupils.

To determine the degree of internal consistency of this sex difference finding, we examined the relationship between the principals' sex and

TABLE 12-6. Mean Scores of Schools Administered by Women and Men Principals on Pupils' Academic Performance ($N = 155$)*

Sex	Mean Score	Standard Deviation	Number of Cases
Women	12.20	2.86	79
Men	10.89	3.23	73

* Data unavailable for 37 of the 189 principals.

  $t = -2.64$; $p < .01$.

TABLE 12-7. Mean Scores of Schools Administered by Women and Men Principals on Pupils' Performance by Socioeconomic Level of Schools

Subclassification*	Women			Men			Direction Predicted Correctly (+) or Incorrectly (-)
	Mean	S.D.	N	Mean	S.D.	N	
Socio-economic Level							
Low	10.19	2.88	25	8.59	3.25	28	+
Middle	11.94	2.40	23	11.27	2.00	25	+
High	14.01	1.93	31	13.64	1.92	20	+

* See Appendix A for the definition of the subclassification categories.

the academic performance of pupils under the following subgroupings of the schools in the sample: region, size of city, size of school, mean age of the teaching staff, average teaching experience of faculty, assessment of staff competence, and the principal's age and marital status. In 21 of the 23 comparisons, the mean Pupils' Academic Performance scores were higher in schools administered by women than in those managed by the men (Table 12-8). This body of additional findings re-enforces our confidence in concluding that schools administered by women outperform those managed by men in terms of the academic performance of pupils.

We now turn to our findings that bear on the reasoning underlying the hypothesis. We had argued that pupils' academic performance would be of a higher quality in schools administered by the women on the assumption that teachers with women principals perform in a more professional manner than do those with men principals.

Do the empirical findings support this line of reasoning? First, we consider whether the variable, teachers' professional performance, which we posited as intervening between the independent variable (sex) and the dependent variable (pupils' academic performance), is related to them. Table 12-9 reveals that in schools administered by women principals, teachers on the average do tend to adhere to higher standards of professional performance than in those managed by men. It also shows that teachers' professional performance is positively related

TABLE 12-8. Mean Scores of Schools Administered by Women and Men Principals on Pupils' Performance for Eight Specified Subclassifications of Schools

Subclassification[#]	Women			Men			Direction Predicted Correctly (+) or Incorrectly (−)
	Mean	S.D.	N	Mean	S.D.	N	
Region							
West	11.86	3.27	9	11.57	3.50	15	+
Midwest	12.27	2.76	26	11.08	2.50	24	+
East	12.51	2.68	29	9.26	3.74	9	+
South	11.70	3.36	15	10.89	3.51	25	+
Size of City							
Small	12.80	2.55	45	11.36	3.16	38	+
Medium	12.02	3.02	24	11.21	2.89	27	+
Large	9.91	2.94	10	7.62	3.20	8	+
Size of School							
Small	12.99	2.49	28	11.02	3.39	21	+
Medium	12.46	2.92	33	11.72	2.84	22	+
Large	10.50	2.78	18	10.20	3.35	30	+
Mean Age of Teachers							
Young	12.17	2.96	30	10.32	3.30	23	+
Middle	12.00	2.58	28	11.11	3.51	22	+
Old	12.50	3.21	21	11.20	3.01	28	+

\# See Appendix A for the definition of the subclassification categories.

to pupils' academic performance. We now inquire whether the zero-order relationship between sex and pupils' academic performance declines when the variable, professional performance of teachers, is held constant. The zero-order correlation between sex and pupils' learning is .21; when the professional performance of teachers is held constant, the relationship drops to .16. We interpret these findings as providing some,

TABLE 12-8. *(Continued)*

Subclassification[#]	Women			Men			Direction Predicted Correctly (+) or Incorrectly (−)
	Mean	S.D.	N	Mean	S.D.	N	
Mean Teacher Experience							
Short	11.24	2.92	26	10.07	3.44	25	+
Medium	12.90	2.11	27	11.32	3.56	24	+
Long	12.48	3.38	25	11.32	2.58	24	+
Competence of Staff							
Low	10.62	3.01	20	9.01	3.54	20	+
Medium	11.92	2.59	28	11.61	3.01	27	+
High	13.79	2.18	29	11.59	2.70	26	+
Age of Principal							
Young	12.55	2.14	10	9.98	3.88	26	+
Middle	11.79	3.46	30	11.88	2.46	23	−
Old	12.43	2.55	39	10.94	2.94	24	+
Marital Status of Principal							
Married	10.59	2.91	20	11.14	3.08	66	−
Single	--	--	52	--	--	4	*
Other	--	--	7	--	--	3	*

\# See Appendix A for the definition of the subclassification categories.

* No comparison made when number of cases in smaller category is less than five.

TABLE 12-9.   Correlation Coefficients for the Relationships Between an Assumed Intervening Variable (Professional Performance of Teachers) and the Independent Variable (Sex) and Dependent Variable (Pupils' Performance) ($N = 155$)

Assumed Intervening Variable	Sex[#] (Point-biserial $\underline{r}$)	Pupils' Performance (Pearsonian $\underline{r}$)
Professional performance of teachers	.21*	.39*

[#] Female = 1; male = 0.

* $p < .05$.

but relatively slight, support for the line of reasoning we used in developing the hypothesis (Table 12-10).

TEACHERS' MORALE

In one phase of the study, we asked the principals how much weight they would assign to 25 different criteria for evaluating schools similar to their own.[8] They assigned the greatest weight to "the morale of the teachers in the school." Is there any relationship between the sex of the principal and this standard for judging schools?

We found ourselves in a perplexing situation as we deliberated about the development of a teachers' morale hypothesis. The reason for our difficulty was that the two arguments we found most convincing for developing a directional hypothesis led to directly contradictory conclusions. The first was that subordinates, whether female or male, would generally prefer men to women as their bosses. In the case of the women teachers in our study, we anticipated that they would share the sentiments that Gardner claimed were widespread in American industry: "For the most part women themselves prefer to be supervised by men, and few express a preference for a woman as their boss."[9] Furthermore, we assumed that most male elementary school teachers would resent or feel discomfort in serving as a subordinate of a woman principal. If we further assume that subordinates will feel or experience displeasure if the gender of their superordinate is not to their liking, and that this in

TABLE 12-10.   Zero-order and First-order Partial Correlation Coefficients for the
Relationships Between Sex and Pupils' Performance ($N = 152$)

	Zero-order $\underline{r}$	First-order Partial $\underline{r}$
Sex and Pupils' Performance	.21	
Holding constant:		
Professional performance of teachers		.16

turn will have an unfavorable effect on their morale, then we would expect that the morale of both men and women teachers would be higher
when their principal was a male and lower when their administrator
was a female.

The second line of reasoning was based on the assumption that staff
morale is a function in part of the ability of superiors to be of service to
their subordinates. If it is further assumed that women principals offer
greater service to their teachers than men because of their greater teaching experience and knowledge of elementary schools, then we would expect staff morale to be higher in schools administered by women. Since

TABLE 12-11.   Mean Teachers' Morale Scores of Schools Administered by
Women and Men Principals ($N = 171$)*

Sex	Mean Score	Standard Deviation	Number of Cases
Women	11.77	4.22	85
Men	11.72	3.73	86

* Data unavailable for 18 of the 189 principals.

$t = 0.09$; $p > .05$.

TABLE 12-12. Mean Teachers' Morale Scores of Schools Administered by Women and Men Principals for Eight Specified Subclassifications of Schools

Subclassification#	Women Mean	N	Men Mean	N	t	Probability less than
Region						
West	11.02	10	12.05	18	-0.52	n.s.
Midwest	11.93	26	11.76	28	0.20	n.s.
East	10.92	31	8.56	11	1.42	n.s.
South	13.42	18	12.67	29	0.88	n.s.
Size of City						
Small	12.07	45	11.92	48	0.21	n.s.
Medium	11.61	29	11.85	28	-0.20	n.s.
Large	10.95	11	10.38	10	0.27	n.s.
Size of School						
Small	11.57	30	13.12	29	-1.27	n.s.
Medium	12.65	36	11.62	26	1.15	n.s.
Large	10.42	19	10.49	31	-0.08	n.s.
Mean Age of Teachers						
Young	11.26	31	10.55	27	0.74	n.s.
Middle	12.05	30	12.27	27	-0.19	n.s.
Old	12.08	24	12.24	32	-0.15	n.s.

#See Appendix A for the definition of the subclassification categories.

these two lines of reasoning lead to contradictory conclusions about the impact of the sex factor on morale, we decided to test the null hypothesis: the sex of principals is not related to the morale of their teachers.

To test the hypothesis, we used a factor score to measure teachers' morale. The data from which the factor score is based were obtained

TABLE 12-12.   *(Continued)*

Subclassification[#]	Women		Men		t	Probability less than
	Mean	N	Mean	N		
Mean Experience of Teachers						
Short	10.38	29	11.07	28	-0.58	n.s.
Medium	12.05	27	12.25	30	-0.21	n.s.
Long	12.81	28	11.79	28	1.05	n.s.
Competence of Staff						
Low	9.62	23	9.73	22	-0.07	n.s.
Medium	11.41	30	12.09	33	-0.81	n.s.
High	14.02	30	12.74	31	1.78	n.s.
Age of Principal						
Young	12.20	11	11.67	32	0.46	n.s.
Middle	11.80	33	12.21	27	-0.41	n.s.
Old	11.63	41	11.28	27	0.31	n.s.
Marital Status of Principal						
Married	10.94	23	11.84	78	-1.07	n.s.
Single	12.06	55	12.55	5	-0.24	n.s.
Other	--	7	--	3	*	

See Appendix A for the definition of the subclassification categories.

* No comparison made when number of cases in smaller category is less than five.

from the responses of the teacher-observers in each school to six questions. We asked: Of the teachers in your school, what per cent:

1. Display a sense of pride in the school.
2. Enjoy working in the school.
3. Display a sense of loyalty to the school.
4. Respect the judgment of the administrators of the school.
5. Accept the educational philosophy underlying the curriculum of the school.
6. Work cooperatively with their fellow teachers.

We then averaged the factor scores of the teachers to obtain the best estimate of teachers' morale for each school.[10]

When we compared the mean Teachers' Morale score of schools administered by men with the score of those supervised by women, the findings supported the null hypothesis: the mean score of the women's schools was 11.77 and of the men's, 11.72; the difference of 0.05 is not statistically significant (Table 12-11).

Our confidence in this conclusion is strengthened by additional analyses that we undertook of the mean score on teachers' morale for schools administered by men and women under the following data subclassifications: region, size of city, size of school, mean age of the teaching staff, their average teaching experience, their competence as assessed by the principal, the age of principals, and their marital status. Of the 24 comparisons we made, none were statistically significant (Table 12-12).[11]

NOTES AND REFERENCES

1.   Department of Elementary School Principals, National Education Association, *The Elementary School Principalship in 1968—A Research Study* (Washington, D.C.: National Education Association, 1968).

2.   For the item means, standard deviations, and weights used in obtaining a summary measure of teachers' professional performance, see Appendix C, Table C-22.

3.   See Chapter 2 for a more extensive discussion of the age differences between the men and women principals.

4.   The measurement of commitment to the principalship was based on the principals' responses to 18 items dealing with six occupational positions which a principal might be offered. For example, with respect to a job offer to accept an administrative position with a reputable textbook company, he was asked if he would or would not accept the job (a) "with the same salary as my present one;" (b) "with a salary $2000 greater than my present one;" (c) "with a salary $4000 greater than my present one." A Commitment Scale was then developed on the basis of a two-step scaling process. The three categories in each of the six areas were scaled with coefficients of reproducibility all in excess of .997. The resulting scale scores were then developed into a six-item Guttman scale.

5.   For a further consideration of this matter, see Neal Gross and Robert E. Herriott, *Staff Leadership in the Public Schools* (New York: John Wiley and Sons, 1965), pp. 40–41. Chapter 3 of this volume considers important methodological problems we encountered.

6.   For the item means, standard deviations, and weights used in obtaining a summary measure of school scores of pupils' performance, see Appendix C, Table C-23.

7.   See Patricia Sexton, *Education and Income* (New York: The Viking Press, 1961), for a study of the relationship between the socioeconomic background of pupils and its influence on their learning activities; and Joseph A. Kahl, *The American Class Structure* (New York: Holt, Rinehart, and Winston, 1961), for a summary of sociological studies bearing on this question.

In our own study, the relationship between indices of socioeconomic status of the pupils as a body and measures of their learning is substantial. For example, the coefficient of linear correlation between the percentage of pupils' parents whose average income was more than $5000 and the percentage of pupils one or more years behind grade level in reading ability (as reported by their teachers) was −.61 for a sample of 152 of the elementary schools. See Gross and Herriott, *op. cit.,* pp. 43–44.

8.   For a description of the procedure used to obtain the principals' assessment of different criteria for evaluating schools, see Chapter 6.

9.   Burleigh B. Gardner, *Human Relations in Industry* (Chicago: Richard D. Irwin, Inc., 1945), p. 270.

10.   For the item means, standard deviations, and weights used to secure a score on teachers' morale for each school, see Appendix C, Table C-24.

11.   A two-tailed test of significance was used for these comparisons since a null hypothesis was being tested.

13

Worry

One reason executives earn more remuneration than those who work under their jurisdiction is that their responsibilities involve problems and decisions that are more difficult, complex, stressful, and anxiety-laden than those dealt with by their subordinates. This circumstance accounts in part for the disinterest in management positions exhibited by many talented individuals in the lower echelons of organizational hierarchies. In their view, although the material benefits to be accrued from occupying an executive suite are enticing, they are not viewed as rewarding enough to compensate for the strains, tensions, and psychic discomforts which executives frequently encounter.

Many stress-provoking organizational problems that school principals encounter in their work are similar in nature to those experienced by managers of banks, business firms, and welfare agencies. All of these officials, for example, must deal with problems that relate to the turnover of personnel, irresponsible or uncommitted staff members, and subordinates who are resistant to promising organizational changes. In addition to these worrisome problems, elementary principals are exposed to others that are firmly rooted in three basic characteristics of their schools as organizations.

The first is that the teachers they are supposed to supervise view themselves as professionals, and hence can be expected to be highly sensitive and resistant to the attempts of a principal to exercise control over their behavior.[1] This circumstance can result in stress and strain for principals when they attempt to improve the quality of teaching and learning in their schools. Furthermore, the manner in which teachers behave reflects on the performance of principals, but as noted, the autonomy of teachers restricts administrative intervention in their activities. This condition serves as a breeding ground for discontent and anxiety among many principals.

The second characteristic of the elementary school as an organization that can expose principals to considerable stress is that its clients are children. As the chief administrator of the school, the principal stands *in loco parentis* and is legally responsible for the safety and welfare of a large body of young children. Moreover, compulsory school attendance laws require public schools to accept all the children who live within their attendance areas, including those with marked emotional problems and learning difficulties. Developing programs or strategies to help these children can be gratifying; however, working with teachers, parents, and school district specialists in implementing them can also be frustrating and exasperating experiences.

The third stress-provoking characteristic of the elementary school for principals is that it is a neighborhood institution. In consequence, the principalship occupies a boundary position located between the school and the community. The principals' primary contacts with people outside the school system are with parents. Because the child clients of the school are minors, parents are viewed as its indirect clients, and hence principals are exposed to and must deal with their legitimate and illegitimate claims and demands. Principals must attempt to satisfy or at least mollify parents whose views about school practices and procedures may be disparate from those held by teachers, the central administration, or the principals themselves. These encounters can be characterized by tension and acrimony.

Do men and women in the principalship vary in their experience of job-related worry? This is the question we examine in this chapter.

THE HYPOTHESIS

The hypothesis we tested, that women principals worry less than men about their work, was based on the following lines of reasoning. We assumed that among incumbents of the same managerial position, those with more experience in the activity they supervise would have less reason to worry about problems associated with their work than those with less experience. The individuals with greater experience, we assumed, would have a more realistic understanding of their problems, be able to view them in perspective, be more aware of alternative strategies to deal with them, and hence be in a position to cope with them more effectively. If we further assume that women principals served as teachers for a longer period than men principals (data presented in Chapter 3, p. 45 support this assumption), then it follows that women in the principalship would worry less than men about their work.

The second line of reasoning is based on an assumption about how an individual's career aspirations influence job-related worry. We assume that among individuals in the same occupational position, the more ambitious will have the greater concern about the effects of their current role performance on their future careers. If we also assume that men principals have higher career aspirations than women (data presented in Chapter 14, p. 206 support this assumption), it follows that women principals will worry less about their work than men administrators.

The third line of reasoning begins with an assumption about the effect of an individual's self-assessment of his ability to perform his organizational tasks on the degree of his worry. Although the principal's managerial tasks are one step removed from the teaching and learning activities of the classroom, they are directly or indirectly concerned with instruction and its facilitation. We reasoned that principals with a higher self-evaluation of their ability as instructional leaders would worry less than those whose assessment of themselves in this respect was lower. Those with a more positive assessment, we reasoned, could be expected to interact with teachers and parents with greater self-assurance and self-confidence. And since we assumed that women would hold a higher evaluation of their competence to supervise instruction than men in view of their longer and more varied teaching experience in the elementary school and their greater familiarity with its recurrent problems (data presented in Chapter 3, p. 46 support this assumption), we anticipated that women principals would worry less than men.

TESTING THE HYPOTHESIS

The replies of the principals to a "Worry Instrument" furnished the data to test the hypothesis. It elicited the frequency ("very frequently," "frequently," "sometimes," "almost never," "never") with which principals worried about 11 problems or situations that arise in their work, for example, the reactions of teachers to their decisions and physical injuries received by pupils in their schools. A six-item Guttman scale with a coefficient of reproducibility of .907 was developed from the principals' responses to the Worry Instrument.[2] When this index of their worry was cross-tabulated with the sex of the administrators, support was found for the hypothesis. Nearly twice the proportion of men as women (22% vs. 12%) received the highest worry scale scores (scores of 6 and 5) and over twice the proportion of women as men (23% vs. 10%) received the lowest scores (scores of 0 and 1). The difference between the mean worry scores of the men (3.12) and that of the women (2.67) is 0.45 units on the worry scale and is statistically significant (Table 13-1).[3] We conclude that on the average men in the elementary principal-ship worry more than women principals.

This relationship could simply be an artifact of school size.[4] That is, if worry is positively related to the size of a principal's school, and since the schools administered by men tend to be larger than those managed by women, then size of school could account for the relationship. We rejected this artifact possibility because, as Table 13-2 indicates, the mean score of the men was higher on the worry scale than that of the women principals in the small, the medium-sized, and the large schools.

TABLE 13-1. Mean, Frequency, and Percentage Distribution of the Scores of Women and Men Principals on the Worry Scale

Worry Scale Score	Women		Men	
	Frequency	Per Cent	Frequency	Per Cent
6	5	5	8	8
5	6	7	14	14
4	14	15	14	14
3	28	31	26	27
2	17	19	26	27
1	9	10	2	2
0	12	13	8	8
	91	100	98	100
Mean Scale Score	2.67		3.12	

t = 1.94; p < .05.

TABLE 13-2. Mean Worry Scores of Women and Men Principals by Size of School

Subclassification[#]	Women			Men			Direction Predicted Correctly (+) or Incorrectly (−)
	Mean	S.D.	N	Mean	S.D.	N	
Size of School							
Small	2.88	1.51	33	3.53	1.50	30	+
Medium	2.51	1.60	37	3.22	1.55	27	+
Large	2.62	1.70	21	2.76	1.59	41	+

[#] See Appendix A for the definition of the subclassification categories.

We next examined the degree to which the finding about sex differences in job-related worry was internally replicated in the sample. The data (Table 13-3) revealed that the mean worry score of the men was higher than that of the women in all regions, in schools with pupils from different socioeconomic backgrounds and in those with differences in teacher competence and average teacher experience. In only 1 of 16 subclassifications, cities of medium size, did the men principals have a lower mean worry score than the women. The fact that the sex difference finding holds up in 15 out of the 16 subclassifications of the data strengthens our confidence in the findings obtained for the total sample.

TEST OF THE REASONING

Is there empirical support for any of the lines of reasoning we used to develop the hypothesis about sex differences in worry? We posited that the women principals would have greater experience in teaching, a lower level of aspiration, and a higher self-evaluation of their ability to supervise instruction than the men, and that of these differences would predispose women to experience less job-related worry than the men. The data required to determine if each of these intervening variables is related to both the independent variable (sex) and the dependent one (worry) in the way we had assumed are presented in Table 13-4. The second column in Table 13-4 reports the relevant empirical findings: (1) women principals have more teaching experience than men; (2) women have lower career aspirations than men; and (3) women evaluate their ability to direct the instructional program more favorably than men. The third column of Table 13-4 shows that level of career aspiration and self-

TABLE 13-3. Mean Worry Scores of Women and Men Principals for Five Specified Subclassifications of Schools

Subclassification*	Women Mean	S.D.	N	Men Mean	S.D.	N	Direction Predicted Correctly (+) or Incorrectly (−)
Region							
West	2.46	1.45	13	3.25	1.61	20	+
Midwest	2.23	1.28	26	3.20	1.40	30	+
East	3.00	1.81	33	3.16	1.81	19	+
South	2.84	1.56	19	2.93	1.57	29	+
Socio-economic Level							
Low	2.86	1.68	29	2.91	1.46	35	+
Middle	2.96	1.79	27	3.23	1.49	35	+
High	2.29	1.28	35	3.25	1.81	28	+
Size of City							
Small	2.38	1.45	45	3.22	1.31	49	+
Medium	3.15	1.79	33	2.90	1.81	30	−
Large	2.46	1.28	13	3.21	1.79	19	+
Mean Teacher Experience							
Low	3.10	1.54	30	3.61	1.82	33	+
Middle	2.32	1.58	28	2.91	1.26	33	+
High	2.48	1.60	31	2.84	1.50	32	+
Competence of Staff							
Low	3.17	1.60	24	3.59	1.39	27	+
Middle	2.73	1.73	33	3.08	1.48	36	+
High	2.13	1.22	32	2.80	1.74	35	+

* See Appendix A for the definition of the subclassification categories.

TABLE 13-4. Correlation Coefficients for the Relationships Between Three Assumed Intervening Variables and the Independent Variable (Sex) and Dependent Variable (Worry) ($N = 189$)

Assumed Intervening Variable	Sex[#] (Point-biserial $\underline{r}$)	Worry (Pearsonian $\underline{r}$)
Years of elementary school teaching experience	.61*	-.06
Level of aspiration	-.37*	.14*
Self-evaluation of ability to direct instructional program	.24*	-.17*

[#] Female = 1; male = 0.

* p < .05.

evaluation are related to worry as we assumed; it also indicates that length of teaching experience is not related to worry and hence falls short of meeting the specifications required for its consideration as an intervening variable.

The next question is: Do the two variables, level of aspiration and self-evaluation, meet the final condition required if they are to be viewed as intervening between sex and worry? That is, when each is held constant, does the magnitude of the relationship between the independent variable (sex) and the dependent one (worry) diminish? Table 13-5 reveals that when level of aspiration is held constant, the first-order partial correlation coefficient between sex and worry is slightly smaller than the zero-order correlation coefficient. A similar finding occurs when the variable, self-evaluation of ability to direct the instructional program, is held constant. When aspiration and self-evaluation are both held constant, the relationship diminishes still more. We interpret these findings as indicating that aspiration and self-evaluation may be operating as intervening variables in the relationship between sex and worry, but that they do not completely explain it.

FURTHER ANALYSES

We now examine the responses of the principals to the 11 questions in the Worry Instrument in order to ascertain which aspects of their work cause them more or less stress and to determine if there are any important sex differences in this respect (Table 13-6).

The *in loco parentis* dimension of the principals' role that makes them legally responsible for the safety and welfare of the young children in their schools constituted the major source of worry for the principals. Nearly 40% reported that they "very frequently" or "frequently" worry about possible physical injury to the children and over one-third reported that they sometimes worry about this matter. It is of interest to note that over twice the proportion of women as men principals (35% vs. 16%) stated that they "never" or "almost never" worry about this possibility.

To what extent do principals feel a sense of anxiety when they relate to parents? Over 60% reported that they worry "sometimes" or more frequently about the impression they make when speaking to groups of parents. Approximately 30% of the administrators indicated that they worried as frequently about having to meet with complaining parents. However, over 80% of the school administrators claimed that they never or almost never "felt nervous" when attending P.T.A. or other parent meetings. Their participation in large gatherings of parents appears to

TABLE 13-5.   Zero-order, First-order, and Higher-order Partial Correlation Coefficients Between Sex and Worry ($N = 189$)

	Zero-order r	First-order Partial r	Higher-order Partial r
Sex and Worry	−.16		
Holding Constant:			
Level of aspiration		−.11	
Self-evaluation of ability to direct instructional program		−.12	
Level of aspiration and self-evaluation of ability to direct instructional program			−.07

TABLE 13-6.   Percentage Distribution and Mean of the Responses of Women and Men Principals to the Items in the Worry Instrument

The Question	The Response Choices	
To what extent does each of these situations occur in your job?	A = I very frequently B = I frequently C = I sometimes	D = I almost never E = I never

Item#		Per Cent of Principals Responding							Direction of Difference
		A (5)	B (4)	C (3)	D (2)	E (1)	N	Mean	
1. Worry about possible physical injuries to individual students while they are at school.*	W	17%	13%	34%	24%	11%	(90)	3.0	M > W
	M	19	28	37	13	3	(98)	3.5	
7. Am concerned about the impression I will make when I have to speak to a group of parents.*	W	3	13	46	24	13	(91)	2.7	M > W
	M	8	19	36	28	8	(98)	3.0	
10. Have anxiety when I deal with "complaining" parents.	W	1	7	39	40	14	(91)	2.4	M > W
	M	0	14	42	34	10	(98)	2.6	
11. Feel nervous when I attend PTA or other parent meetings.	W	1	1	13	36	48	(91)	1.7	M > W
	M	0	1	18	49	31	(98)	1.9	
8. Am concerned about the impression I will make when I have to speak to a group of teachers.*	W	3	19	36	23	17	(91)	2.7	M > W
	M	7	20	35	29	9	(98)	2.9	

Items are numbered according to their position in the 11-item research instrument.

* Item was included in Worry Scale.

be less stressful for most principals than interacting with them in small groups or as individuals. In each of these types of contact with parents, the women again reported that they experienced worry less frequently than the men.

Do principals also worry about their relationships with teachers? Approximately 60% of the principals reported that they worry "sometimes" or with greater frequency about the impression they make when they are required to speak to a group of teachers and nearly one-half reported some degree of concern about the possibility that their

TABLE 13-6.   (*Continued*)

The Question	The Response Choices
To what extent does each of these situations occur in your job?	A = I very frequently D = I almost never B = I frequently E = I never C = I sometimes

Item #		Per Cent of Principals Responding							Direction of Difference
		A (5)	B (4)	C (3)	D (2)	E (1)	N	Mean	
3. Am concerned that what I do or say may cause me to be disliked by my teachers.	W	2%	7%	34%	34%	23%	(91)	2.3	M > W
	M	3	10	42	33	11	(97)	2.6	
9. Find myself worrying whether I have made the right decision on a matter with which I have just dealt.	W	3	9	42	37	9	(91)	2.6	M > W
	M	5	11	50	30	3	(98)	2.8	
4. Worry about what an individual or group may do if I make a decision contrary to their wishes.*	W	1	5	26	41	25	(91)	2.2	M > W
	M	0	1	42	45	12	(98)	2.3	
2. Worry about the possible occurrence of a "disaster" (e.g., serious fire, food poisoning, etc.) at my school.	W	7	6	19	35	34	(91)	2.2	M > W
	M	5	9	33	39	13	(98)	2.5	

Items are numbered according to their position in the 11-item research instrument.

* Item was included in Worry Scale.

performance or statements would be viewed with displeasure by their faculty. Nearly twice as many women as men claimed never to worry about either of these two possible sources of stress.

Approximately three out of five of the elementary school administrators reported that they at times find themselves worrying about whether they have made "right" decisions, and nearly two out of five said they worry at times about what an individual or group may do if their decisions run contrary to their wishes. For both types of occurrences, the women, again, reported less frequency of worry than the men.

A majority of the principals reported that they "never" or "almost never" worry about the possible occurrence of some type of "disaster"

TABLE 13-6. *(Continued)*

The Question	The Response Choices	
To what extent does each of these situations occur in your job?	A = I very frequently B = I frequently C = I sometimes	D = I almost never E = I never

Item#		Per Cent of Principals Responding						Mean	Direction of Difference
		A (5)	B (4)	C (3)	D (2)	E (1)	N		
5. Worry about what is going on in my school when I am away from it for any length of time during school hours.*	W	3%	12%	16%	41%	27%	(91)	2.2	M > W
	M	4	13	30	33	20	(98)	2.5	
6. Am kept awake at night thinking about problems associated with my job.*	W	2	1	35	37	24	(91)	2.2	M = W
	M	3	3	28	41	24	(98)	2.2	

Items are numbered according to their position in the 11-item research instrument.

* Item was included in Worry Scale.

striking their school or what is happening in their building when they are away from it for any length of time during school hours. Women again reported that they worry less frequently about these two matters than the men.

Finally, over three-fifths of the principals indicated that they "never" or "almost never" were kept awake at night thinking about problems associated with their job. There was no sex difference in response to this item. For each of the other 10 items in the Worry Instrument, the men reported greater frequency of worry than the women.

Are the situations that the men and women principals worry most and least about similar or different? To examine this question, we assigned weights ranging from 5 to 1 to the response categories in the Worry Instrument, computed a mean score for the men and the women on each item, and then ranked the items by frequency of worry for the two groups. As Table 13-7 indicates, the rank order of the items for the female and male administrators is highly similar. We conclude that the areas of relatively great and slight worry are approximately the same for the women and men principals.

TABLE 13-7. Rank Ordering of the Responses of Women and Men Principals to the Eleven Items in the Worry Scale

Item*	Rank Order of Responses	
	Women	Men
1. Worry about possible physical injuries to individual students while they are at school.	1	1
7. Am concerned about the impression I will make when I have to speak to a group of parents.	2	2.5
8. Am concerned about the impression I will make when I have to speak to a group of teachers.	3.5	2.5
9. Find myself worrying whether I have made the right decision on a matter with which I have just dealt.	3.5	4
3. Am concerned that what I do or say may cause me to be disliked by my teachers.	5	5.5
10. Have anxiety when I deal with "complaining" parents.	6	5.5
5. Worry about what is going on in my school when I am away from it for any length of time during school hours.	8.5	7.5
2. Worry about the possible occurrence of a "disaster" (e.g., serious fire, food poisoning, etc.) at my school.	8.5	9
4. Worry about what an individual or group may do if I make a decision contrary to their wishes.	8.5	9
6. Am kept awake at night thinking about problems associated with my job.	8.5	10
11. Feel nervous when I attend PTA or other parent meetings.	11	11

* Items are numbered according to their position in the 11-item Worry Instrument.

NOTES AND REFERENCES

1. As noted in Chapter 8, the conflict of authority inherent in the close supervision of professionals is one type of major problem that confronts the principal. Positions within organizations are differentially subject to the critical problems that confront the organization and consequently are characterized by different intensities of stress and worry. See Robert L. Kahn et al., *Organizational Stress: Studies in Role Conflict and Ambiguity* (New York: John Wiley and Sons, 1964), Chapters 6-9.

2. See Appendix C, Table C-2, for the technical details of the construction of the Worry Scale.

3. As with the Level of Aspiration Scale (Chapter 14), in using the *t*-test as the test of significance in comparing the mean scores of the men and women principals, we have treated the Worry Scale as though it were an interval scale. Applying a chi-square test to the data in Table 13-1 results in the same conclusion: women in general receive lower scores on the Scale than men. The mean scale scores of the sex groups are used to facilitate a comparison of the findings for the total sample with those for the subsamples presented in Tables 13-2 and 13-3.

4. While age and marital status were viewed as possible confounding variables in other chapters, they will not be treated that way in this chapter. Age might have been used as an indirect indicator of one of the intervening variables postulated as linking sex and worry, namely, length of experience. Instead, a more direct index, described later in the chapter, was employed. Conceptually, marital status, specifically "marriedness," could not be viewed as an intervening or confounding variable because it has different effects on men and women. That is, being married may predispose men to worry more because of the greater number of economic dependents they have as compared with single men. However, married women principals generally represent a secondary source of economic support for their families, so there is less pressure on them related to the financial dependence of others than there probably is for single women.

14

Career Aspirations

The upward and downward movement of individuals in the world of work—their vertical occupational mobility—has been the subject of extensive sociological research. These studies shed considerable light on the rates and mechanisms of occupational mobility in American society and other nations. Their primary focus has been on intergenerational mobility, that is, the degree to which the occupational status of a son differs from that of his father.[1] Less attention has been directed to intragenerational mobility,[2] which is concerned with the rise or fall in the occupational status of individuals during the course of their own work careers. Our knowledge is especially limited about the circumstances that account for the varying aspirations for occupational advancement of persons at the same point in their career line.[3] In this chapter, we examine this issue with special reference to the impact of the gender of school principals on their career aspirations.

The organizational charts displayed in the central administrative offices of school systems and other large-scale enterprises are designed to outline their division of labor and their structure of formal authority. The small square boxes with their connecting lines delineate who is formally responsible to whom and who is supposed to perform different tasks. They also fulfill another and less frequently recognized purpose: the specification of available routes of advancement for those who aspire to climb up the organizational ladder.

As noted in Chapter 4, all of the men and women principals in our study had already climbed one or more steps in the status hierarchy of school systems during their professional careers. Over half of them (55%) had moved up directly from classroom teaching to the principalship. The job sequence followed by the remainder consisted primarily of serving first as a teacher, then in an administrative capacity such as an assistant or vice-principalship, and then moving up to the principal-ship.

Like lower-level administrators in other types of organizations, prin-cipals vary in their occupational aspirations. Some aspire to the top administrative positions of their profession and harbor ambitions of be-coming a school superintendent or a deputy superintendent. Other prin-cipals have lower mobility targets in mind. They hope to achieve a job such as the director of curriculum or personnel for a school district or to secure a principalship with greater responsibilities or prestige.

The organizational chart of a school system, however, does not depict all the ways in which principals can obtain increased prestige or greater rewards during the course of their educational careers. They may, for example, aspire to enhance their reputation among their professional colleagues, hold office in national educational associations, or become a college professor of educational administration. The possibility should also be recognized that some principals may have largely acheived their occupational ambitions when they were appointed to an elementary prin-cipalship.

We now turn to the hypothesis we tested in our examination of whether the career aspirations of principals are related to their gender.

THE HYPOTHESIS

Since women who become principals have followed a career sequence largely identical to that of men who serve in this capacity, it could be argued that their aspirations for occupational advancement would ap-proximate those of their male colleagues. However, all of the other argu-ments we examined led us to anticipate that the level of aspiration of men in the elementary principalship would be higher than that of women. This hypothesis is based on three lines of reasoning.

The first is rooted in an assumption of reference group theory[4] and two of its key concepts, *relative deprivation* and *relative gratification*, that Stouffer used to account for several perplexing findings that he presented in *The American Soldier*. He invoked reference group theory to explain why individuals who had experienced the same rate of ad-vancement in the army assessed it differently.

> ... *relative rate of advancement can be based on different standards by different classes of the Army population.* For example, a grade school man

who became a corporal after a year of service would have had a more rapid rate of promotion compared with most of his friends at the same educational level than would a college man who rose to this same grade in a year. Hence we would expect, at a given rank and a given longevity, that the better educated would be more likely than others to complain of the slowness of promotion.[5]

What does reference group theory imply for a hypothesis dealing with the relationship of the sex factor to career aspirations? If we assume that women principals use as their reference group in evaluating their occupational achievement the cohort of women college graduates in their age group in the occupational structure and that the men principals employ as their reference group male college graduates of comparable age in the labor force, we would expect that women principals would have a higher evaluation of their occupational accomplishment than the men. In the case of the women, they would perceive their vocational advancement with a relatively high degree of gratification in view of the relatively few females in managerial or executive positions with income and prestige as high as their own. For the men, they would perceive their career mobility as relatively low in view of the relatively large number of males who occupy managerial or executive positions with higher economic and social status than the principalship. If we assume further that among a set of individuals who occupy the same position, those who assess their previous mobility as relatively high will feel less need to strive for even higher status than those who assess theirs as relatively low, it follows that women in the principalship would have a lower level of aspiration than men.

The second line of reasoning begins with the assumption that individuals who have achieved the same amount of social mobility in a particular occupational hierarchy will vary in the length of time it took them to attain their current position; this circumstance, in turn, will have consequences for the amount of time remaining in their careers in which they can achieve further occupational advancement. We further assumed that among the incumbents of the same organizational position, their career aspirations will be positively related to the number of years prior to their retirement. Other things being equal, we would anticipate that those principals who had served a relatively long time as teachers prior to achieving their present administrative post would tend to have lower career aspirations than those who had spent less time in the teaching ranks. If we assume that on the average the female principals served as teachers longer than the men before becoming principals (data in support of this assumption are presented in Chapter 3, p. 45), then it would follow that the career aspirations of women in the principalship would be lower than those of the men.[6]

The third line of reasoning is based on the idea that in American society men experience greater exposure to pressure for achieving success in the occupational sphere than women. Success in another realm, the family and the home, receives greater stress for women. The different referents of success applied to men and women also lead us to anticipate that men will express a greater desire for occupational advancement than women.

To test the career aspirations hypothesis, 6 of the 13 items presented in Table 14-5 were combined to form a 6-item Guttman scale having a coefficient of reproducibility of .920.[7] When the scores of the men and women principals on this index of Level of Career Aspiration were compared, the evidence supported the hypothesis: over three times the proportion of men as women (53% vs. 16%) received the highest scale scores (scores of 6, 5, and 4) and over three times the proportion of women as men (36% vs. 12%) obtained the lowest scale scores (scores of 0 and 1). The difference between the mean score of the men (3.30) and that of the women (2.03) is 1.27 units on the Career Aspirations Scale (Table 14-1) and is statistically significant.[8]

It could be maintained that the difference in the mean career aspiration scores of the men and women principals simply is an artifact of one or more "confounding" third variables, for example, academic ability or self-evaluation of professional performance. If academic ability were operating in this fashion, then the men's academic ability would need to be greater than that of the women principals. However, we presented findings in Chapter 3 that indicated that the women principals reported receiving higher grades than the men in both high school and in college. In Chapter 7 we reported the finding that the women principals held a higher self-evaluation of their professional performance than the men. Therefore, neither of these variables can "explain away" the relationship between sex and career aspirations.[9]

To determine whether this sex difference finding for the total sample holds up under various subgroupings of the data, we classified the men and women principals in four different ways: by region, size of city, size of school, and by the average socioeconomic status of pupils in their schools. We then computed the mean career aspiration scores of the

TABLE 14-1. Mean, Frequency, and Percentage Distribution of Women and Men Principals on the Level of Aspiration Scale

Level of Aspiration Scale Score	Women (N=90)			Men (N=98)		
	Frequency	Per Cent	Cumulative Per Cent	Frequency	Per Cent	Cumulative Per Cent
6 (High)	4	4	4	8	9	9
5	5	6	10	11	11	20
4	5	6	16	32	33	53
3	8	9	25	15	15	68
2	35	39	64	20	20	88
1	20	22	86	7	7	95
0 (Low)	13	14	100	5	5	100
No. of Cases	90	100%		98	100%	
Mean Scale Score	2.03			3.30		

$t = 5.61$; $p < .001$.

TABLE 14-2.   Mean Scores of Women and Men Principals on Level of Aspiration Scale by Four Specified Subclassifications of Schools

Subclassification*	Women			Men			Direction Predicted Correctly (+) or Incorrectly (−)
	Mean	S.D.	N	Mean	S.D.	N	
Region							
West	2.46	1.78	13	3.15	1.71	20	+
Midwest	2.20	1.44	25	2.80	1.28	30	+
East	1.88	1.57	33	3.89	1.55	19	+
South	1.79	1.24	19	3.52	1.48	29	+
Size of City							
Small	1.73	1.36	45	3.12	1.45	49	+
Medium	1.94	1.46	33	3.20	1.68	30	+
Large	3.42	1.55	12	3.89	1.37	19	+
Size of School							
Small	2.18	1.59	33	3.53	1.45	30	+
Medium	1.76	1.19	37	2.70	1.61	27	+
Large	2.30	1.85	20	3.51	1.45	41	+
Socio-economic Level							
Low	2.14	1.41	28	3.31	1.55	35	+
Middle	1.74	1.62	27	3.34	1.49	35	+
High	2.17	1.50	35	3.21	1.59	28	+

* See Appendix A for the definition of the subclassification categories.

men and women in each of the subclassifications. The findings, which are reported in Table 14-2, show that in each of the resulting subclassifications of the data, the mean career aspiration score for the men was higher than that obtained by the women principals. The persistence of this sex difference finding under various subclassifications of the data increases our confidence in the finding for the total sample.

TEST OF THE REASONING

Now we examine whether evidence available from our study offers support for the lines of reasoning we used in developing the hypothesis about a sex difference in level of aspiration. We had reasoned that three intervening variables link sex to aspiration: satisfaction with progress in career, length of time in teaching prior to becoming a principal, and "felt" pressure for occupational advancement.

The following procedures were used to obtain indicators of the assumed intervening variables: (a) The indicator of the principals' evaluation of their occupational achievement was obtained from their responses to the following question: "How satisfied do you feel about the amount of progress which you have made in your professional career?" The response categories and the weights assigned to them were as follows: (6) very satisfied; (5) moderately satisfied; (4) slightly satisfied; (3) slightly dissatisfied; (2) moderately dissatisfied; and (1) very dissatisfied. (b) The total number of years of service as a teacher prior to becoming a principal was obtained from the administrators' responses to questions included in a job history instrument which constituted an important part of the Personal and School Background Questionnaire. (c) The index of "felt" pressure for occupational advancement was based on their replies to the following question: "How desirous are you to take every opportunity to advance your own career?" The five response categories and their weights were: (5) extremely anxious to; (4) would very much like to; (3) have some desire to; (2) not especially anxious to; and (1) would not want to.

The findings with respect to the relationships between these three variables and the independent (sex) and dependent (career aspiration) variables are presented in Table 14-3. They show that two of the three posited intervening variables are related to both the independent and dependent variables as we had assumed: women principals on the average had served as teachers longer than the men and length of teaching experience is negatively related to level of aspiration; the women expressed less felt pressure for occupational advancement than the men, and this variable was positively associated with level of aspiration.[10] However, although "satisfaction with progress in career" was, as anticipated, negatively related to career aspiration, it was not related to the principals' gender. Therefore, this variable does not meet the required specifications of an intervening variable.

The zero-order correlation between sex and career aspiration is reported in column 2 of Table 14-4. The first-order partial correlation coefficients between these two variables, when each of the two assumed intervening variables is held constant individually, are presented in column 3 of Table 14-4. Only one of the presumed "explanatory" varia-

TABLE 14-3. Correlation Coefficients of the Relationships Between Three Assumed Intervening Variables and the Independent Variable (Sex) and Dependent Variable (Level of Aspiration) ($N = 188$)

Assumed Intervening Variable	Sex[#] (Point-biserial r)	Level of Aspiration (Pearsonian r)
Satisfaction with progress in career[1]	.09	−.21*
Total number of years in teaching	.47*	−.29*
Pressure for occupational advancement[2]	−.12*	.43*

[#] Female = 1; male = 0.

* $p < .05$.

[1]See text, p. 209 for the way this variable was measured

[2]See text, p. 209 for the way this variable was measured

TABLE 14-4. Zero-order, First-order, and Higher-order Partial Correlation Coefficients Between Sex and Level of Aspiration ($N = 188$)

	Zero-order r	First-order Partial r	Higher-order Partial r
Sex and Level of Aspiration	−.38		
Holding constant:			
Total number of years in teaching		−.28	
Pressure for occupational advancement		−.35	
Total years in teaching and pressure for occupational advancement			−.17

bles, years as a teacher, has any appreciable bearing on the relationships between the independent and dependent variables. The other one, felt pressure for occupational advancement, has only a negligible effect. However, column 4 reveals that when both of these variables are held constant simultaneously, the correlation between sex and level of aspiration diminishes appreciably, from −.38 to −.17. The findings, in combination, thus indicate that two of the three lines of reasoning underlying the hypothesis appear to have some factual basis; the third, however, does not.[11]

FURTHER ANALYSES

Additional light on sex differences in occupational aspirations among elementary school administrators may be obtained by examining the responses of the male and female administrators to individual questions in the Level of Career Aspiration Instrument (Table 14-5).

Of the five questions pertaining to vertical mobility within school systems to which the principals responded, two were quite general in nature: "How desirous are you to obtain a higher administrative position in your *present* school system?" and "How desirous are you to obtain a higher administrative position in *another* school system?" More than twice the proportion of women as of men (34% vs. 13%) indicated *no* desire to ascend the hierarchy *in their own school system,* and over twice the proportion of men as women expressed a definite interest in achieving a higher administrative position in it (item 1, Table 14-5). The replies of the men and women to the question about their aspirations for an administrative position in school systems *other than their own* (item 2) revealed the same general response pattern: men much more frequently expressed a desire for an administrative position of this kind than did women principals (23% vs. 7%). A comparison of the principals' responses to items 1 and 2 reveals that both men and women are more interested in moving into the higher ranks of their own school district than into another school system. This finding undoubtedly reflects such matters as their greater familiarity with the formal and informal organization of their own school system, attachments to their local community, and seniority and pension rights.

What do the data reveal about the interest of men and women principals in top level positions in educational administration such as superintendent of schools or deputy or assistant superintendent?

TABLE 14-5. Percentage Distribution of the Responses of Women and Men Principals to the 13 Items in the Level of Aspiration Instrument

		Per Cent of Principals Responding			
Item		Would Not Want to	Not Especially Anxious to	Have Definite Desire to[#]	(N)
How desirous are you to:					
1. Obtain a higher administrative position in my present school system.*	W	34%	41%	25%	91
	M	13	28	59	98
2. Obtain a higher administrative position in some other school system.*	W	69	24	7	90
	M	44	33	23	98
3. Become an assistant or deputy superintendent of schools in a large city system.*	W	81	12	7	91
	M	38	36	26	98
4. Become the school superintendent of a large city system.	W	90	9	1	91
	M	61	26	13	98
5. Become the school superintendent of a small school system.	W	89	9	1	91
	M	61	27	12	98
6. Obtain a principalship that has greater responsibilities than my present position.	W	42	43	15	91
	M	19	39	42	98
7. Obtain a principalship that would carry more prestige than my present position.*	W	39	43	18	91
	M	17	50	33	98
8. Obtain a principalship which would pay more money tham my present position.*	W	18	52	30	91
	M	9	32	59	98

Includes the following three response categories: "have some desire to," "would very much like to," and "am extremely anxious to."

* Item included in Level of Aspiration Scale.

TABLE 14-5. (*Continued*)

		Per Cent of Principals Responding			
Item		Would Not Want to	Not Especially Anxious to	Have Definite# Desire to#	(N)

How desirous are you to:

Item		Would Not Want to	Not Especially Anxious to	Have Definite Desire to	(N)
9. Establish an outstanding reputation among my professional colleagues.	W	12%	36%	52%	91
	M	8	21	71	98
10. Take a more important role in professional educational organizations.*	W	26	35	39	91
	M	16	29	55	98
11. Some day be president of a state association of principals.	W	58	36	6	91
	M	41	38	21	98
12. Some day be president of a national association of principals.	W	77	21	2	90
	M	55	33	12	97
13. Become a college professor of education.	W	65	15	20	90
	M	40	22	38	98

Includes the following three response categories: "have some desire to," "would very much like to," and "am extremely anxious to."

* Item included in Level of Aspiration Scale.

The percentage of both men and women principals who aspired to these positions (items 3, 4, 5) was much smaller than the percentage who indicated a desire for higher administrative jobs "in general" (items 1 and 2). The proportion of women principals who reported an interest in jobs of this kind was, again, considerably less than the proportion of men principals with such interests: 4 out of 5 of the women, in comparison to 2 out of every 5 men, expressed no interest in becoming an assistant or deputy superintendent of a large city school system. And 9 out of 10 women, in comparison to 6 out of 10 men, stated that they had no desire to obtain a school superintendency in either a large or small school system. The responses of some women principals to this set of questions probably reflect their assessment of the possibilities of achieving a top level position. The replies of most men also bespoke a measure of realism: twice as many of the male principals evinced interest in an *assistant* superintendency as in the superintendency.

The responsibilities, prestige, and salaries associated with different principalships vary considerably. A high school principalship generally entails greater responsibilities than one at an elementary school; high school principals generally receive larger salaries than principals of junior high schools, who in turn, usually receive more remuneration than administrators of elementary schools. In many school systems the salary of principals is determined by the number of pupils enrolled in their school. In responding to three questions concerned with their interest in obtaining other principalships, the men expressed higher career aspirations than women in each instance (items 6, 7, 8). Two other interesting findings emerged from this set of responses: first, both men and women exhibited much greater interest in a principalship with a higher salary than one with greater responsibility or prestige; second, a greater proportion of the men than the women expressed a clear cut interest in obtaining a principalship that had greater responsibilities or more prestige than the one that they presently hold.

To discover if there were sex differences in the principals' concern for recognition from professional colleagues, we asked them to respond to four questions that dealt with their desire (1) to establish an outstanding professional reputation among their colleagues, (2) to take a more active role in professional educational associations, (3) to be president of a state association of principals, and (4) to serve as president of a national association of principals. The men evinced a greater interest in each of these types of professional recognition than the women (items 9–12).

A principal may also aspire to become a professor of education in an institution of higher learning. Many faculty members in schools of education at one time served as a principal of an elementary or secondary school. Is there also a sex difference in this respect? The data indicated that there is: 65% of the women, in contrast to 40% of the men, indicated no desire for this type of position.

NOTES AND REFERENCES

1. For reviews or appraisals of the large body of literature on social mobility, see Pitirim A. Sorokin, *Social Mobility* (New York: Harper & Bros., 1927); David V. Glass (Ed.), *Social Mobility in Britain* (London: Routledge and Kegan Paul, 1954); Raymond

W. Mack, Linton Freeman, and Seymour Yellin, *Social Mobility: Thirty Years of Research and Theory* (Syracuse: Syracuse University Press, 1957); Seymour Martin Lipset and Reinhard Bendix, *Social Mobility in Industrial Society* (Berkeley and Los Angeles: University of California Press, 1959); and Thomas Fox and S. M. Miller, "Occupational Stratification and Mobility: Intra-Country Variations," *Studies in Comparative International Development*, I, (1), (1965).

2. See Robin M. Williams, Jr., *American Society: A Sociological Interpretation*, Second Edition, Revised (New York: Alfred A. Knopf, 1961), Chapter 5.

3. Two important studies that report findings on intragenerational mobility in American cities are Percy E. Davidson and H. Dewey Anderson, *Occupational Mobility in an American Community* (Stanford: Stanford University Press, 1937); and Lipset and Bendix, *op. cit.*, pp. 156–181.

4. For an excellent treatment of reference group theory, see Robert K. Merton, *Social Theory and Social Structure* (Glencoe, Ill.: The Free Press, 1957), (Revised and enlarged edition), pp. 281–386.

5. Samuel A. Stouffer et al., *The American Soldier: Adjustment During Army Life*, Vol. 1 (Princeton: Princeton University Press, 1949), p. 250.

6. Another circumstance in the occupational world of principals deserves note: opportunities for advancement to top level administrative positions in large city school systems unquestionably have been much greater for men than women. Although almost 4 out of 10 elementary principals were women in 1960, the proportion of females in key administrative roles dropped sharply at top levels of the public school systems. Thus, no woman was superintendent of any of the 41 larger city school systems in our study, and in nearly all of them the great majority of secondary school principals and higher administrators were men. If we assume that women administrators of elementary schools took these facts into account in their career planning, it also would lead to their having lower occupational aspirations than men principals. Since we have no data indicating whether women in fact take this condition into account in their career orientations, this line of reasoning must be viewed as speculative.

7. See Appendix C, Table C-1 for the technical details of the construction of the Level of Aspiration Scale.

8. In using the t-test as the test of significance in comparing the mean scores of the men and women principals, we have treated the Level of Aspiration Scale as if it were an interval scale. A chi-square test applied to the data in Table 14-1 leads to the same conclusion, namely that men on the average receive higher scores on the Scale than do women. We focus on the mean scale scores of the two sex groups in order to facilitate an easy comparison of the findings for the total sample with those for subsamples that are presented in Table 14-2.

9. Two other factors, age and marital status, deserve comment at this point. In a number of analyses in earlier chapters we treated them as possible confounding variables. We use another strategy in this chapter. We could have used age and marital status as indicators of two of the intervening variables we have proposed as links between sex and level of aspiration. Thus, the age of principals could serve as an index of the length of time available to them for occupational advancement prior to retirement and "marriedness" could have been used as an index of high economic pressure for men principals and low economic pressure for women principals. We preferred to use more direct indices of these intervening variables. Those that we will employ are described later in the chapter.

10. The findings about the association between sex and the assumed intervening variables are based on point-biserial correlation coefficients and those between the assumed intervening variables and level of aspiration are based on Pearsonian correlation coefficients (see Table 14-3).

11.   On several occasions we have employed the point-biserial correlation to ascertain the relationship between sex and other variables. In this connection it deserves note that the magnitude of the coefficients of correlation based on the point-biserial correlation analyses are almost identical to those obtained from the use of Kendall's Tau. For example, the correlation coefficient between sex and level of aspiration that is presented in Table 14-3 using Kendall's Tau was − .38 when we computed the point-biserial correlation; if we had used Kendall's Tau instead of point-biserial correlation to measure the zero-order relationship reported in Table 14-3, the coefficient of correlation would have changed only slightly. For a discussion of the use and calculation of Kendall's Tau and other distribution-free statistical techniques, see Keith Smith, "Distribution-free Statistical Methods and the Concept of Power Efficiency," in Leon Festinger and Daniel Katz (Eds.), *Research Methods in the Behavioral Sciences* (New York: The Dryden Press, 1953), pp. 536–577.

15

Summary and Implications

Our inquiry was conducted with four major objectives in mind: first, to determine if there are differences in the career histories of men and women principals of public elementary schools; second, to ascertain if sex differences exist in their orientations and reactions to this position; third, to find out if the role performance of men and women principals vary; and fourth, to determine if schools administered by men and women principals differ in their functioning and educational productivity. The data employed to examine these issues were obtained from a national cross-section of 189 elementary school principals in 41 large school systems in the United States as well as from their teachers. In this final chapter we present a brief summary of our major findings, consider some of their educational and social science implications, and comment on their relevance for women who have speculated about careers in educational administration.

SUMMARY OF MAJOR FINDINGS

Our findings showed that the sex of principals had a bearing in a number of important respects on their career decisions and occupational histories. We found that women considered and made up their minds to become teachers at a much earlier age than men, but that men gave serious consideration to becoming a principal at a much earlier stage in their careers than women. Our findings revealed that most men, but only a minority of the women, claimed that they had no strong motivation to become school teachers and that teaching was the first-choice vocation for the great majority of the women, but for only half of the men. We also found that men and women were exposed to different amounts and types of encouragement and discouragement in their career decisions. Moreover, our data revealed that the age at which individuals attain the principalship and the length of time it took them to become a principal were both influenced by the sex factor: over twice the proportion of men as women were under 36 years of age when they first became principals and over four times the proportion of men than women became principals within 10 years after they became teachers. Furthermore, although only minor sex differences existed with reference to their system-wide and in-school administrative experience prior to their first principalship, the men and women did differ greatly in the type and quantity of teaching experience they brought to the elementary principalship: 34% of the men as compared to 3% of the women had never taught in an elementary school; furthermore, the mean years of elementary teaching experience of women was over three times as great as the men's (14.7 vs. 4.6 years). We conclude from these findings that the sex factor did have a bearing on the timing, context, and motivation of the career decisions of elementary school principals and that it also had a direct influence on the amount and kinds of educational experience they brought to their administrative roles.

In our examination of the influence of the sex factor on the principals' reactions to their work, we found that the women principals had lower aspiration for professional advancement and tended to worry less about their work than the men. In regard to sex differences in their orientation to their role and responsibilities, our findings indicated that the women place greater emphasis on three criteria for evaluating an elementary school: its concern with individual differences among its pupils, the social and emotional development of its pupils, and its efforts to help "deviant" pupils. We found no sex differences in the importance that the principals placed on the academic performance of pupils or on the ability of a school to maintain pupil discipline. With respect to criteria for evaluating teachers, the data revealed that women placed more emphasis than men on the technical skills of teachers and the extent to which they fulfill their organizational responsibilities.

The findings also showed that women on the average evaluated their performance more highly on, and derived more satisfaction from, supervising instruction than did men, but that there was no sex difference for the entire sample in the importance they attributed to it. In regard to the management of routine administrative affairs, we found that the men and women did not differ in the importance they assigned to it or in the evaluation of their ability to perform it; however, the men derived more satisfaction from this component of their work than the women. On the basis of these findings, we conclude that the sex factor also influences in importance respects the way principals view and react to their work.

The study also revealed that the sex factor had a bearing on the principals' performance and the operation of their schools. We found that women exerted greater control over their teachers' professional activities than men and that the women associated more frequently with members of the faculty outside of school than the men. Although sex differences of a conditional nature were identified on certain dimensions of their performance, no sex differences were found for the entire sample in the following aspects of their performance: support of teachers in situations involving teacher-pupil conflict, stress placed on teachers offering maximum service to pupils, social distance from teachers in school, and involvment of parents in school affairs. Finally, our findings showed that the professional performance of teachers and pupils' learning were higher on the average in the schools administered by women than by men; however, staff morale was not associated with the gender of the principal.

IMPLICATIONS FOR EDUCATION

Selection of Principals

One of the basic objectives of our inquiry was to ascertain if the sex of principals had any bearing on the functioning and performance of schools. As noted, the findings revealed that the quality of pupil learning and the professional performance of teachers were higher on the average in the schools administered by the women, but that teachers' morale was not associated with the sex of their principal (Tables 12-1, 12-6, and 12-11). What do these findings imply for urban school systems in their selection of elementary school administrators?

They challenge the validity of the widespread practice followed by many school districts of giving preference to men in filling vacancies in the principalship. Three arguments have been invoked to justify this common practice. The first is that schools with men principals outperform those in which women serve as their administrators. If pupil learning and the professional performance of teachers are viewed as legitimate criteria for assessing organizational performance, then our findings indicate that this argument has no factual basis. The calibre of the performance of both pupils and teachers was on the average of a higher quality in schools administered by women than in those managed by men.

The second is that the elementary principalship should be reserved for men in order to meet the need of men teachers for occupational advancement and to make public education a more attractive vocational area for men. This argument assumes that the sex of a principal has no bearing on the functioning and performance of schools and therefore, that no significant educational consequences will follow from giving preference to the men. However, the evidence from our inquiry indicates that this assumption is not in accord with the facts.

The third argument offered is that teachers, whether male or female, generally prefer to work in a school administered by a male rather than a female principal. This view is typically based on invidious distinctions between men and women school administrators, for example, that female principals tend to be more emotional, more petty, more evasive, and less decisive than male administrators. If teachers in elementary school in fact prefer men to women as principals, then we would expect to find that the morale of teachers would be higher in schools administered by males. Our findings, however, indicated that there was no significant difference in teacher morale in the schools administered by men and in those with women principals. This argument, too, does not appear to be supported by the evidence.

In short, our findings undercut the arguments generally used to support the male preference policy in selecting elementary school principals. They also imply that one of its unanticipated and unrecognized educational consequences has been that the learning of pupils and the quality of performance of teachers has been adversely affected in many school districts throughout the nation.

The male preference policy undoubtedly accounts in large part for the tilting of the sex ratio in the principalship that has been in evidence for over thirty years. It also is directly relevant to the reversal of the sex ratio in teaching and in administration at the elementary school level: 85% of the nation's elementary school teachers in 1971 were female, but 79% of the elementary school principals were males. These sex-ratio differences are especially noteworthy when it is recalled that the pool from which elementary principals are drawn consists primarily of elementary teachers. Our findings, then, suggest that school systems that have been following a male preference policy should give serious consideration to abandoning it and to replacing it with one designed to provide equal opportunities for women to become elementary school principals. They also imply that implementing this proposal would have beneficial effects for the functioning of schools.

Improving the Performance of Principals

Our findings revealed that the men evaluated their performance in supervising the instructional program less positively than women and that the professional performance of teachers and pupil learning was lower on the average in schools administered by male than female principals. One possible explanation for these sex differences might be that men, generally, attribute less importance to their instructional responsibilities than women. However, this explanation must be discarded in view of our finding that men attribute as much importance as women principals to this aspect of their work. What could account for these differences? Our inquiry suggests that its explanation may lie in the differences in the type and amount of teaching experience that the men and women principals had prior to becoming principals. Our data revealed that the women had taught on the average at the elementary school level over three times as long as the men and uncovered the fact that over one-third of the males, in comparison to 3% of the women, had never taught at all in an elementary school.

These sex difference findings imply that many men in the principalship lack the knowledge and skills required to offer professional direction to the instructional programs of their schools. They are being asked to serve as instructional leaders, but they lack the capabilities required to validate this important aspect of their administrative role. This circumstance could also account for our finding that men generally derive less gratification from instructional activities than women.

On the basis of these findings we submit that school systems with a strong interest in upgrading the quality of their instructional programs would be well advised to develop intensive in-service training programs in instructional leadership for male principals with limited teaching experience. These programs should be designed so that they will provide them with the knowledge, skills, and type of experiences they need to supervise, and give professional leadership to, the school's instructional programs and to work with their teachers in a constructive, productive, and nonthreatening manner. At present, the vogue in many school systems is to place considerable emphasis on modern business management techniques in their in-service programs for administrators. Staff development efforts of this kind undoubtedly have some utility for educational administrators. We submit, however, that instituting programs designed to increase the capabilities of male principals who possess limited teaching experience to serve as instructional leaders of their schools may constitute a more productive way to utilize funds allocated to in-service training programs. Activities of this nature could constitute a relatively inexpensive mechanism to upgrade the academic productivity of schools.

Improving the Performance of Schools

Our findings about sex differences in the performance of principals and in their orientations and reactions to their work imply that school systems may not be maximizing the skills and talents of their female administrators. A case in point is the general practice of appointing men as principals of elementary schools located in the lowest socioeconomic areas. The academic achievement of pupils in these schools is usually the lowest among all the elementary schools in the city and their truancy rates are among the highest. A problem that continues to perplex school superintendents and their staffs is how they can upgrade the quality and quantity of learning of pupils in low SES schools.

One strategy for coping with this very complex problem that has been largely ignored in the social science and educational literature concerned with it is to provide low SES schools with the type of leadership that can revitalize their instructional programs, can motivate teachers, and can create the type of learning environment conducive to rewarding educational and personal experiences for children.

Most school systems assign men to serve as principals of low SES schools. They assume that male administrators will perform more effectively than women in managing schools of this kind. Our findings imply that this assumption is probably erroneous. We found that in low SES schools, pupils' learning and the professional performance of teachers were lower on the average when men served as their principals. The data revealed that men and women principals in these schools did not differ in the importance they assigned to supervising instruction.

However, they also disclosed that the men derived less gratification from this task than the women. Furthermore, they showed that male administrators of low SES schools displayed on the average less concern for individual differences among children and for their social and emotional development than the women principals.

These findings in combination raise serious questions about the common practice of assigning men to these "difficult" schools. They imply that it needs to be discarded. As noted, the quality of leadership offered by the principal of a low SES school may be one of the most critical factors influencing the performance of its teachers and the educational achievement of its pupils. Our findings imply that assigning more women to low SES schools may be one method of upgrading the quality of leadership offered to their teachers and pupils.

A problem of concern to numerous school districts is how to provide inexperienced teachers with the techniques and skills essential for carrying out their teaching responsibilities in an imaginative and professional manner. Our findings strongly imply that women principals, because of their greater experience in teaching and their greater concern with, and involvement in, the instructional program of their schools generally provide new teachers with the help and support they need more readily than men administrators. In short, assigning new teachers to schools with women principals may constitute an efficacious way to improve the teaching skills of neophyte teachers.

We noted in Chapter 1 that it is widely believed in many circles that when men and women occupy the identical managerial position, men will do the better job. Our findings indicate that with respect to the elementary school principalship this belief is incorrect. The performance of schools administered by women principals was on the average superior to those managed by men, and teacher morale in their schools was not significantly different. Whether our findings would be replicated in other types of organizations is an open question. Our findings, however, imply that the view that men generally outperform women in managerial or executive roles needs to be sharply questioned.

Our findings also strongly suggest that women in teaching and other females with an interest in becoming educational administrators need have no fear about the influence of their gender on their performance. As noted, the quality of performance of teachers and pupils was generally of higher quality when the principal was a woman. Women reported less worry than men in the principalship. Women derived greater satisfaction from supervising the instructional program than the men and the women had the higher evaluation of their performance in this essential aspect of their work. Furthermore, contrary to a widely held view, the morale of teachers did not differ in schools administered by women or men. These and related findings indicate that women have no reason to consider their gender as a disadvantage in performing the functions of a principal. It appears to be an advantage. They do, however, need to be aware that their gender at the present time constitutes a barrier to procuring a principalship in many school districts. Furthermore, they need to recognize that the decline in the size of the elementary school population predicted by demographers will curtail the number of vacancies in elementary principalships. The growing pressure for equality in the employment of women and the efforts of women in education to remove sex discrimination in the schools, however, can be expected to decrease this type of bias in the selection of elementary principals in the years ahead.

SOCIOLOGICAL IMPLICATIONS OF THE STUDY

Our study has examined a problem area that has been largely ignored in the sociological literature: ways in which the gender of role incumbents in identical positions may influence their performance, their reactions to work, their career patterns, and organizational performance. Our findings provide considerable evidence to support the proposition that the gender of the administrators of elementary schools does make a difference in how they behave as administrators, in their feelings about their work, in their career patterns, and in the operation of their schools. The results of our inquiry suggest that sociologists who study complex organizations may find it profitable to give serious consideration to the advisability of including sex identity as an independent variable in their inquiries.[1]

In addition to replication studies, there is also the need for inquiries that examine the impact of the sex factor on the performance, attitudes and beliefs of individuals who occupy other types of managerial positions in school systems and who serve as executives of other types or organizations. In the case of educational systems, there appear to be no published studies that have determined if the sex factor has any bearing on the performance of top level officials such as associate superintendents, directors of curriculum and instruction, or officials in charge of the psychological services program of a school district. With respect to other types of organizations such as social work agencies, government agencies, and business firms, the question of whether men and women who serve in the same managerial capacity vary in their role orientations and performance remains unanswered. The influence of the sex factor on university administration is also a relatively unexplored issue. For example, is the morale or productivity of the faculty in departments of a university influenced by the gender of their "chairperson"? What are the organizational consequences of appointing a man or a woman to a deanship? It also should be noted that the question of the influence of the sex factor on the functioning of organizations becomes more complicated, but also more interesting, when the gender of both the superordinate and subordinates are taken into account in the analyses. Studies of these kinds constitute a sample of the types of inquiries required if our understanding of how the sex factor influences specific aspects of organizational functioning in different kinds of settings is to be materially increased.

Sociologists generally assume that sex roles influence the behavior of persons primarily because of the social expectations attached to them. Our findings suggest another way in which they may influence conduct. We found that the women principals had considerably more teaching experience than the men prior to their becoming principals and that this circumstance accounted in part for sex differences in their role performance and in their reaction to their work. These findings, in combination, suggest that for men and women who are incumbents of the identical occupational position, their gender may largely account for differences in the types of experience they bring to their work. And these differences in their earlier work experiences may carry over and directly influence their present role performance. In short, sex roles influence earlier career experiences and opportunities of individuals and they, in turn, may account in part for differences in the performance and attitudes of men and women who serve in identical positions.

We have emphasized that most studies of organizations have ignored the fact that their members have a gender. The implicit assumption underlying their design appears to be that although individuals simultaneously occupy several positions, they activate each of them singly at any given moment of time. In Linton's terms, certain statuses and roles are active while the others are latent or passive.[2] In the case of school principals, it would be assumed that their managerial role would be active whereas their sex role would be latent. Our findings suggest that the notion of the single activation of positions needs to be challenged. The differences we found in the attitudes and behavior of women and men principals can be attributed to the influence of their sex identities on their administrative roles, for example, in the women's greater concern for individual differences among children and their greater emphasis on the school's responsibility for the social and emotional development of the child. We are suggesting that the social reality is that individuals frequently activate *multiple* positions simultaneously and that they are also reacted to as incumbents of *multiple* positions. If this is indeed the case, then we need to take into account the *multiple* positions that are simultaneously occupied by individuals in organizations and in other social settings, rather than assume that they invariably activate roles singly. In addition to sex, individuals in organizations have identifications based on their age, religion, marital status, political affiliation, and additional attributes. We are suggesting that instead of assuming that these identities or positions are dormant, it may be more heuristic to assume that for many aspects of their behavior, they are influencing their organizational behavior and hence organizational functioning.

In view of the differences in age and marital status of the men and women principals in our inquiry and the possibility that these variables, rather than the sex factor, might account for certain of our findings, we frequently reexamined relationships between the gender of the principal and dependent variables, holding age and marital status constant. These analyses suggest the possible utility of deriving a more complex measure from the combination of sex, age, and marital status—a life cycle variable. Invoking it, as an explanatory variable rather than each of the variables separately, might be more fruitful in the analysis of many types of problems. For example, a complex factor that included the age, marital status, and sex of elementary school administrators would probably account for a greater portion of the variance of the variable, level of career aspiration, than if gender were used as the only independent variable. In short, we are maintaining that a "life cycle variable" may be a more powerful predictor of dependent variables like career aspiration than sex, age, or marital status individually.

We feel it important to emphasize again that our findings have reference to *group*, not *individual*, differences between men and women in the principalship. To conclude, for example, that women *invariably* exercise greater control over the performance of their teachers from our finding that women *on the average* tend to exert the greater control, would constitute a serious misinterpretation of the findings.

We conclude that sex, indeed, does make a difference in the operation and management of schools. While conducting our inquiry we became acutely aware of how restricted our knowledge is of the personal and organizational effects of the sex factor. Rhetoric abounds but there is a paucity of inquiries about these issues. Since the proportion of women who will occupy managerial and other types of positions will undoubtedly increase in the decades ahead, research investigations that increase our understanding of the organizational and personal consequences of the sex factor will have important practical as well as sociological implicatons. It is our hope that our explorations into this intriguing problem area will serve as a catalyst for studies of this kind.

NOTES AND REFERENCES

1. See Alvin W. Gouldner, "Organizational Analysis," in Robert K. Merton, Leonard Broom, and Leonard S. Cottrell, Jr., (Eds.), *Sociology Today* (New York: Basic Books, Inc., 1959), pp. 412–413.

2. For a critique of Linton's formulations of the concepts of status and role, see Neal Gross, Ward S. Mason, and Alexander W. McEachern, *Explorations in Role Analysis: Studies of the School Superintendency Role* (New York: John Wiley and Sons, 1958), Chapter 2.

Definition of the Subclassifications of Variables Used in "Third Variable Analyses"

A number of tables presented in this book compare women and men in the elementary principalship on some specified variable (for example, level of aspiration or worry) under subclassifications of various characteristics of the principals or their schools (for example, age of principal or size of school). Tables of this type are used to introduce third variables into the analysis for one of the three following purposes: (1) to determine if findings for the total sample are "internally replicated" in selected subclassifications of the sample; (2) to examine the possibility of conditional relationships; and (3) to ascertain if a relationship found between the sex of principals and a particular variable could be "explained away" by a confounding third variable. This appendix defines the subclassifications of the variables used in these tables and reports the number of elementary principals in each subclassification.

TABLE A-1. Definition of the Subclassifications of Variables Used in "Third Variable Analyses"

Subclassification	Number of Principals in the Subcategory
Characteristics of Principals	
Age	
Young – Under 46 years of age	48
Medium – 46 – 55 years of age	69
Old – 56 years of age or older	72
Marital Status	
Married	115
Single	62
Other (widowed or divorced)	12
Characteristics of Schools	
Size of School	
Small – Under 541 pupils	63
Medium – 541 to 750 pupils	64
Large – Over 750 pupils	62
Size of City	
Small – Population of 50,000 to 249,999	89
Medium – Population of 250,000 to 999,999	68
Large – Population of 1,000,000 and over	32
Mean Age of Teachers	
Young – 24.2 to 38.9 years	65
Middle – 39.0 to 43.4 years	60
Old – 43.5 to 52.5 years	63

TABLE A-1. *(Continued)*

Subclassification	Number of Principals in the Subcategory
Characteristics of Schools (Cont.)	
Mean Experience of Teachers	
Short - 2.8 to 11.2 years	63
Medium - 11.3 to 15.1 years	61
Long - 15.2 to 23.2 years	63
Variance in Teachers' Ages (σ^2)	
Low - 1.6 to 17.7 years	62
Medium - 17.8 to 24.6 years	63
High - 24.7 to 51.0 years	62
Proportion of Men Teachers (of the total teaching faculty)	
Low - Under 7 per cent	58
Medium - 8 to 15 per cent	68
High - 16 to 42 per cent	63
Percentage of Staff Viewed as Competent by Principal	
Low - 70 per cent or under	51
Medium - 71 to 89 per cent	69
High - 90 to 100 per cent	67
Region (Based on 1960 U.S. Census classification)	
West - Mountain, Pacific States	33
Midwest - East North Central, West North Central States	56

Subclassification	Number of Principals in the Subcategory
Characteristics of Schools (Cont.)	
Region (Cont.)	
East - New England, Middle Atlantic States	52
South - South Atlantic, East South Central, West South Central States	48
Average Socio-economic Level of Parents of Pupils in a School*	
Low - S.E.S. factor scores 7.91 to 8.80	64
Middle - S.E.S. factor scores 8.81 to 10.25	62
High - S.E.S. factor scores 10.26 to 14.41	63

*Determined by an S.E.S. factor score for each school derived from factor loadings applied to the principals' responses to the following six questions: "What percentage of the students in your school:"

1. Come from homes where at least one parent is a college graduate.

2. Come from homes where neither parent has gone to school beyond high school.

3. Come from homes where the father is a professional person, business executive, or manager.

4. Come from homes where the father is an unskilled or semi-skilled worker.

5. Come from homes where the parents have a combined family income of $10,000 or more.

6. Come from homes where the parents have a combined family income of less than $5,000.

Specimen Research Instruments

The multiple objectives of the National Principalship Study required the collection of a large body of data from the three types of school personnel who participated in it: principals, teachers, and top officials. Instruments of special relevance to our study are exhibited here.

The following instruments used in the present inquiry to obtain data were presented in Neal Gross and Robert E. Herriott, *Staff Leadership in Public Schools: A Sociological Inquiry* (New York: John Wiley & Sons, 1965): questionnaires concerned with the job history and personal and social background of the principals, the self-evaluation instrument, the part of the interview schedule dealing with the importance principals attach to various aspects of their work.

We present below four other instruments used to obtain measures of central variables examined in the study of men and women as elementary principals: their worry (B-1), the weight they assign different criteria for evaluating teachers (B-2), the satisfaction they derive from various aspects of their work (B-3), and their role performance (B-4).

TABLE B-1. Worry Instrument

Instructions	**Question 18**
Listed below are a number of things that sometimes trouble principals. Please answer Question 18 by *circling* the *one* letter that best represents your reply.	To what extent does each of the following occur in your situation? A = I very frequently B = I frequently C = I sometimes D = I almost never E = I never

1.	Worry about possible physical injuries to individual students while they are at school.	A	B	C	D	E
2.	Worry about the possible occurrence of a "disaster" (e.g., serious fire, food poisoning, etc.) at my school.	A	B	C	D	E
3.	Am concerned that what I do or say may cause me to be disliked by my teachers.	A	B	C	D	E
4.	Worry about what an individual or group may do if I make a decision contrary to their wishes.	A	B	C	D	E
5.	Worry about what is going on in my school when I am away from it for any length of time during school hours.	A	B	C	D	E
6.	Am kept awake at night thinking about problems associated with my job.	A	B	C	D	E
7.	Am concerned about the impression I will make when I have to speak to a group of parents.	A	B	C	D	E
8.	Am concerned about the impression I will make when I have to speak to a group of teachers.	A	B	C	D	E
9.	Find myself worrying whether I have made the right decision on a matter with which I have just dealt.	A	B	C	D	E
10.	Have anxiety when I deal with "complaining" parents.	A	B	C	D	E
11.	Feel nervous when I attend PTA or other parent meetings.	A	B	C	D	E

TABLE B-2. Instrument Used to Determine the Weight Principals Apply to Different Criteria for Evaluating Teachers

Instructions

Listed below are some factors which are frequently used in the evaluation of teachers. Please answer Question 2 and Question 3 by *circling* the letter and number which best represent your judgment.

Question 2

In your judgment, what weight *should be given* to each of the following factors in evaluating how well a teacher is carrying out his or her job?

A = very great weight
B = considerable weight
C = some weight
D = little weight
E = no weight at all

Question 3

In evaluating the teachers in your school, what weight *do you give?*

1 = very great weight
2 = considerable weight
3 = some weight
4 = little weight
5 = no weight at all

Factors

Factor	Question 2	Question 3
1. Attendance at PTA or parent meetings.	A B C D E	1 2 3 4 5
2. Participation in civic affairs.	A B C D E	1 2 3 4 5
3. Cooperation with school administration.	A B C D E	1 2 3 4 5
4. Interest in social and emotional development of students.	A B C D E	1 2 3 4 5
5. Willingness to serve on committees of the school.	A B C D E	1 2 3 4 5
6. Ability to maintain good relations with fellow teachers.	A B C D E	1 2 3 4 5
7. Participation in extra-curricular school activities.	A B C D E	1 2 3 4 5

8.	Dress and general appearance.	A	B	C	D	E	1	2	3	4	5
9.	Ability to maintain classroom discipline.	A	B	C	D	E	1	2	3	4	5
10.	Comprehensiveness of lesson plans.	A	B	C	D	E	1	2	3	4	5
11.	Knowledge of subject matter.	A	B	C	D	E	1	2	3	4	5
12.	Ability to make subject matter interesting to students.	A	B	C	D	E	1	2	3	4	5
13.	Attendance at state educational conventions.	A	B	C	D	E	1	2	3	4	5
14.	Popularity with the student body.	A	B	C	D	E	1	2	3	4	5
15.	Willingness to stay after school to help students with their difficulties.	A	B	C	D	E	1	2	3	4	5
16.	Ability to maintain good relations with parents.	A	B	C	D	E	1	2	3	4	5
17.	Academic progress of students.	A	B	C	D	E	1	2	3	4	5
18.	Cooperation with staff specialists.	A	B	C	D	E	1	2	3	4	5
19.	Willingness to participate in in-service training programs.	A	B	C	D	E	1	2	3	4	5
20.	Contributions to faculty meetings.	A	B	C	D	E	1	2	3	4	5
21.	Extent to which they write articles for professional journals.	A	B	C	D	E	1	2	3	4	5
22.	Willingness to give up free time for good of the school.	A	B	C	D	E	1	2	3	4	5
23.	Attractiveness of classroom displays.	A	B	C	D	E	1	2	3	4	5
24.	Social habits in the community.	A	B	C	D	E	1	2	3	4	5
25.	Degree of promptness in getting to classes.	A	B	C	D	E	1	2	3	4	5

TABLE B-2 (*Continued*)

Instructions	Question 2	Question 3
Listed below are some factors which are frequently used in the evaluation of teachers. Please answer Question 2 and Question 3 by *circling* the letter and number which best represent your judgment.	In your judgment, what weight *should be given* to each of the following factors in evaluating how well a teacher is carrying out his or her job? A = very great weight B = considerable weight C = some weight D = little weight E = no weight at all	In evaluating the teachers in your school, what weight *do you give?* 1 = very great weight 2 = considerable weight 3 = some weight 4 = little weight 5 = no weight at all
26. Enthusiasm for the school.	A B C D E	1 2 3 4 5
27. Loyalty to the school administration.	A B C D E	1 2 3 4 5
28. Degree of promptness in submitting reports.	A B C D E	1 2 3 4 5
29. Extent to which they keep informed on new educational practices.	A B C D E	1 2 3 4 5
30. Ability to adequately cover assigned course material during school year.	A B C D E	1 2 3 4 5
31. Extent to which students respect the teachers.	A B C D E	1 2 3 4 5

TABLE B-3. Instrument Used to Determine the Satisfaction Principals Derive from Various Aspects of Their Work

Instructions

The role of the *PRINCIPAL* is a varied one, involving many different tasks and calling for the application of many different skills. Most principals find that they enjoy these different aspects of their role to varying degrees.

Please answer the question to the right for each of the aspects of the principal's role given below. In answering this question, *circle* the *one* code letter which best represents your answer.

Question 25

To what degree do you enjoy each of the following aspects of a principal's role?

I enjoy . . .

A = A great deal
B = Very much
C = Somewhat
D = Very little
E = Not at all
N = Aspect not relevant in my particular situation

Aspects of a Principal's Role

1.	Handling administrative routine.	A	B	C	D	E	N
2.	Supervising the instructional program.	A	B	C	D	E	N
3.	Allocating the school budget.	A	B	C	D	E	N
4.	Talking with individual parents about a problem concerning their child.	A	B	C	D	E	N
5.	Serving on committees with parents.	A	B	C	D	E	N
6.	Talking with a group of parents about a school problem.	A	B	C	D	E	N
7.	Working primarily with teachers, rather than with pupils.	A	B	C	D	E	N
8.	Working with "exceptionally able" teachers.	A	B	C	D	E	N
9.	Working with "average" teachers.	A	B	C	D	E	N
10.	Working with new teachers.	A	B	C	D	E	N
11.	Working with youngsters who are having a hard time adjusting to a school situation.	A	B	C	D	E	N
12.	Having a vacation from work periodically during the school year.	A	B	C	D	E	N

Instructions

The role of the *PRINCIPAL* is a varied one, involving many different tasks and calling for the application of many different skills. Most principals find that they enjoy these different aspects of their role to varying degrees.

Please answer the question to the right for each of the aspects of the principal's role given below. In answering this question, *circle* the *one* code letter which best represents your answer.

Question 25

To what degree do you enjoy each of the following aspects of a principal's role?

I enjoy . . .

A = A great deal
B = Very much
C = Somewhat
D = Very little
E = Not at all
N = Aspect not relevant in my particular situation

Aspects of a Principal's Role

13.	Conducting teachers' meetings.	A	B	C	D	E	N
14.	Evaluating teacher performance.	A	B	C	D	E	N
15.	Having the freedom to schedule one's own time.	A	B	C	D	E	N
16.	Working with community agencies.	A	B	C	D	E	N
17.	Handling public relations.	A	B	C	D	E	N
18.	Supervising custodial personnel.	A	B	C	D	E	N
19.	Supervising office personnel.	A	B	C	D	E	N
20.	Supervising large groups of students.	A	B	C	D	E	N
21.	Having to reprimand teachers.	A	B	C	D	E	N
22.	Having to discipline pupils.	A	B	C	D	E	N
23.	Preparing staff bulletins or announcements.	A	B	C	D	E	N
24.	Working with guidance personnel.	A	B	C	D	E	N
25.	Working with curriculum specialists.	A	B	C	D	E	N
26.	Preparing reports to the higher administration.	A	B	C	D	E	N

TABLE B-4. Section of Teacher Questionnaire Used to Obtain Teachers' Observations of the Role Performance of their Principal

Instructions	Question 3 (Col. I)	Question 4 (Col. II)
Listed below are some activities in which a PRINCIPAL can engage. Please answer Question 3 and Question 4 by *writing* in Col. I the *LETTER* and in Col. II the *NUMBER* which best represent your replies.	Do you feel the *PRINCIPAL OF YOUR SCHOOL* should engage in the following activities? I feel that the principal of my school . . . A = Absolutely must B = Preferably should C = May or may not D = Preferably should not E = Absolutely must not N = This activity not relevant to my school	How frequently does your principal do this? My principal . . . does this. 1 = Always 2 = Almost always 3 = Occasionally 4 = Almost never 5 = Never N = This activity not relevant to my school
13. Use interested parents as an advisory group when making out the course of study.	☐	☐
14. Attempt to restrict as much as possible the part parents play in school affairs.	☒	☒
16. Discourage parental questioning of educational beliefs of faculty members.	☐	☐
17. Encourage a group of parents to discuss and help formulate the educational philosophy to be used in the school.	☒	☐
18. Encourage parental attendance at school assemblies.	☐	☒

TABLE B-4 (Continued)

240

Instructions	Question 3 (Col. I)	Question 4 (Col. II)
Listed below are some activities in which a PRINCIPAL can engage. Please answer Question 3 and Question 4 by *writing* in Col. I the *LETTER* and in Col. II the *NUMBER* which best represent your replies.	Do you feel the *PRINCIPAL OF YOUR SCHOOL* should engage in the following activities? I feel that the principal of my school . . . A = Absolutely must B = Preferably should C = May or may not D = Preferably should not E = Absolutely must not N = This activity not relevant to my school	How frequently does your principal do this? My principal . . . does this. 1 = Always 2 = Almost always 3 = Occasionally 4 = Almost never 5 = Never N = This activity not relevant to my school

20. Encourage parents to help during school hours on school or class trips or projects.

☐   ☐

21. Devote considerable effort to developing or maintaining an active parents' organization in his school.

☐   ☐

22. Encourage interested parent groups to evaluate how well the school is achieving its curricular objectives.

☐ x   ☐ x

24. Attempt to "redirect" the activities of the PTA or similar organizations that are beginning to question school practices.

☐   ☐

(813)

25. Use interested parents as volunteer part-time "teacher helpers."

☐   ☐

(814)

11. Give additional free time to teachers who are trying out new ideas in their classes.

13. Attempt to secure teachers in the school who are interested in experimenting with new educational ideas.

14. Encourage the introduction of curricular changes which he believes in even though there is little proof that the new curriculum will do a better job than the old one.

15. Encourage the staff to learn about and try out some of the "new ideas" coming from schools of education.

16. Encourage teachers to consider adopting new educational ideas which have been tried out in other communities and found to be successful.

17. Resist the introduction of a new educational method when he believes the current method is reasonably satisfactory.

18. Go slowly in introducing new techniques recommended by curriculum specialists.

19. Encourage schools of education to conduct experimental research in the school.

20. Make only those changes in teaching methods which are being introduced on a systemwide basis.

23. Seek out new ideas to introduce into the school's program.

11. Closely supervise new teachers in the school.

12. Require that teachers' classroom behavior conform to the principal's standards.

(815) (816)

241

TABLE B-4 (Continued)

Instructions	Question 3 (Col. I)	Question 4 (Col. II)
Listed below are some activities in which a PRINCIPAL can engage. Please answer Question 3 and Question 4 by *writing* in Col. I the *LETTER* and in Col. II the *NUMBER* which best represent your replies.	Do you feel the *PRINCIPAL OF YOUR SCHOOL* should engage in the following activities? I feel that the principal of my school . . . A = Absolutely must B = Preferably should C = May or may not D = Preferably should not E = Absolutely must not N = This activity not relevant to my school	How frequently does your principal do this? My principal . . . does this. 1 = Always 2 = Almost always 3 = Occasionally 4 = Almost never 5 = Never N = This activity not relevant to my school

13. Visit classes on a regular schedule to determine how well teachers are carrying out their jobs.

  Col. I: □ □xx   Col. II: □ □xx

16. Check to see that teachers prepare written lesson plans.

17. Ask teachers to report all major conferences with parents to the principal.

  Col. I: □x   Col. II: □x

19. Closely direct the work of teachers who are likely to experience difficulty.

  Col. I: □   Col. II: □

20. Require that teachers discuss their major classroom problems with the principal.

  Col. II: □

21. Limit supervisory activities primarily to those teachers with classroom problems.

22. Know what is taking place in most classrooms during most of the day.

26. Require teachers to keep the principal informed about "problem" children in their classrooms.

28. Determine what the objectives of the guidance program should be in the school.

11. Support a teacher's discipline decision that the principal believes is grossly unfair to the child.

14. Insist that students obey teacher's instructions first, and complain about them later.

15. Side with the teacher when a student complains about the teacher's behavior, even if the student's complaint is legitimate.

16. Be tolerant of older teachers if their teaching techniques are "poor."

17. Encourage worthwhile student activities that would require additional work by teachers.

18. Avoid curricular changes that would strengthen the educational program, when the majority of the teachers oppose them.

22. Back the teacher in any public controversy between teacher and student.

23. Encourage teachers to give extra help in their "free" periods to students needing that help.

TABLE B-4 *(Continued)*

Instructions

Listed below are some activities in which a PRINCIPAL can engage. Please answer Question 3 and Question 4 by *writing* in Col. I the *LETTER* and in Col. II the *NUMBER* which best represent your replies.

Question 3 (Col. I)

Do you feel the *PRINCIPAL OF YOUR SCHOOL* should engage in the following activities?

I feel that the principal of my school . . .

A = Absolutely must
B = Preferably should
C = May or may not
D = Preferably should not
E = Absolutely must not
N = This activity not relevant to my school

Question 4 (Col. II)

How frequently does your principal do this?

My principal . . . does this.

1 = Always
2 = Almost always
3 = Occasionally
4 = Almost never
5 = Never
N = This activity not relevant to my school

#	Activity	Question 3 (Col. I)	Question 4 (Col. II)
24.	Correct a teacher in front of the students when he sees the teacher dealing with students unwisely.	☐ x	☐ x
26.	Put the student's welfare above that of the teacher's when the two are opposed.	☐ (819)	☐ (820)
11.	Avoid social involvement with groups of teachers.	☐	☐
12.	Spend an occasional evening with faculty members.	☐ x	☐ x
14.	Encourage all teachers to call him by his first name, when students are not present.	☐	☐

15. Make it a practice to have lunch frequently with the teachers in his school.

16. Discourage teachers from treating him as "one of the gang" at informal gatherings of teachers.

17. Follow the policy of not having members of the faculty as close personal friends.

19. Refrain from joining a social club to which a number of his teachers belong.

23. Discourage social invitations from faculty members.

24. Avoid first-name relationships with his teachers.

25. Insist, tactfully, that teachers show due respect for his position as principal.

11. Reprimand a faculty member who criticizes another faculty member or administrator in front of students.

12. Insist that arguments and dissensions among school staff members be kept within the school family.

13. Expect an "off-duty" teacher to step in and help another teacher preserve order in an assembly or class group, when the teacher on duty is having some difficulty.

15. Require another teacher to fill in for a teacher who is late for school.

16. Expect that faculty members will stand behind the principal when he is under attack by parents on school matters.

(821)

(822)

TABLE B-4 *(Continued)*

Instructions

Listed below are some activities in which a PRINCIPAL can engage. Please answer Question 3 and Question 4 by *writing* in Col. I the *LETTER* and in Col. II the *NUMBER* which best represent your replies.

Question 3 (Col. I)

Do you feel the *PRINCIPAL OF YOUR SCHOOL* should engage in the following activities?

I feel that the principal of my school . . .

A = Absolutely must
B = Preferably should
C = May or may not
D = Preferably should not
E = Absolutely must not
N = This activity not relevant to my school

Question 4 (Col. II)

How frequently does your principal do this?

My principal . . . does this.

1 = Always
2 = Almost always
3 = Occasionally
4 = Almost never
5 = Never
N = This activity not relevant to my school

	Question 3 (Col. I)	Question 4 (Col. II)
17. Require that all teachers share in non-teaching duties.	xx	xx
20. Require teachers to stay after school occasionally to work on school projects unrelated to their teaching duties, but of benefit to the whole school.		
21. Reprimand a teacher who publicly takes issue with school policies.		
22. Insist that a teacher participate in a school program favored by a majority of teachers, even if the teacher has disagreed with it.	x	x

24. Request a teacher who has a legitimate complaint against another teacher to do nothing about it, since it might create dissension in the school.

☐ (823)   ☐ (824)

11. Share with teachers the responsibility for determining the minimum level of satisfactory student performance in your school.

☐   ☐

12. Share with teachers the responsibility for evaluating how good a job the school is doing.

☐   ☐

13. Share with teachers the responsibility for determining how teachers should be supervised.

☐   ☐

14. Share with teachers the responsibility for developing a policy for handling student discipline problems.

☐   ☐

Guttman Scales and Factor Weights
Used in Measurement of Selected Variables

We present here the Guttman scales used in this study and the factor weights of items (as well as their means and standard deviations) used in computing scores for variables descriptive of the principals' educational values, their reactions to role functions, their performance, and the functioning of their schools.

For the Guttman scales (Tables C-1 and C-2) we present the item number, the definition of a positive response, the percentage of positive responses, and the frequency and percentage of item error for the entire sample of 501 principals in the National Principalship Study. We also present the number and percentage of cases assigned to each perfect scale type. Although the distributions of nonscale types were tallied and checked for evidence of nonrandomness, we do not report them here (there are seven perfect and 57 nonscale types for a 6-item scale). The distribution of responses to items in the Worry and Level of Aspiration Instruments for the 189 elementary principals were presented in Chapters 13 and 14.

The other tables in the Appendix (Tables C-3 to Table C-24) present the wording of items, item means, standard deviations, and factor weights derived from factor analyses that were applied to the responses of principals or teachers to obtain scores to measure (1) the principals' educational values, (2) their reactions to their role functions, (3) their performance, and (4) organizational characteristics of their schools. The scores to measure the principals' educational values and reactions to work were based on factor weights derived from factor analyses of correlation matrices of the responses of the 501 principals in the National Principalship Study. The correlation matrices on which the factor analyses were based resulting in the factor weights used in developing the measures of the principals' performance were reported in Chapter 1, pp. 14 to 15; the correlation matrices on which the factor analyses were based resulting in the factor weights used in developing school scores on

Operational Definition of Scale

m*	Definition of Positive Response*	Per Cent Positive Marginal	Frequency of Item Error (e)	Per Cent of Item Error
	C, D, E	76.4	50.3	10.1
	C, D, E	71.8	56.4	11.3
	D, E	62.8	43.7	8.7
	D, E	41.0	52.5	10.5
	D, E	26.8	33.1	6.6
	E	20.6	42.1	8.4

Coefficient of Reproducibility $= 1 - \dfrac{\Sigma e}{m\,(N)} = 1 - \dfrac{278}{3000} = .907$

Distribution of Scale Scores

Response ern	Score	Frequency	Per Cent
+ + +	6	49	9.8
+ + −	5	50	10.0
+ − −	4	85	17.0
− − −	3	116	23.2
− − −	2	111	22.2
− − −	1	41	8.2
− − −	0	48	9.6

ording of items and response alternatives see Table 13-6

organizational characteristics were reported in Chap
tion matrices that were factored and the details of
the varimax rotations, as well as the computation o!
cients are not presented here in order to keep th
reasonable limits and because of the highly technica
search activities.

TABLE C-1. Level of Aspiration Scale: Technical Details

Number of Usable Cases (N) = 501   Number of It

I. Operational Definition of Scale

Item*	Definition of Positive Response*	Per Cent Positive Marginal	Frequ Item E
11	B, D, D, E	80.2	
2	B, C, D, E	70.8	
7	B, C, D, E	58.0	
4	C, D, E	44.0	
5	D, E	27.6	
6	C, D, E	18.4	

Coefficient of Reproducibility = $1 - \dfrac{\Sigma e}{m(N)}$ = 1 –

II. Distribution of Scale Scores

Ideal Response Pattern	Score	Freque
+ + + + + +	6	54
+ + + + + -	5	51
+ + + + - -	4	85
+ + + - - -	3	113
+ + - - - -	2	10(
+ - - - - -	1	4
- - - - - -	0	5

*For wording of items and response alternatives se

TABLE C-3. Item Means, Standard Deviations, and Factor Weights Applied to the Responses of 185 Principals Used to Compute Factor Scores for Their Concern with Individual Differences among Pupils

Item*	Mean	Standard Deviation	Factor Weight
In evaluating a school such as yours, how much importance [(1) great importance, (2) some importance, (3) little importance, (4) no importance] should be given to such a criterion?			
1. The degree to which special provisions are made for the "slow learner."	1.37	0.55	−0.484
2. The degree to which special provisions are made for the "gifted child."	1.49	0.69	−0.442
3. The degree to which teaching materials in addition to textbooks are being used.	1.36	0.52	−0.422
4. The degree to which students work up to their capacities.	1.22	0.50	−0.296

*Items ordered in terms of decreasing magnitude of factor weight.

TABLE C-4. Item Means, Standard Deviations, and Factor Weights Applied to the Responses of 185 Principals Used to Compute Factor Scores for the Importance They Attribute to the Academic Performance of Pupils

Item*	Mean	Standard Deviation	Factor Weight
In evaluating a school such as yours, how much importance [(1) great importance, (2) some importance, (3) little importance, (4) no importance] should be given to such a criterion?			
1. The success of former students in whatever educational institution they go to next.	1.65	0.72	0.579
2. The proportion of students who eventually go on to college.	2.19	1.02	0.527
3. The degree of student mastery of subject matter fundamentals.	1.33	0.56	0.465
4. The achievement test scores of students.	1.66	0.73	0.438

*Items ordered in terms of decreasing magnitude of factor weight.

TABLE C-5. Item Means, Standard Deviations, and Factor Weights Applied to the Responses of 185 Principals Used to Compute Factor Scores for Their Concern for the Social and Emotional Development of the Child

Item*	Mean	Standard Deviation	Factor Weight
In evaluating a school such as yours, how much importance [(1) great importance, (2) some importance, (3) little importance, (4) no importance] should be given to such a criterion?			
1. The degree to which students exhibit emotional maturity.	1.77	0.86	−0.710
2. The degree to which students exhibit social maturity.	1.69	0.80	−0.678
3. The degree of tolerance toward fellow students of differing social backgrounds exhibited by students.	1.45	0.72	−0.451

*Items ordered in terms of decreasing magnitude of factor weight.

TABLE C-6. Item Means, Standard Deviations, and Factor Weights Applied to the Responses of 185 Principals Used to Compute Factor Scores for Their Emphasis on the Ability to Maintain Pupil Discipline

Item*	Mean	Standard Deviation	Factor Weight
In evaluating a school such as yours, how much importance [(1) great importance, (2) some importance, (3) little importance, (4) no importance] should be given to such a criterion?			
1. The degree to which teachers are able to maintain discipline in their classes.	1.20	0.42	−0.608
2. The degree to which students have respect for the teachers.	1.27	0.51	−0.469
3. The degree to which students exercise self-discipline.	1.28	0.52	−0.397

*Items ordered in terms of decreasing magnitude of factor weight.

TABLE C-7. Items Means, Standard Deviations, and Factor Weights Applied to the Responses of 185 Principals Used to Compute Factor Scores for Their Emphasis They Place on Extent of Pupil Deviant Behavior

Item*	Mean	Standard Deviation	Factor Weight
In evaluating a school such as yours, how much importance [(1) great importance, (2) some importance, (3) little importance, (4) no importance] should be given to such a criterion?			
1. The proportion of students engaging in vandalism.	1.99	0.99	0.637
2. The proportion of students who are constant discipline problems.	1.92	0.95	0.633
3. The amount of student truancy.	1.91	0.88	0.588
4. The proportion of students who cheat.	1.91	0.97	0.576
5. The drop-out rate in the school.	1.86	0.87	0.505

*Items ordered in terms of decreasing magnitude of factor weight.

TABLE C-8. Item Means, Standard Deviations, and Factor Weights Applied to the Responses of 189 Principals Used to Compute Factor Scores for the Importance They Attribute to the Technical Skills of Teachers

Item*	Mean	Standard Deviation	Factor Weight
In your judgment, what weight [(1) very great weight, (2) considerable weight, (3) some weight, (4) little weight, (5) no weight at all] should be given to each of the following factors in evaluating how well a teacher is carrying out his or her job?			
1. Ability to make subject matter interesting to students.	1.32	0.51	−0.538
2. Comprehensiveness of lesson plans.	1.90	0.80	−0.428
3. Knowledge of subject matter.	1.38	0.54	−0.425

*Items ordered in terms of decreasing magnitude of factor weight.

TABLE C-9. Item Means, Standard Deviations, and Factor Weights Applied to the Responses of 189 Principals Used to Compute Factor Scores for the Importance They Attribute to the Organizational Responsibility of Teachers

Item*	Mean	Standard Deviation	Factor Weight
In your judgment, what weight [(1) very great weight, (2) considerable weight, (3) some weight, (4) little weight, (5) no weight at all] should be given to each of the following factors in evaluating how well a teacher is carrying out his or her job?			
1. Cooperation with school administration.	1.42	0.55	−0.592
2. Degree of promptness in submitting reports.	2.19	0.75	−0.574
3. Degree of promptness in getting to classes.	1.65	0.67	−0.548
4. Loyalty to the school administration.	1.79	0.79	−0.537
5. Dress and general appearance.	2.14	0.70	−0.517
6. Willingness to serve on committees of the school.	1.94	0.66	−0.463
7. Ability to maintain good relations with fellow teachers.	1.76	0.64	−0.456
8. Ability to maintain classroom discipline.	1.33	0.50	−0.424

*Items ordered in terms of decreasing magnitude of factor weight.

TABLE C-10. Items Means, Standard Deviations, and Factor Weights Applied to the Responses of 186 Principals Used to Compute Factor Scores for the Importance They Assign to the Supervision of Instruction

Item*	Mean	Standard Deviation	Factor Weight
How important [(1) extremely important, (2) very important, (3) of moderate importance, (4) of little importance, (5) of no importance] do you view this activity in carrying out your job as principal of your school?			
1. Working on the improvement of the curriculum.	1.43	0.59	0.504
2. Introducing new teaching ideas.	1.64	0.67	0.488
3. Counselling pupils.	1.61	0.68	0.479
4. Carrying on in-service training programs for teachers.	1.68	0.73	0.458
5. Dealing with classroom problems of teachers.	1.45	0.61	0.451
6. Evaluating the performance of students.	1.74	0.79	0.433
7. Coordinating the work of teachers.	1.73	0.68	0.414
8. Conferring with individual teachers.	1.41	0.55	0.367

*Items ordered in terms of decreasing magnitude of factor weight.

TABLE C-11. Item Means, Standard Deviations, and Factor Weights Applied to the Responses of 186 Principals Used to Compute Factor Scores for the Importance They Assign to Administrative Tasks

Item*	Mean	Standard Deviation	Factor Weight
How important [(1) extremely important, (2) very important, (3) of moderate importance, (4) of little importance, (5) of no importance] do you view this activity in carrying out your job as principal of your school?			
1. Keeping school records.	1.84	0.78	0.687
2. Checking school attendance.	2.01	0.86	0.651
3. Taking inventory of equipment.	2.63	0.80	0.616
4. Ordering or distributing supplies.	2.38	0.88	0.560
5. Preparing reports for the higher administration of the school system.	1.98	0.80	0.468
6. Checking grade sheets or report cards.	2.37	0.90	0.440
7. Planning students' schedules or class plans.	1.68	0.82	0.428
8. Dealing with correspondence.	2.30	0.79	0.428
9. Keeping a watch on the school budget.	1.89	0.82	0.426
10. Managing the school office.	2.17	0.81	0.425
11. Supervising the custodial staff.	2.40	0.83	0.356

*Items ordered in terms of decreasing magnitude of factor weight.

TABLE C-12. Item Means, Standard Deviations, and Factor Weights Applied to the Responses of 189 Principals Used to Compute Factor Scores for Their Self-evaluation of Their Ability to Supervise the Instructional Program

Item*	Mean	Standard Deviation	Factor Weight
How would you rate your performance [(1) outstanding, (2) excellent, (3) good, (4) fair, (5) poor, (6) very poor] in each of the following areas?			
1. Getting experienced teacher to upgrade their performance.	3.10	0.83	−0.648
2. Improving the performance of inexperienced teachers.	2.79	0.79	−0.617
3. Getting teachers to use new educational methods.	2.96	0.74	−0.609
4. Giving leadership to the instructional program.	2.74	0.80	−0.592
5. Communicating the objectives of the school program to the faculty.	2.56	0.77	−0.565
6. Getting teachers to coordinate their activities.	2.78	0.71	−0.561
7. Knowing about the strengths and weaknesses of teachers.	2.36	0.77	−0.545
8. Maximizing the different skills found in a faculty.	2.59	0.81	−0.537

*Items ordered in terms of decreasing magnitude of factor weight.

TABLE C-13. Item Means, Standard Deviations, and Factor Weights Applied to the Responses of 189 Principals Used to Compute Factor Scores for Their Self-assessment of Their Administrative Abilities

Item*	Mean	Standard Deviation	Factor Weight
How would you rate your performance [(1) outstanding, (2) excellent, (3) good, (4) fair, (5) poor, (6) very poor] in each of the following areas?			
1. Keeping the school office running smoothly.	2.48	0.78	−0.674
2. General planning for the school.	2.37	0.74	−0.609
3. Directing the work of administrative assistants.	2.54	0.79	−0.472
4. Cutting "red-tape" when fast action is needed.	2.23	0.85	−0.398
5. Publicizing the work of the school.	2.97	0.93	−0.377

*Items ordered in terms of decreasing magnitude of factor weight.

TABLE C-14. Item Means, Standard Deviations, and Factor Weights Applied to the Responses of 189 Principals Used to Compute Factor Scores for the Satisfaction They Derive from Supervising the Instructional Program

Items*	Mean	Standard Deviation	Factor Weight
To what degree do you enjoy [(1) a great deal, (2) very much, (3) somewhat, (4) very little, (5) not at all] each of the following aspects of a principal's role?			
1. Working with "exceptionally able" teachers.	1.57	0.67	0.625
2. Working with "average" teachers.	2.04	0.70	0.622
3. Working with new teachers.	1.62	0.68	0.541
4. Supervising the instructional program.	1.76	0.68	0.488
5. Working with curriculum specialists.	2.03	0.81	0.446
6. Having the freedom to schedule one's own time.	1.79	0.72	0.360
7. Having a vacation from work periodically during the school year.	1.71	0.80	0.340

*Items ordered in terms of decreasing magnitude of factor weight.

TABLE C-15.   Item Means, Standard Deviations, and Factor Weights Applied to the Responses of 189 Principals Used to Compute Factor Scores for the Satisfaction They Derive from Performing Administrative Tasks

Item*	Mean	Standard Deviation	Factor Weight
To what degree do you enjoy [(1) a great deal, (2) very much, (3) somewhat, (4) very little, (5) not at all] each of the following aspects of a principal's role?			
1. Supervising office personnel.	2.61	0.80	0.635
2. Supervising custodial personnel.	3.05	0.89	0.610
3. Preparing reports to the higher administration.	3.07	0.94	0.601
4. Preparing staff bulletins or announcements.	2.87	0.84	0.498
5. Handling administrative routine.	2.30	0.99	0.486
6. Allocating the school budget.	2.84	0.94	0.469
7. Evaluating teacher performance.	2.83	0.97	0.460

*Items ordered in terms of decreasing magnitude of factor weight.

TABLE C-16. Item Means, Standard Deviations, and Factor Weights Applied to the Responses of 1303 Elementary School Teachers Used to Compute Factor Scores for Their Reports of Their Principals' Control over Teachers' Professional Activities

Item*	Mean	Standard Deviation	Factor Weight
How frequently [always (5), almost always (4), occasionally (3), almost never (2), never (1)] does your principal:			
1. Require that teachers discuss their major classroom problems with the principal.	3.76	0.85	0.630
2. Ask teachers to report all major conferences with parents to the principal.	3.55	0.90	0.593
3. Require teachers to keep the principal informed of "problem" children in their classrooms.	3.69	0.89	0.586
4. Closely direct the work of teachers who are likely to experience difficulty.	4.24	0.72	0.500
5. Require that teachers' classroom behavior conform to the principal's standards.	3.54	0.90	0.497
6. Check to see that teachers prepare written lesson plans.	3.58	0.93	0.463
7. Know what is taking place in most classrooms during most of the day.	3.72	0.82	0.393
8. Determine what the objectives of the guidance program should be in the school.	4.13	0.89	0.383

*Items ordered in terms of decreasing magnitude of factor wieght.

TABLE C-17. Item Means, Standard Deviations, and Factor Weights Applied to the Responses of 1303 Elementary School Teachers Used to Compute Factor Scores for Their Reports of Their Principals' Emphasis on Concern for Maximizing Teachers' Service to Pupils

Item*	Mean	Standard Deviation	Factor Weight
How frequently [always (5), almost always (4), occasionally (3), almost never (2), never (1)] does your principal:			
1. Encourage teachers to give extra help in their "free" periods to students needing that help.	2.03	0.84	0.413
2. Put the student's welfare above that of the teachers when the two are opposed.	2.35	1.12	0.410
3. Encourage worthwhile student activities that would require additional work by teachers.	2.30	0.77	0.406

*Items ordered in terms of decreasing magnitude of factor weight.

TABLE C-18.   Item Means, Standard Deviations, and Factor Weights Applied to the Responses of 1303 Elementary School Teachers Used to Compute Factor Scores for Their Reports of Their Principals' Support of Teachers in Cases of Conflict with Pupils

	Mean	Standard Deviation	Factor Weight
How frequently [always (5), almost always (4), occasionally (3), almost never (2), never (1)] does your principal:			
1. Side with the teacher when a student complains about the teacher's behavior, even if the student's complaint is legitimate.	2.97	1.12	0.693
2. Support a teacher's discipline decision that the principal believes is grossly unfair to the child.	2.41	1.15	0.580
3. Back the teacher in any public controversy between teacher and student.	3.94	0.88	0.572
4. Insist that students obey teacher's instructions first, and complain about them later.	4.06	0.92	0.373

*Items ordered in terms of decreasing magnitude of factor weight.

TABLE C-19. Item Means, Standard Deviations, and Factor Weights Applied to the Responses of 1303 Elementary School Teachers Used to Compute Factor Scores for Their Reports of Their Principals' Social Distance in the School

	Mean	Standard Deviation	Factor Weight
How frequently [always (5), almost always (4), occasionally (3), almost never (2), never (1)] does your principal:			
1. Discourage teachers from treating him as "one of the gang" at informal gatherings of teachers.	2.34	1.05	0.579
2. Encourage all teachers to call him by his first name when students are not present.	3.51	0.95	−0.522
3. Make it a practice to have lunch frequently with the teachers in his school.	2.07	0.76	−0.470
4. Insist, tactfully, that teachers show due respect for his position as principal.	2.93	1.27	0.312

*Items ordered in terms of decreasing magnitude of factor weight.

TABLE C-20. Item Means, Standard Deviations, and Factor Weights Applied to the Responses of 1303 Elementary School Teachers Used to Compute Factor Scores for Their Reports of Their Principals' Social Distance Outside the School

Item*	Mean	Standard Deviation	Factor Weight
How frequently [always (5), almost always (4), occasionally (3), almost never (2), never (1)] does your principal:			
1. Discourage social invitations from faculty members.	2.50	0.94	0.638
2. Avoid social involvement with groups of teachers.	3.07	1.12	0.583
3. Refrain from joining a social club to which a number of his teachers belong.	2.51	1.01	0.577
4. Follow the policy of not having members of the faculty as close personal friends.	2.99	1.04	0.490
5. Spend an occasional evening with faculty members.	2.45	0.77	−0.437

*Items ordered in terms of decreasing magnitude of factor weight.

TABLE C-21. Item Means, Standard Deviations, and Factor Weights Applied to the Responses of 1303 Elementary School Teachers Used to Compute Factor Scores for Their Reports of Their Principals' Involvement of Parents in School Affairs

Item*	Mean	Standard Deviation	Factor Weight
How frequently [always (5), almost always (4), occasionally (3), almost never (2), never (1)] does your principal:			
1. Encourage a group of parents to discuss and help formulate the educational philosophy to be used in the school.	3.35	1.01	0.609
2. Use interested parents as volunteer part-time "teacher helpers."	2.59	1.01	0.605
3. Encourage parents to help during school hours on school or class trips or projects.	3.66	0.88	0.598
4. Use interested parents as an advisory group when making out the course of study.	3.13	0.95	0.548
5. Encourage interested parent groups to evaluate how well the school is achieving its curricular objectives.	3.46	0.98	0.476
6. Encourage parental attendance at school assemblies.	3.63	0.78	0.441

*Items ordered in terms of decreasing magnitude of factor weight.

TABLE C-22. Item Means, Standard Deviations, and Factor Weights Applied to the Responses of 1235 Elementary School Teachers Used to Compute Factor Scores for Their Reports of the Professional Performance of Teachers in Their School

Item*	Mean	Standard Deviation	Factor Weight
Of the teachers in your school, what percent . . .			
1. Are committed to doing the best job of which they are capable.	78.6	11.8	0.806
2. Maintain a professional attitude towards their work.	81.3	9.7	0.803
3. Maintain an interest in improving the educational program of the school.	73.0	14.7	0.803
4. Maintain effective discipline in their classes.	80.5	9.5	0.692
5. Usually "drag their feet" when new ideas are introduced into the school program.	22.9	11.4	−0.690
6. Try new teaching methods in their classrooms.	59.6	16.4	0.663
7. Do "textbook" teaching only.	24.7	13.6	−0.662
8. Waste a lot of time in their classroom activities.	18.9	11.1	−0.598

*Items ordered in terms of decreasing magnitude of factor weight.

TABLE C-23. Item Means, Standard Deviations, and Factor Weights Applied to the Responses of 964 Elementary School Teachers Used to Compute Factor Scores from Their Reports of Pupils' Performance.

Item*	Mean	Standard Deviation	Factor Weight
Of the pupils you teach, what percent . . .			
1. Are one or more years behind grade level in reading ability.	30.9	17.4	−0.802
2. Are not mastering the subject matter or skills you teach at the minimum level of satisfactory performance.	20.3	11.2	−0.787
3. Are not interested in academic achievement.	28.5	14.1	−0.771
4. Were not adequately prepared to do the grade level work expected of them when they entered your class(es).	31.2	14.9	−0.769
5. Work up to their intellectual capacities.	43.5	15.2	0.482

*Items ordered in terms of decreasing magnitude of factor weight.

TABLE C-24. Item Means, Standard Deviations, and Factor Weights Applied to the Responses of 1235 Elementary School Teachers Used to Compute Factor Scores for Their Reports of Teachers' Morale.

Item*	Mean	Standard Deviation	Factor Weight
Of the teachers in your school, what percent . . .			
1. Display a sense of pride in the school.	80.0	14.0	0.858
2. Enjoy working in the school.	79.5	13.6	0.825
3. Display a sense of loyalty to the school.	82.5	11.8	0.823
4. Respect the judgment of the administrators of the school.	76.1	14.8	0.782
5. Accept the educational philosophy underlying the curriculum of the school.	82.1	11.2	0.750
6. Work cooperatively with their fellow teachers.	84.7	8.5	0.689

*Items ordered in terms of decreasing magnitude of factor weight.

Author Index

Abegglen, James, 33
Adams, Stuart, 34
Anastasi, Anne, 54
Anderson, H. Dewey, 215

Barter, Alice S., 17, 18
Baudler, Lucille, 69
Becker, Howard, S., 33, 171
Bendix, Reinhard, 69, 215
Benney, Mark, 161
Bernard, Jessie, 33
Blalock, Hubert M., 19
Blau, Peter M., 139
Bowman, G. W., 18
Broom, Leonard, 18, 227

Caplow, Theodore, 11, 18, 19, 81
Carr-Saunders, A. M., 139
Charters, W. W., Jr., 33, 34
Clark, Burton R., 171
Cook, Stuart W., 19
Cottrell, Leonard S., Jr., 18, 227
Cussler, Margaret, 81

Davidson, Percy E., 215
Davis, James A., 55
Degler, Carl N., 7, 18
Deutsch, Martin, 19
Dodd, Peter C., 19
Dreeben, Robert, 19

Erikson, Erik H., 70

Festinger, Leon, 216
Fiedler, Fred E., 161
Fox, Thomas, 215
Frederiksen, Norman, 17
Freeman, Linton, 215

Gage, N. L., 33

Gardner, Burleigh B., 5, 18, 184, 189
Glass, David V., 214
Goode, William J., 19
Gouldner, Alvin W., 2, 18, 227
Greyser, S. A., 18
Griffith, Daniel E., 17
Grobman, Hulda G., 17
Gross, Edward, 33, 139
Gross, Neal, 15, 19, 171, 188, 189,
    227, 232

Harman, Harry H., 14, 19
Hatt, Paul K., 19, 69
Hemphill, John K., 17, 33
Henderson, A. M., 161
Herriott, Robert E., 15, 19, 188, 189,
    232
Hughes, Everett C., 10, 19, 144, 149,
    154-155, 161, 171
Hynes, Vynce A., 17

Jahoda, Marie, 19
Janowitz, Morris, 33

Kadushin, Charles, 151, 161
Kahl, Joseph A., 188
Kahn, Robert L., 202
Kaiser, Henry F., 14, 19
Kaplan, Frances B., 18
Katz, Daniel, 216
Kendall, Patricia L., 19, 33

Lazarsfeld, Paul F., 19
Linton, Ralph, 225, 227
Lipset, Seymour M., 69, 215
Lyon, Catherine D., 18

McEachern, Alexander W., 227
McGuire, Carson, 33
Mack, Raymond W., 214, 215

271

Subject Index